CODI-CRAC 2021 Shared Task on Anaphora, Bridging, and Discourse Deixis in Dialogue (CODI-CRAC 2021)

Punta Cana, Dominican Republic
10 November 2021

ISBN: 978-1-7138-9173-4

Printed from e-media with permission by:

Curran Associates, Inc.
57 Morehouse Lane
Red Hook, NY 12571

Some format issues inherent in the e-media version may also appear in this print version.

Association for Computational Linguistics
209 N. Eighth Street
Stroudsburg, Pennsylvania 18360

Phone: 1-570-476-8006
Fax: 1-570-476-0860

acl@aclweb.org

Additional copies of this publication are available from:

Curran Associates, Inc.
57 Morehouse Lane
Red Hook, NY 12571 USA
Phone: 845-758-0400
Fax: 845-758-2633
Email: curran@proceedings.com
Web: www.proceedings.com

CODI-CRAC 2021

The CODI-CRAC 2021 Shared Task on Anaphora, Bridging, and Discourse Deixis in Dialogue

Proceedings of the Workshop

November 10, 2021
Punta Cana, Dominican Republic

Message from the Program Chairs

This shared task represents the collaborative efforts of a diverse team of researchers, across countries, institutional types, research areas, and career stages. The idea emerged through a Discourse Analysis breakout session at SIGDIAL 2020. The goal was to foster a more active partnership between the discourse and dialogue communities and to offer, not just a competition, but an opportunity to identify the next great challenges for the area of coreference.

Since that initial discussion at the Spring 2020 conference, the core organizing team has met almost weekly to build a vision for this shared task as the initial event out of what is hoped to become a series of such events, and situated in partnership with other related efforts, such as the Universal Anaphora effort. The team is excited to host this shared task, jointly with the CODI and CRAC workshops, co-located with EMNLP 2021. Each of the organizing team's members are also grateful to their respective institutions for providing the kind of environment that facilitates such international collaborations.

The team is grateful for funding committed by the Heidelberg Institute for Theoretical Studies and the Dali Project at Queen Mary University (both of which supported annotation for this shared task event) and Carnegie Mellon University (slated to support annotation for next year's event), as well as resources provided by Intel (especially in connection with the CODALAB infrastructure). The annotation team managed by Queen Mary University worked tirelessly to produce the annotated data, without which this shared task would not be a shared task at all! The team is also grateful for the synergistic efforts of the broader ACL community, for providing an environment in which the vision for this shared task could be realized and situated within this vibrant EMNLP milieu.

Organizing Committee

- Sopan Khosla, Amazon, USA
- Ramesh Manuvinakurike, Intel, USA
- Vincent Ng, University of Texas at Dallas, USA
- Massimo Poesio, Queen Mary University, UK
- Michael Strube, Heidelberg Institute for Theoretical Studies, Germany
- Carolyn Rosé, Carnegie Mellon University, USA

Table of Contents

Workshop Program

Wednesday, November 10, 2021

09:05–09:30 Session 1: Welcome

09:05–09:30 *The CODI-CRAC 2021 Shared Task on Anaphora, Bridging, and Discourse Deixis in Dialogue*
Sopan Khosla, Juntao Yu, Ramesh Manuvinakurike, Vincent Ng, Massimo Poesio, Michael Strube and Carolyn Rosé

09:30–10:30 Session 2: System Talks (part 1)

09:30–09:45 *Neural Anaphora Resolution in Dialogue*
Hideo Kobayashi, Shengjie Li and Vincent Ng

09:45–10:00 *Anaphora Resolution in Dialogue: Description of the DFKI-TalkingRobots System for the CODI-CRAC 2021 Shared-Task*
Tatiana Anikina, Cennet Oguz, Natalia Skachkova, Siyu Tao, Sharmila Upadhyaya and Ivana Kruijff-Korbayova

10:00–10:15 *The Pipeline Model for Resolution of Anaphoric Reference and Resolution of Entity Reference*
Hongjin Kim, Damrin Kim and Harksoo Kim

10:15–10:30 *An End-to-End Approach for Full Bridging Resolution*
Joseph Renner, Priyansh Trivedi, Gaurav Maheshwari, Rémi Gilleron and Pascal Denis

10:30–11:00 Coffee Break

11:00–11:15 Session 3: System Talks (part 2)

11:00–11:15 *Adapted End-to-End Coreference Resolution System for Anaphoric Identities in Dialogues*
Liyan Xu and Jinho D. Choi

Wednesday, November 10, 2021 (continued)

11:15–11:45 Session 4: Analysis Papers

11:15–11:30 *Anaphora Resolution in Dialogue: Cross-Team Analysis of the DFKI-TalkingRobots Team Submissions for the CODI-CRAC 2021 Shared-Task*
Natalia Skachkova, Cennet Oguz, Tatiana Anikina, Siyu Tao, Sharmila Upadhyaya and Ivana Kruijff-Korbayova

11:30–11:45 *The CODI-CRAC 2021 Shared Task on Anaphora, Bridging, and Discourse Deixis Resolution in Dialogue: A Cross-Team Analysis*
Shengjie Li, Hideo Kobayashi and Vincent Ng

11:45–12:00 Session 5: Visioning and Discussion

The CODI-CRAC 2021 Shared Task on Anaphora, Bridging, and Discourse Deixis in Dialogue

Sopan Khosla[1,7]*, **Juntao Yu**[2], **Ramesh Manuvinakurike**[3], **Vincent Ng**[4], **Massimo Poesio**[5], **Michael Strube**[6], and **Carolyn Rosé**[1]

[1]Canegie Mellon Univ., USA; [2]Univ. of Essex, UK; [3]Intel Labs, USA; [4]UT Dallas, USA; [5]Queen Mary Univ., UK; [6]HITS, Germany; [7]AWS AI, Amazon, USA

sopankh@amazon.com; j.yu@essex.ac.uk; ramesh.manuvinakurike@intel.com; vince@hlt.utdallas.edu; m.poesio@qmul.ac.uk; Michael.Strube@h-its.org; cprose@cs.cmu.edu

Abstract

In this paper, we provide an overview of the CODI-CRAC 2021 Shared Task. The shared task focuses on detecting anaphoric relations in different genres of conversations. Using five conversational datasets, four of which have been newly annotated with a wide range of anaphoric relations: identity, bridging references and discourse deixis, we defined multiple tasks focusing individually on these key relations. We discuss the evaluation scripts used to assess the system performance on these tasks, and provide a brief summary of the participating systems and the results obtained across 115 runs from six teams, with most submissions achieving significantly better results than our baseline methods.

1 Introduction

The performance of models for single-antecedent anaphora resolution on the aspects of anaphoric interpretation annotated in the standard ONTONOTES dataset (Pradhan et al., 2012) has greatly improved in recent years (Wiseman et al., 2015; Lee et al., 2017, 2018; Kantor and Globerson, 2019; Joshi et al., 2020). So the attention of the community has started to turn to more complex cases of anaphora not found or not properly tested in ONTONOTES.

Well-known examples of this trend are work on the cases of anaphora whose interpretation requires some form of commonsense knowledge tested by benchmarks for the Winograd Schema Challenge (Rahman and Ng, 2012; Liu et al., 2017; Sakaguchi et al., 2020), or the pronominal anaphors that cannot be resolved purely using gender, for which benchmarks such as GAP have been developed (Webster et al., 2018). GAP, however, still focused on identity coreference.

In addition, more research has been carried out on aspects of anaphoric interpretation that go beyond identity anaphora but are covered by datasets such as ARRAU (Poesio et al., 2018; Uryupina et al., 2020). These include, e.g., bridging reference (Clark, 1977; Hou et al., 2018; Hou, 2020; Yu and Poesio, 2020; Kobayashi and Ng, 2021), discourse deixis (Webber, 1991; Marasović et al., 2017; Kolhatkar et al., 2018) or split-antecedent anaphora (Eschenbach et al., 1989; Vala et al., 2016; Zhou and Choi, 2018; Yu et al., 2020b, 2021).

There has been interest in other genres apart from news. This includes substantial research on annotating and resolving coreference in biomedical and other scientific domains (Cohen et al., 2017; Lu and Poesio, 2021) as well as in literary documents (Bamman et al., 2020). There are, however, language genres still understudied in the literature on anaphoric reference. Arguably the most important among these is conversational language in dialogue. Anaphora resolution in dialogue requires systems to handle grammatically incorrect language suffering from disfluencies. Dialogue involves much more deictic reference, vaguer anaphoric and discourse deictic reference, speaker grounding of pronouns and long-distance conversation structure. These are complexities that are often missing in news or Wikipedia articles, which form a large chunk of current datasets for coreference resolution. There has been some research on coreference in dialogue (Byron, 2002; Eckert and Strube, 2001; Müller, 2008), but very limited in scope (primarily related to pronominal interpretation), due to the lack of suitable corpora. The one language for which substantial corpora of coreference in dialogue exist is French: the ANCOR corpus (Muzerelle et al., 2014) has enabled the development of an end-to-end neural model for coreference interpretation in dialogue by Grobol (2020). For English, the one resource we are aware of fully annotated for anaphoric reference is the TRAINS corpora included in the ARRAU corpus (Uryupina et al., 2020).

The objective of the CODI-CRAC 2021 Shared

*Work done when the author was a student at CMU

Proceedings of the CODI-CRAC 2021 Shared Task on Anaphora, Bridging, and Discourse Deixis in Dialogue, pages 1–15
Punta Cana, Dominican Republic, November 10, 2021.

Task in Anaphora Resolution in Dialogue[1] was to provide participants with the opportunity to develop automated approaches for coreference resolution that tackle less studied forms of anaphora and generalize on different types of conversational setups. Specifically, the shared task is divided in three tasks that individually tackle a particular anaphoric relation: identity, bridging, and discourse deixis. To evaluate the participating systems, we provide development and test sets consisting of four conversational datasets from different domains newly annotated with the above-mentioned relations. This lack of in-domain training data also poses research challenges related to transfer learning and out-of-domain generalization of learned representations. To accommodate for systems that use gold/predicted mentions for bridging and discourse deixis tasks, we set up separate leaderboards for the two settings.

Our goal in this paper is to present an overview of the CODI-CRAC 2021 shared task. We begin by providing some background in Section 2 and introducing the new CODI-CRAC 2021 corpus in Section 3. We then provide an extensive overview of the different CODI-CRAC 2021 tasks, markable settings, and evaluation metrics in Section 4, and submission details in Section 5. This is followed by details of the baselines in Section 6 and participating systems in Section 7. We present a discussion of the performance of the systems on different tasks and sub-corpora in Section 8, and finally conclude this paper in Section 9.

2 Background

2.1 Beyond Identity Coreference

Most modern anaphoric annotation projects cover basic identity anaphora as in (1).

(1) [Mary]$_i$ bought [a new dress]$_j$ but [it]$_j$ didn't fit [her]$_i$.

However, many other types of identity anaphora exist, as well as other types of anaphoric relations that are not annotated in ONTONOTES but are annotated in other corpora.

Split-antecedent anaphora In ONTONOTES, plural reference is only marked when the antecedent is mentioned by a single noun phrase. However, **split-antecedent anaphors** are also possible (Eschenbach et al., 1989; Kamp and Reyle, 1993), as in (2). These are also cases of plural identity coreference, but to sets composed of two or more entities introduced by separate noun phrases. Such references are annotated in, e.g., ARRAU (Uryupina et al., 2020), GUM (Zeldes, 2017) and *Phrase Detectives* (Poesio et al., 2019).

(2) [John]$_1$ met [Mary]$_2$. [He]$_1$ greeted [her]$_2$. [They]$_{1,2}$ went to the movies.

Discourse deixis In ONTONOTES, **event anaphora**, a subtype of **discourse deixis** (Webber, 1991; Kolhatkar et al., 2018) is marked, as in (3) (where *[that]* arguably refers to the event of a white rabbit with pink ears running past Alice) but not the whole range of abstract anaphora, illustrated by, e.g., (4), where again arguably *[this]* refers to the fact that the Rabbit was able to talk. (Both examples from the *Phrase Detectives* corpus (Poesio et al., 2019).)

(3) So she was considering in her own mind (as well as she could, for the hot day made her feel very sleepy and stupid), whether the pleasure of making a daisy-chain would be worth the trouble of getting up and picking the daisies, when suddenly a White Rabbit with pink eyes ran close by her. There was nothing so VERY remarkable in [that]; nor did Alice think it so VERY much out of the way to hear the Rabbit say to itself, 'Oh dear! Oh dear! I shall be late!' (when she thought it over afterwards, it occurred to her that she ought to have wondered at this, but at the time it all seemed quite natural); ...

(4) There was nothing so VERY remarkable in that; nor did Alice think it so VERY much out of the way to hear the Rabbit say to itself, 'Oh dear! Oh dear! I shall be late!' (when she thought it over afterwards, it occurred to her that she ought to have wondered at [this], but at the time it all seemed quite natural); but when the Rabbit actually TOOK A WATCH OUT OF ITS WAISTCOAT-POCKET, and looked at it, and then hurried on, Alice started to her feet, for it flashed across her mind that she had never before seen a rabbit with either a waistcoat-pocket, or a watch to take out of it, and burning with curiosity, she ran across the field after it, and fortunately was

[1] https://competitions.codalab.org/competitions/30312

just in time to see it pop down a large rabbit-hole under the hedge.

Bridging references There are other forms of anaphoric reference besides identity, and there are now a number of corpora annotating (a subset of) these forms. Possibly the most studied of non-identity anaphora is **bridging reference** or **associative anaphora** (Clark, 1977; Hawkins, 1978; Prince, 1981) as in (5), where bridging reference / associative anaphora *the roof* refers to an object which is related to / associated with, but not identical to, the *hall*. We also take bridging reference to cover *other* anaphora as in (6), as well as other cases of association such as identity of sense anaphora, etc. (Poesio, 2016).

(5) There was not a moment to be lost: away went Alice like the wind, and was just in time to hear it say, as it turned a corner, 'Oh my ears and whiskers, how late it's getting!' She was close behind it when she turned the corner, but the Rabbit was no longer to be seen: she found herself in [a long, low hall, which was lit up by a row of lamps hanging from [the roof]].
There were doors all round the hall, but they were all locked; and when Alice had been all the way down one side and up the other, trying every door, she walked sadly down [the middle], wondering how she was ever to get out again.

(6) There was not a moment to be lost: away went Alice like the wind, and was just in time to hear it say, as it turned a corner, 'Oh my ears and whiskers, how late it's getting!' She was close behind it when she turned the corner, but the Rabbit was no longer to be seen: she found herself in a long, low hall, which was lit up by a row of lamps hanging from the roof.
There were doors all round the hall, but they were all locked; and when Alice had been all the way down [one side] and up [the other], trying every door, she walked sadly down the middle, wondering how she was ever to get out again.

2.2 The CRAC 2018 Shared Task

The more general types of anaphoric reference just discussed are now routinely annotated in a number of corpora, including ANCORA (Recasens and Martí, 2010), ARRAU (Uryupina et al., 2020), GNOME (Poesio, 2004), GUM (Zeldes, 2017), ISNOTES (Markert et al., 2012), the Prague Dependency Treebank (Nedoluzhko, 2013), and TÜBA-DZ (Versley, 2008). (See Poesio et al. (2016) for a more detailed survey and Nedoluzhko et al. (2021) for a more recent, extensive update.)

Some of these resources are of a sufficient size to support shared tasks. In particular, the ARRAU corpus was used as the dataset for the Shared Task on Anaphora Resolution with ARRAU in the CRAC 2018 Workshop (Poesio et al., 2018). That shared task was articulated around three tasks: identity coreference (including identification of non-referring expressions), bridging references, and discourse deixis. The organization of the shared task resulted in the development of an extended version of the Coreference Reference Scorer (Pradhan et al., 2014), which also scores non-referring expressions. Separate scorers were developed for bridging reference resolution, carrying out both mention-based evaluation and entity-based evaluation of bridging references, as done by Hou et al. (2018), and for discourse deixis, based on Kolhatkar and Hirst (2014). The present shared task was modeled on that.

2.3 Universal Anaphora

In order to enable further progress in the empirical study of anaphora by coordinating the many existing efforts to annotate not just identity coreference, but all aspects of anaphoric interpretation from identity of sense anaphora to bridging to discourse deixis; and not just for English, but all languages, the **Universal Anaphora** (UA) initiative was launched in 2020.[2] Progress so far includes a first proposal concerning the range of phenomena to be covered, as well as a survey of the range of existing anaphoric annotations and a proposal for a markup format extending the CONLL-U format developed by the **Universal Dependencies** initiative[3] with mechanisms for marking up the range of anaphoric information covered by UA. Crucially, a scorer able to evaluate all types of anaphoric reference in the scope of the proposal was also developed, which we used in this shared task. The scorer is briefly discussed in Section 4.2.

[2] https://universalanaphora.github.io/UniversalAnaphora/

[3] https://universaldependencies.org/

2.4 Datasets of Anaphora in Dialogue

A limitation of most resources annotated for anaphora is that they mostly focus on expository text. The one substantial dataset of anaphoric relations in dialogue is ANCOR for French (Muzerelle et al., 2014), in which identity and bridging anaphora are annotated. Among the small number of English corpora that cover dialogue include ONTONOTES (Pradhan et al., 2012), which contains a small number of conversations annotated for identity anaphora and a small subtype of discourse deixis (as discussed earlier). ARRAU's (Poesio and Artstein, 2008; Uryupina et al., 2020) TRAINS sub-corpus consists of task-oriented dialogues for identity, bridging, and discourse deixis. We include TRAINS in CODI-CRAC 2021 training data. The more recently released ONTOGUM (Zhu et al., 2021) builds upon the ONTONOTES schema and adds several new genres (including more spoken data) to the ONTONOTES family. Both identity anaphora and bridging are annotated in the dataset.

3 The CODI-CRAC 2021 Corpus

One of the objectives of the CODI-CRAC 2021 Shared Task was to annotate new data for studying anaphora in dialogue. The only existing dataset covering the full range of phenomena and with some coverage of dialogue, the ARRAU data used for the CRAC 2018 Shared Task, was used as training material. In addition, new data from dialogue corpora were annotated for development and testing using the same annotation scheme used in ARRAU.

3.1 ARRAU: Corpus and Annotation Scheme

Genres The ARRAU corpus[4] (Poesio and Artstein, 2008; Uryupina et al., 2020) was designed to cover a variety of genres. It includes a substantial amount of news text in a sub-corpus called RST, consisting of the entire subset of the Penn Treebank (Marcus et al., 1993) that was annotated in the RST treebank (Carlson et al., 2003). In addition to the news data, ARRAU includes three more sub-corpora. The TRAINS sub-corpus includes all the task-oriented dialogues in the TRAINS-93 corpus[5] as well as the pilot dialogues in the so-called TRAINS-91 corpus. The PEAR sub-corpus consists of the complete collection of spoken narratives in the Pear Stories that provided some of the early evidence on salience and anaphoric reference (Chafe, 1980), and the GNOME sub-corpus covers documents from the medical and art history genres covered by the GNOME corpus (Poesio, 2004). The same coding scheme was used for all sub-corpora, but separate guidelines were written for the textual and the spoken dialogue sub-corpora. RST, TRAINS-93 and PEAR were used for the CRAC 2018 shared task. For this year's shared task, TRAINS-91 was used for development in the trial phase, whereas all other datasets were used for training.[6]

Annotation scheme The original annotation scheme used for Release 1 (Poesio and Artstein, 2008) is distributed with the dataset and is also available from the ARRAU corpus page. For the second release (Uryupina et al., 2020), the guidelines for bridging were extended and genericity was also annotated using the GNOME guidelines, but a complete new manual was not produced. However, a fairly extensive description can be found in Uryupina et al. (2020). Following the CRAC 2018 shared task, the guidelines for bridging, semantic category and genericity were further revised as part of the work on ARRAU Release 3, which is almost ready, and a full revision of the annotation manual was also started. These guidelines were used in the current annotation. A brief summary follows.

Markable definition Many, especially among the older, anaphorically annotated corpora impose syntactic, semantic or discourse-based restrictions on markables. For instance, in ONTONOTES neither expletives nor singletons are annotated (for a discussion of the state of the art in anaphoric annotation, see Poesio et al. (2016)). By contrast, in ARRAU *all* NPs are considered as markables, including non-referring expressions (e.g., expletives such as *it* or predicative NPs such as *a busy place*) in (7), and expressions do not corefer with any other markable and thus form a singleton coreference chain. Moreover, in ARRAU non-referring markables are manually sub-classified into expletives, predicative, and quantifiers. In addition, all generic references are marked, including premodifiers when the entity referred to is mentioned again, e.g., in the case of

[4]http://www.arrauproject.org

[5]http://www.ldc.upenn.edu/Catalog/catalogEntry.jsp?catalogId=LDC95S25

[6]The original intention had been to use the soon-to-be-released ARRAU 3, but as the work on this version was still under way by the time the training data had to be released, ARRAU 2 was used instead–i.e., the exact same version used for the CRAC 2018 shared task.

the proper name *US* in (8), and premodifiers that refer to a kind, like *exchange-rate* in (9).

(7) [It] seems to be [a busy place]

(8) ...The Treasury Department said that the $[\text{US}]_1$ trade deficit may worsen next year after two years of significant improvement... The statement was the $[\text{US}]_1$'s government first acknowledgment of what other groups, such as the International Monetary Fund, have been predicting for months.

(9) The Treasury report, which is required annually by a provision of the 1988 trade act, again took South Korea to task for its $[\text{exchange-rate}]_1$ policies. "We believe there have continued to be indications of $[\text{exchange-rate}]_1$ manipulation ...

Types of anaphoric relations marked The ARRAU guidelines support annotation of different types of anaphoric relations. All referring markables are marked as either `discourse new` or `discourse old`. Discourse new mentions introduce new entities and thus are not marked as being coreferent with an entity already introduced (**antecedent**). For discourse-old mentions, an antecedent can be identified, either of type `phrase` (if the antecedent was introduced using a nominal markable) or `segment` (not introduced by a nominal markable, for **discourse deixis**).[7] In addition, referring NPs can be marked as **related** to a previously mentioned discourse entity to identify them as examples of associative (**bridging**) anaphora.

Bridging references Annotating — indeed, even identifying — bridging references in a reliable way is difficult, which is one of the reasons why so few large-scale corpora for anaphora include this type of annotation (Poesio et al., 2016; Kobayashi and Ng, 2020). The ARRAU guidelines for bridging anaphora are based on experiments that were started by Vieira and Poesio (Poesio and Vieira, 1998) and continued in the GNOME project (Poesio, 2004). The ARRAU Release 1 guidelines followed the GNOME guidelines, but with an extension and a simplification. Annotators were asked to mark a markable as `related` to a particular antecedent if it stood to that antecedent in one of the relations identified in GNOME (indeed, the same examples were used), and in addition, if they stood in two additional relations (but without testing the reliability of this annotation):

- `other`, for *other* NPs, broadly following the guidelines in Modjeska (2003);
- an `undersp-rel` relation for 'obvious cases of bridging that didn't fit any other category'.

Discourse deixis Discourse deixis in its full form is a very complex form of reference, both to annotate (Kolhatkar et al., 2018) and to resolve. Very few anaphoric annotation projects have attempted to annotate discourse deixis in its entirety (Kolhatkar et al., 2018). More typical is a partial annotation, as in (Byron and Allen, 1998; Navarretta, 2000), who annotated pronominal reference to abstract objects; in ONTONOTES, where event anaphora was marked (Pradhan et al., 2007); and in the work of Kolhatkar and Hirst (2014), which focused on so-called shell nouns. In ARRAU, A coder specifying that a referring expression is discourse-old is asked whether its antecedent was introduced using a `phrase` (markable) or a `segment` (discourse segment). Coders who choose `segment` have to mark a sequence of *predefined* clauses.

3.2 New Data

The annotated corpus prepared for the CODI-CRAC 2021 shared task consists of conversations from four well-known conversational datasets: the AMI corpus (Carletta, 2006), the LIGHT corpus (Urbanek et al., 2019), the PERSUASION corpus (Wang et al., 2019) and SWITCHBOARD (Godfrey et al., 1992). For each of these datasets, documents for about 15K tokens were annotated for development, and about the same number of tokens were annotated for testing, according to the ARRAU annotation scheme.

Switchboard SWITCHBOARD[8] (Godfrey et al., 1992) is one of the best known dialogue corpora. It consists of 1,155 five-minute spontaneous telephone conversations between two participants not previously acquainted with each other. In these conversations, callers question receivers on provided topics, such as child care, recycling, and news media. 440 speakers participate in these 1,155 conversations, producing 221,616 utterances. It was

[7] Identity anaphora also includes split antecedent plural anaphoric reference.

[8] `https://catalog.ldc.upenn.edu/LDC97S62`

annotated for dialogue acts by Stolcke et al. (1997)[9] and for information status by Nissim et al. (2004).

AMI The AMI corpus[10] (Carletta, 2006) is a collection of 100 hours of meeting recordings between several participants. The recordings include signals from close-talking and far-field microphones, individual and room-view video cameras, and output from a slide projector and an electronic whiteboard. Several types of annotation were carried out, including dialogue acts, topics, summaries, named entities, and focus of attention.

Light Amazon, Facebook, Google, and other AI companies have all created dialogue corpora in recent years to support their research on conversational agents. LIGHT (Urbanek et al., 2019) is one of the many recently created corpora available on the `Parl.ai` platform.[11] LIGHT is a large-scale fantasy text adventure game research platform for training agents that can both talk and act, interacting either with other models or with humans. The LIGHT corpus was entirely created through crowdsourcing at different levels. In the first round, workers created a number of settings (the King's palace, the dark forest, etc); then in a second round workers created fitting characters for each scenario, providing information about their background history, their personality, etc. Finally, in a third round, workers created dialogues between these characters.

Persuasion The Persuasion for Good corpus[12] (Wang et al., 2019) is a collection of online conversations generated by Amazon Mechanical Turk workers, where one participant (the persuader) tries to convince the other (the persuadee) to donate to a charity. 1017 conversations were collected in total, along with demographic data and responses to psychological surveys from users. Several speaker-level annotations were marked, including, e.g., demographics, the big five personality traits, etc.

3.3 Annotation

The dataset was annotated using the same MMAX2 tool (Müller and Strube, 2006) – indeed, almost exactly the same MMAX style – and by the same two annotators from the DALI team at Queen Mary University and University of Essex, Dr. Maris Camilleri and Dr. Paloma Carretero Garcia, who annotated and checked ARRAU Release 3, which is currently being prepared for release. However, due to time constraints, each document was only annotated by a single annotator, with spot checks carried out by the other annotator and Massimo Poesio (in ARRAU 3 each document was looked at by both annotators, and most documents were also independently checked by Massimo Poesio).

To prepare the data for the shared task, mentions were automatically extracted using the mention detector from Yu et al. (2020a), and the output converted into MMAX XML format.

3.4 The Corpus

Some basic statistics about the CODI-CRAC 2021 dataset are provided in Table 1. For each dataset, the Table reports number of documents, size in tokens, number of markables, and how many of these are Discourse Old (Identity Coreference) anaphors (DO), bridging references, and discourse deixis. With a total of 147,725 tokens and 41,807 markables, the CODI-CRAC 2021 dataset is to our knowledge the largest dataset annotated for anaphoric interpretation in dialogue, almost twice the size of ARRAU's TRAINS sub-corpus in tokens and more than twice its size in markables.

After annotation, the documents were converted into the CONLL-UA 'Extended' format used by the scorer, described by a document on the Universal Anaphora site.[13]

AMI, LIGHT and PERSUASION are freely available from the Shared Task Codalab site. ARRAU and SWITCHBOARD are distributed by LDC.[14]

4 Task Description

Following the structure of the CRAC 2018 Shared Task, CODI-CRAC 2021 was articulated around three tasks covering three key aspects of anaphoric interpretation: identity anaphora, bridging anaphora, and discourse deixis. Participants or groups could participate in one or more tasks.

[9] This version is available from https://convokit.cornell.edu/documentation/switchboard.html

[10] https://groups.inf.ed.ac.uk/ami/corpus/

[11] https://parl.ai/projects/light/

[12] https://convokit.cornell.edu/documentation/persuasionforgood.html

[13] https://github.com/UniversalAnaphora/UniversalAnaphora/blob/main/UA_CONLL_U_Plus_proposal_v1.0.md

[14] ARRAU is also freely available to any group that purchased the Penn Treebank and TRAINS-93 corpora from LDC.

		Docs	Tokens	Markables	DO	Bridging	Disc. Deix
AMI	dev	7	33741	8935	4400	850	230
	test	3	18260	4879	2300	633	118
LIGHT	dev	20	11495	3877	2120	381	62
	test	21	11824	3931	2174	415	80
PERSUASION	dev	22	9757	2929	1191	242	94
	test	28	12629	3839	1605	288	123
SWITCHBOARD	dev	11	14992	4025	1664	602	127
	test	22	35027	9392	3992	1190	263
Totals		134	147,725	41,807	19,446	4601	1097

Table 1: Statistics about the CODI-CRAC 2021 corpus (new datasets only)

4.1 Markable Settings

Bridging reference resolution and discourse deixis are very difficult tasks. In consideration of this, the Bridging (Task 2) and Discourse Deixis (Task 3) tasks were further divided into system and gold settings, according to whether the markables would be predicted by the system or provided by the organizers. The two settings were run in order – the gold setting became available after the runs under the system setting had been submitted. The two settings were scored separately and independently.

4.2 The Universal Anaphora Scorer

The new Universal Anaphora (UA) scorer was used to evaluate the systems. This is a Python scorer for the varieties of anaphoric reference covered by the Universal Anaphora guidelines, which include identity reference, split antecedent plurals, identification of non-referring expressions, bridging reference, and discourse deixis.

The scorer builds on the original Reference Coreference scorer[15] (Pradhan et al., 2014) developed for use in the CONLL 2011 and 2012 shared tasks on the ONTONOTES corpus (Pradhan et al., 2012) and its reimplementation in Python by Moosavi[16], which was already extended to evaluate non-referring expressions evaluation and cover singletons for the CRAC 2018 shared task (Poesio et al., 2018). The scorer reports scores for identity reference (with and without singletons and non-referring expressions – in the modality without singletons and non referring expressions the scorer is compatible with the original Coreference Reference scorer – split antecedents, bridging reference, and discourse deixis). For identity reference, the scorer reports the MUC, B^3, CEAF, CONLL (the unweighted average of MUC, B^3, and CEAF) (Pradhan et al., 2014), BLANC (Recasens and Hovy, 2011), and LEA (Moosavi and Strube, 2016) scores. The same scores are also computed for discourse deixis, which is treated as a generalized case of event coreference. For split antecedents, a generalization of these metrics following Paun et al. (2021) was developed. Entity F1 is computed for bridging–i.e., a system's interpretation is deemed correct as long as any mention of the correct anchor is found, as done e.g., in Hou et al. (2018).

4.3 Setting of the Scorer used in the Shared Task

The UA scorer can be run in a number of ways. The following settings were used for the individual tasks.[17]

Task 1 For Task 1, the Evaluating coreference relations (including split-antecedents) and singletons modality was used. Non-referring expressions identification were not scored.

```
python ua-scorer.py key system
```

Task 2 For Task 2, the scorer was called using the command:

```
python ua-scorer.py key system \
    keep_bridging
```

[15] https://github.com/conll/reference-coreference-scorers

[16] https://github.com/ns-moosavi/coval

[17] For a full description of the task(s), see https://github.com/sopankhosla/codi2021_scripts/blob/main/2021_CODI_CRAC_Introduction.md

Task 3 Finally, for Task 3, the scorer was called using the command:

```
python ua-scorer.py key system \
     evaluate_discourse_deixis
```

5 Submission Details

We used CodaLab to evaluate submissions and distribute the datasets. In the development phase, the participants only had access to out-of-domain training data (e.g., the ARRAU corpus) and in-domain validation data. They could submit results to the public leaderboard to evaluate their systems. In addition, we also released the scoring script on Github to reduce the dependency on CodaLab during model development. During the evaluation phase, we released the unseen test set across four sub-corpora. The submissions were evaluated on each sub-corpus individually and the final ranking for each task was performed by taking the mean of the four scores. Due to the lack of in-domain training data, the participants were allowed to use additional resources.

6 Baselines

We released one baseline system for each task. We derive the baselines for identity and bridging anaphora from current state-of-the-art methods, and set up a simple yet effective method for discourse deixis.

For Task 1, we used Xu and Choi (2020)'s coreference resolution model but without any higher-order inference.[18] We used the ONTONOTES (English) dataset for training and development. This model is then evaluated on CODI-CRAC 2021 datasets.

For Task 2, the baseline was derived from (Yu and Poesio, 2020). We used their single-task variant that is only trained on bridging annotations. We evaluated their best-performing model, which was trained on the RST sub-corpus of ARRAU, on CODI-CRAC 2021 data.[19]

The baseline for Task 3 leverages a simple heuristic that only considers demonstrative pronouns (*this*, *that*) as anaphors and considers the immediately preceding clause/utterance in the conversation to be their antecedent. Although simplistic, the algorithm achieves respectable scores on the CODI-CRAC 2021 development corpus. The performance of each baseline on different sub-corpora is shown in Tables 3, 4, and 5.

To help participants interested in building upon these baselines, we released the scripts used in the baseline pipeline to convert the CODI-CRAC 2021 data from the CONLL-UA format to JSON structure and vice-versa for each task.[20] The scripts contain modules that can also be used independently to transform conversations into a format compatible with different transformer-based encoders, allowing participants to set optional arguments to specify the *segment_size* and *tokenizer* for the conversion.

7 Participating Systems

A total of 55 individual participants registered for the CODI-CRAC 2021 shared task on CodaLab.[21] Among them, five teams submitted results for Task 1, three submitted results for Task 2, and two submitted results for Task 3. Teams UTD_NLP, KU_NLP, DFKI_TalkingRobots, Emory_NLP, and INRIA submitted system description papers. We summarize their approaches below (and in Table 2):

UTD_NLP participated in all three tasks. For identity anaphora, they deployed a pipeline architecture consisting of a mention detection component and an entity coreference component. The coreference component extends Xu and Choi (2020)'s implementation of Lee et al. (2018) by modifying the objective so that it can output singleton clusters, and enforces dialogue-specific constraints. They setup a similar architecture for discourse deixis. However, they slightly modified the objective function in Xu and Choi (2020) by classifying each span as a candidate anaphor, a candidate antecedent, or a non-mention in the mention detection stage, and resolving only candidate anaphors to candidate antecedents later. The team used a multi-pass sieve approach for bridging resolution to target same-head bridging links, with Yu and Poesio (2020)'s model as one of the sieves. In the gold setting, they trained an additional anaphor detection model (adapted from Yu and Poesio (2020)) to first identify the bridging anaphors from the gold markables before sending them to the sieves.

KU_NLP submitted results for tasks 1 and 2. For identity anaphora, they leveraged Cui and Zhang (2019)'s model with an ELECTRA-large backbone

[18] https://github.com/lxucs/coref-hoi/

[19] https://github.com/juntaoy/dali-bridging

[20] The necessary scripts are available from https://github.com/sopankhosla/codi2021_scripts

[21] Participants were allowed to create teams.

Track	Team	Baselines	Framework	Markable ID	Train. Data	Dev. Data
Anaphora Resolution	UTD_NLP	Xu and Choi (2020)	Pipeline of mention detection and entity coreference components. Modifies baseline to handle singleton clusters and enforce dialogue-specific constraints.	Adapted from Xu and Choi (2020)	CODI-CRAC 2021	CODI-CRAC 2021
	KU_NLP	-	(Cui and Zhang, 2019) with ELECTRA-large for mention detection. A pointer-network (Vinyals et al., 2015) based model for resolution.	Cui and Zhang (2019) + ELECTRA-large	CODI-CRAC 2021	CODI-CRAC 2021
	DFKI	-	(1) Workspace Coreference System incrementally clusters mentions using semantic similarity based on embeddings and lexical features; (2) Mention-to-Mention system pairs same entity mentions	SpaCy / BiLSTM-CRF	CODI-CRAC 2021	CODI-CRAC 2021
	Emory	Joshi et al. (2020)	Adapts the baseline to recognize singletons and encode speakers for all turns.	Joshi et al. (2020) + Singleton Recognition	CODI-CRAC 2021 + OntoNotes (Pradhan et al., 2012) + BOLT (Li et al., 2016)	CODI-CRAC 2021
Bridging Resolution	UTD_NLP	Yu and Poesio (2020)	A multi-pass sieve approach which used the baseline as one of the sieves and consists of a set of learning-based sieves (trained using SVMs) to target same-head bridging links.	Multi-task learning and SVM-based sieves	CODI-CRAC 2021	CODI-CRAC 2021
	KU_NLP	-	Solved as an MRC problem. Model takes query ("*What is related of ENTITY?*") and the conversation as input, and outputs the answer entity span.	Obtained as a part of the MRC system	CODI-CRAC 2021 + QUOREF	CODI-CRAC 2021
	INRIA	Joshi et al. (2019)	Leverage baseline's architecture to find the correct bridging antecedent in the gold setting.	Joshi et al. (2019)	CODI-CRAC 2021	CODI-CRAC 2021
Discourse Deixis Resolution	UTD_NLP	Xu and Choi (2020)	Builds upon the baseline by classifying each span into candidate anaphor, a candidate antecedent, or a non-mention. Only resolves candidate anaphors to candidate antecedents.	Obtained as part of joint mention detection and deixis resolution	CODI-CRAC 2021	CODI-CRAC 2021
	DFKI	-	A Siamese Network to detect discourse anaphor-antecedent pairs.	SpaCy	CODI-CRAC 2021	CODI-CRAC 2021

Table 2: Summary of the Participating Systems

Team	LIGHT	AMI	PERS.	SWBD.	Avg.
			Eval AR		
Emory	**80.33 (1)**	**63.98 (1)**	**78.41 (1)**	**74.49 (1)**	**74.3 (1)**
UTD_NLP	79.56 (2)	57.38 (3)	77.50 (2)	72.64 (2)	71.8 (2)
KU_NLP	69.16 (3)	57.59 (2)	71.09 (3)	65.67 (3)	65.9 (3)
DFKI (1)	64.99 (4)	43.93 (4)	59.93 (4)	53.55 (4)	55.6 (4)
SCIR[22]	55.92 (6)	39.46 (5)	52.25 (6)	51.63 (5)	49.8 (5)
Baseline	52.45 (7)	36.11 (6)	51.97 (7)	45.80 (7)	46.6 (6)
DFKI (2)	61.26 (5)	00.00 (7)	59.20 (5)	51.24 (6)	42.9 (7)

Table 3: Performance on Task 1 (Evaluation Phase) – Identity Anaphora (CoNLL Avg. F1)

Team	LIGHT	AMI	PERS.	SWBD.	Avg.
		Eval Br (Gold)			
UTD_NLP	**19.73**	**19.65**	**31.40**	**21.10**	**23.0**
KU_NLP	16.67	15.30	18.79	18.33	17.3
INRIA	9.35	6.00	16.28	7.79	9.9
Baseline	6.35	6.21	13.77	5.39	7.9
		Eval Br (Pred)			
UTD_NLP	**13.98**	**13.33**	**21.92**	**15.26**	**16.1**
KU_NLP	13.46	10.25	12.32	10.99	11.8
Baseline	6.01	4.94	9.34	3.78	6.0

Table 4: Performance on Task 2 (Evaluation Phase) – Bridging Anaphora (Entity F1)

Team	LIGHT	AMI	PERS.	SWBD.	Avg.
		Eval DD (Gold)			
UTD_NLP	**43.44**	**36.91**	**52.09**	**40.44**	**43.2**
		Eval DD (Pred)			
UTD_NLP	**42.70**	**35.35**	**39.64**	**35.43**	**38.3**
DFKI	20.97	17.43	23.76	23.86	21.5
Baseline	12.12	15.75	18.27	13.55	14.9

Table 5: Performance on Task 3 (Evaluation Phase) – Discourse Deixis (CoNLL Avg. F1)

for mention detection. The resulting mention representation, created from the constituent token representations, is then fed to a pointer-network (Vinyals et al., 2015) based coreference resolution model for clustering. They solved the bridging resolution problem using a machine reading comprehension framework, where they constructed a query for each entity of the form – *"What is related of ENTITY?"*. The input of their model is the query and the document (i.e., all utterances of dialogue), and the output is the entity span that is the answer for the query.

DFKI_TalkingRobots (DFKI) put forward two systems as their final submissions for the identity anaphora task. The Workspace Coreference System (WCS) attempts to incrementally cluster mentions using semantic similarity based on embeddings combined with lexical feature heuristics, whereas their Mention-to-Mention (M2M) architecture only focuses on mention pairs to make the decision. WCS and M2M use SpaCy and BiLSTM-CRF based mention detection components, respectively. For discourse deixis, the team deployed a Siamese Network to detect discourse anaphor-antecedent pairs. They only focused on demonstrative pronouns (as anaphors), which they detected using the SpaCy NLP pipeline.

Emory_NLP (Emory) only participated in the identity anaphora task. Their system was adapted from the end-to-end neural coreference resolution model of Joshi et al. (2020). They recognized singletons, encoded speakers for all turns, and leveraged other out-of-domain datasets during training.

INRIA submitted an end-to-end transformer-based model fine-tuned for the bridging resolution task. They formulated the bridging problem as antecedent selection, and leveraged Lee et al. (2018); Joshi et al. (2019)'s architecture to find the correct antecedent.

8 Results and Discussion

In this section, we report the results of all systems submitted for each task and discuss the differences among these approaches.

[22]Team SCIR did not submit a system description paper.

8.1 Task 1 – Identity Anaphora

Task 1 saw the highest interest as five teams submitted a total of 36 runs to the official leaderboard. As discussed earlier, we report the CoNLL Avg. F1 score for each sub-corpus separately.

The results on different sub-corpora are reported in Table 3. All five runs outperform the baseline in terms of the CoNLL Avg. F1 score. The best run on all four sub-corpora was submitted by *lxucs* (the Emory team) achieving around 75% or more CoNLL Avg. F1 on LIGHT, PERSUASION, and SWITCHBOARD, and the rankings across the four datasets remained relatively stable. AMI proved to be the toughest sub-corpus with the highest score being around 64%, which is 10 percentage points below that of SWITCHBOARD. This is in line with the organizers' expectations, as AMI proved the most difficult corpus to annotate, with lots of uncertainty and ambiguity. Also, the conversations in AMI are substantially longer than the other three datasets and hence require systems to consider long-distance relationships between mentions. Despite the differences in absolute performance on each sub-corpus, the best-performing system improved over the baseline by an impressive 30 CoNLL Avg. F1 percentage points.

8.2 Task 2 – Bridging Anaphora

Three teams participated in Task 2 with *INRIA* only participating in the gold mention setting. We report Entity F1 scores for each sub-corpora and calculate rankings based on the mean score across the four datasets.

Table 4 summarizes the performance of each run. For the predicted setting Eval-Br (Pred), where the systems need to take a raw conversation as input during the inference time and perform both markable identification and bridging resolution, *UTD_NLP* performs the best across all four sub-corpora. Although both participating systems perform similarly across SWITCHBOARD, AMI, and LIGHT (10 – 15 Entity F1 points), *UTD_NLP* achieves an unusually high score on the PERSUASION dataset (for this task), reaching an Entity F1 of 21.92 percentage points. We see a similar trend in the gold setting (Table 2), where *UTD_NLP* and *INRIA* score 8–10 absolute percentage points higher on PERSUASION (31.40 and 16.28 respectively) as compared to their scores on the other three datasets. Finally, the performance of the runs in the gold setting is substantially higher than that in the predicted setting for both *UTD_NLP* and *KU_NLP* even though the gold setting does not distinguish between the markables that are relevant for the three tasks in the competition.

8.3 Task 3 – Discourse Deixis

We received 25 runs for Task 3. Two teams (*UTD_NLP*, *DFKI_TalkingRobots*) submitted to the predicted mention setting with *UTD_NLP* achieving performance around 35–42 CoNLL Avg. F1 percentage points on the different sub-corpora, almost doubling the score of the second team. For the gold setting, where we released the gold markables, the system submitted by *UTD_NLP* did not improve their scores substantially on LIGHT, AMI, or SWITCHBOARD from the predicted setting. However, they managed a jump of more than 12 CoNLL Avg. F1 points on PERSUASION. All teams outperform the baseline system on all sub-corpora. The performance of both teams on Task 3 is summarized in Table 5.

8.4 Discussion

In retrospect, organizing this shared task required tackling a few too many issues in a short time, from annotating the data to developing a new scorer to devising fair ways to use the scorer to assess systems, to be able to address all of them in a completely satisfactory way. This is why we decided to run the same task again next year, with new test data but maintaining the same genres and annotation guidelines. The ARRAU 3 data and annotation manual should also be available, addressing some of the concerns raised by the participants.

It would be premature to infer too much about the tasks or the genres on the basis of this first experience, but some interesting issues are already emerging from the analysis papers, such as the complex use of first and second person pronouns in these datasets. We do hope it will be possible to carry out a more extensive analysis of the differences between these dialogue datasets and datasets based on written text and annotated for the same phenomena, such as the RST subcorpus of ARRAU.

We would also like to congratulate all participants for gallantly tackling these relatively new tasks and new datasets yet generally outperforming the baselines, some of which were non-trivial.

9 Conclusion and Future Work

We presented a general overview of the CODI-CRAC 2021 shared task. As the first instance in this series, CODI-CRAC 2021 focused on resolving three types of anaphoric relations in dialogues: identity, bridging references, and discourse deixis. In addition, we described the CODI-CRAC 2021 corpus, which contains sub-corpora from different conversation genres newly annotated for the above-mentioned relations. While the teams were encouraged to create systems with generalizable representations using other out-of-domain state-of-the-art coreference datasets during training, only the best-performing team for the entity coreference track did so. Finally, we included a brief summary of the different approaches used by the participants to tackle different tasks within the shared-task.

For the shared-task's next installment, we plan to release the full annotation guidelines to reduce the ambiguity about annotation principles. Based on suggestions from participating teams (Team *DFKI*), we will introduce separate tracks to fairly evaluate the systems trained on the provided data vs. systems (pre-)trained on additional data, and discuss the possibility of using more fine-grained evaluation metrics to differentially evaluate cases of coreference based on their difficulty levels. (E.g., *a black cat* and *the black cat* are much easier to resolve compared to *a black cat* and *the dark and furry creature*.)

Acknowledgments

We are very grateful to Maris Camilleri and Paloma Carretero Garcia, who annotated the dataset very quickly, and to the Linguistic Data Consortium, who very generously made the ARRAU and SWITCHBOARD data available to the participants to the competition. We would also like to thank Team *DFKI* for their suggestions for the future of the shared task.

Massimo Poesio wishes to thank Sharid Loáiciga, Anja Nedoluzhko, Arndt Riester, Amir Zeldes, and several other participants in the Universal Anaphora initiative for discussions about anaphoric annotation and anaphoric annotation in dialogue in particular. The work of Massimo Poesio and Juntao Yu was funded by the the DALI project, ERC Grant 695662. The annotation was funded in part by DALI, in part by HITS Heidelberg.

References

David Bamman, Olivia Lewke, and Anya Mansoor. 2020. An annotated dataset of coreference in english literature. In *Proc. of LREC*. European Language Resources Association (ELRA), Association for Computational Linguistics (ACL).

Donna Byron. 2002. Resolving pronominal references to abstract entities. In *Proc. of the ACL*, pages 80–87.

Donna Byron and James Allen. 1998. Resolving demonstrative anaphora in the trains-93 corpus. In *Proc. of the Second Colloquium on Discourse, Anaphora and Reference Resolution*. University of Lancaster.

Jean Carletta. 2006. Announcing the AMI meeting corpus. *The ELRA Newsletter*, 11(1):3–5.

Lynn Carlson, Daniel Marcu, and Mary Ellen Okurowski. 2003. Building a discourse-tagged corpus in the framework of rhetorical structure theory. In J. Kuppevelt and R. Smith, editors, *Current Directions in Discourse and Dialogue*, pages 85–112. Kluwer.

Wallace L. Chafe. 1980. *The Pear Stories: Cognitive, Cultural and Linguistic Aspects of Narrative Production*. Ablex, Norwood, NJ.

Herbert H. Clark. 1977. Bridging. In P. N. Johnson-Laird and P.C. Wason, editors, *Thinking: Readings in Cognitive Science*, pages 411–420. Cambridge University Press, London and New York.

Kevin Bretonnel Cohen, Arrick Lanfranchi, Miji Joo-young Choi, Michael Bada, William A. Baumgartner Jr., Natalya Panteleyeva, Karin Verspoor, Martha Palmer, and Lawrence E. Hunter. 2017. Coreference annotation and resolution in the Colorado Richly Annotated Full Text (CRAFT) corpus of biomedical journal articles. *BMC Bioinformatics*, 18(372).

Leyang Cui and Yue Zhang. 2019. Hierarchically-refined label attention network for sequence labeling. In *Proceedings of the 2019 Conference on Empirical Methods in Natural Language Processing and the 9th International Joint Conference on Natural Language Processing (EMNLP-IJCNLP)*, pages 4115–4128.

Miriam Eckert and Michael Strube. 2001. Dialogue acts, synchronising units and anaphora resolution. *Journal of Semantics*.

Carola Eschenbach, Christopher Habel, Michael Herweg, and Klaus Rehkämper. 1989. Remarks on plural anaphora. In *Proceedings of the fourth conference on European chapter of the Association for Computational Linguistics*, pages 161–167. Association for Computational Linguistics.

John J. Godfrey, Edward C. Holliman, and Jane McDaniel. 1992. Switchboard: telephone speech corpus for research and development . acoustics,. In *IEEE International Conference on Speech, and Signal Processing, ICASSP-92*, volume 1, pages 517–520.

Loïc Grobol. 2020. *Coreference resolution for spoken French*. Ph.D. thesis, Université Sorbonne Nouvelle.

John A. Hawkins. 1978. *Definiteness and Indefiniteness*. Croom Helm, London.

Yufang Hou. 2020. Bridging anaphora resolution as question answering. In *Proceedings of the 58th Annual Meeting of the Association for Computational Linguistics*, pages 1428–1438, Online. Association for Computational Linguistics.

Yufang Hou, Katja Markert, and Michael Strube. 2018. Unrestricted bridging resolution. *Computational Linguistics*, 44(2):237–284.

Mandar Joshi, Danqi Chen, Yinhan Liu, Daniel S Weld, Luke Zettlemoyer, and Omer Levy. 2020. Spanbert: Improving pre-training by representing and predicting spans. *Transactions of the Association for Computational Linguistics*, 8:64–77.

Mandar Joshi, Omer Levy, Luke Zettlemoyer, and Daniel Weld. 2019. BERT for coreference resolution: Baselines and analysis. In *Proceedings of the 2019 Conference on Empirical Methods in Natural Language Processing and the 9th International Joint Conference on Natural Language Processing (EMNLP-IJCNLP)*, pages 5803–5808, Hong Kong, China. Association for Computational Linguistics.

Hans Kamp and Uwe Reyle. 1993. *From Discourse to Logic*. D. Reidel, Dordrecht.

Ben Kantor and Amir Globerson. 2019. Coreference resolution with entity equalization. In *Proceedings of the 57th Annual Meeting of the Association for Computational Linguistics*, pages 673–677, Florence, Italy. Association for Computational Linguistics.

Hideo Kobayashi and Vincent Ng. 2020. Bridging resolution: A survey of the state of the art. In *Proceedings of the 28th International Conference on Computational Linguistics*, pages 3708–3721, Barcelona, Spain (Online). International Committee on Computational Linguistics.

Hideo Kobayashi and Vincent Ng. 2021. Bridging resolution: Making sense of the state of the art. In *Proceedings of the 2021 Conference of the North American Chapter of the Association for Computational Linguistics: Human Language Technologies*, pages 1652–1659, Online. Association for Computational Linguistics.

Varada Kolhatkar and Graeme Hirst. 2014. Resolving shell nouns. In *Proc. of EMNLP*, pages 499–510, Doha, Qatar.

Varada Kolhatkar, Adam Roussel, Stefanie Dipper, and Heike Zinsmeister. 2018. Anaphora with non-nominal antecedents in computational linguistics: a Survey. *Computational Linguistics*, 44(3):547–612.

Kenton Lee, Luheng He, Mike Lewis, and Luke Zettlemoyer. 2017. End-to-end neural coreference resolution. In *Proceedings of the 2017 Conference on Empirical Methods in Natural Language Processing*, pages 188–197, Copenhagen, Denmark. Association for Computational Linguistics.

Kenton Lee, Luheng He, and Luke Zettlemoyer. 2018. Higher-order coreference resolution with coarse-to-fine inference. In *Proceedings of the 2018 Conference of the North American Chapter of the Association for Computational Linguistics: Human Language Technologies, Volume 2 (Short Papers)*, pages 687–692.

Xuansong Li, Martha Palmer, Nianwen Xue, Lance Ramshaw, Mohamed Maamouri, Ann Bies, Kathryn Conger, Stephen Grimes, and Stephanie Strassel. 2016. Large multi-lingual, multi-level and multi-genre annotation corpus. In *Proceedings of the Tenth International Conference on Language Resources and Evaluation (LREC'16)*, pages 906–913, Portorož, Slovenia. European Language Resources Association (ELRA).

Quan Liu, Hui Jiang, Andrew Evdokimov, Zhen-Hua Ling, Xiaodan Zhu, Si Wei, and Yu Hu. 2017. Cause-effect knowledge acquisition and neural association model for solving a set of winograd schema problems. In *Proceedings of the Twenty-Sixth International Joint Conference on Artificial Intelligence, IJCAI-17*, pages 2344–2350.

Pengcheng Lu and Massimo Poesio. 2021. Coreference resolution for the biomedical domain: A survey. In *Proc. of the CRAC Workshop*.

Ana Marasović, Leo Born, Juri Opitz, and Anette Frank. 2017. A mention-ranking model for abstract anaphora resolution. In *Proceedings of the 2017 Conference on Empirical Methods in Natural Language Processing*, pages 221–232, Copenhagen, Denmark. Association for Computational Linguistics.

Mitchell P. Marcus, Beatrice Santorini, and Mary Ann Marcinkiewicz. 1993. Building a large annotated corpus of english: the Penn Treebank. *Computational Linguistics*, 19(2):313–330.

Katja Markert, Yufang Hou, and Michael Strube. 2012. Collective classification for fine-grained information status. In *Proc. of the ACL*, Juju island, Korea.

Natalia N. Modjeska. 2003. *Resolving other anaphors*. Ph.D. thesis, University of Edinburgh.

Nafise S. Moosavi and Michael Strube. 2016. A proposal for a link-based entity aware metric. In *Proc. of ACL*, pages 632–642, Berlin.

Mark-Christoph Müller. 2008. *Fully Automatic Resolution of It, This And That in Unrestricted Multy-Party Dialog*. Ph.D. thesis, Universität Tübingen.

Mark-Christoph Müller and Michael Strube. 2006. Multi-level annotation of linguistic data with mmax2. In S. Braun, K. Kohn, and J. Mukherjee, editors, *Corpus Technology and Language Pedagogy. New Resources, New Tools, New Methods*, volume 3 of *English Corpus Linguistics*, pages 197–214. Peter Lang.

Judith Muzerelle, Anaïs Lefeuvre, Emmanuel Schang, Jean-Yves Antoine, Aurore Pelletier, Denis Maurel, Iris Eshkol, and Jeanne Villaneau. 2014. Ancor_centre, a large free spoken french coreference corpus. In *Proc. of LREC*.

Costanza Navarretta. 2000. Abstract anaphora resolution in Danish. In *Proc. of the 1st SIGdial Workshop on Discourse and Dialogue*, pages 56–65. ACL.

Anna Nedoluzhko. 2013. Generic noun phrases and annotation of coreference and bridging relations in the prague dependency treebank. In *Proc. of LAW*, pages 103–111.

Anna Nedoluzhko, Michal Novák, Martin Popel, Zdeněk Žabokrtský, and Daniel Zeman. 2021. Coreference meets universal dependencies – a pilot experiment on harmonizing coreference datasets for 11 languages. ÚFAL Technical Report TR-2021-66, Charles University, Prague.

Malvina Nissim, Shipra Dingare, Jean Carletta, and Mark Steedman. 2004. An annotation scheme for information status in dialogue. In *Proc. of LREC*.

Silviu Paun, Juntao Yu, Nafise Moosavi, and Massimo Poesio. 2021. Scoring coreference chains with split-antecedent anaphors and other entities constructed from a discourse model. Submitted.

Massimo Poesio. 2004. Discourse annotation and semantic annotation in the GNOME corpus. In *Proc. of the ACL Workshop on Discourse Annotation*, pages 72–79, Barcelona.

Massimo Poesio. 2016. Linguistic and cognitive evidence about anaphora. In M. Poesio, R. Stuckardt, and Y. Versley, editors, *Anaphora Resolution: Algorithms, Resources and Applications*, chapter 2. Springer.

Massimo Poesio and Ron Artstein. 2008. Anaphoric annotation in the ARRAU corpus. In *Proc. of LREC*, Marrakesh.

Massimo Poesio, Jon Chamberlain, Udo Kruschwitz, Silviu Paun, Alexandra Uma, and Juntao Yu. 2019. A crowdsourced corpus of multiple judgments and disagreement on anaphoric interpretation. In *Proc. of NAACL*, page 1778–1789, Minneapolis. Association for Computational Linguistics (ACL).

Massimo Poesio, Yulia Grishina, Varada Kolhatkar, Nafise Moosavi, Ina Roesiger, Adam Roussel, Fabian Simonjetz, Alexandra Uma, Olga Uryupina, Juntao Yu, and Heike Zinsmeister. 2018. Anaphora resolution with the ARRAU corpus. In *Proceedings of the First Workshop on Computational Models of Reference, Anaphora and Coreference*, pages 11–22, New Orleans, Louisiana. Association for Computational Linguistics.

Massimo Poesio, Sameer Pradhan, Marta Recasens, Kepa Rodriguez, and Yannick Versley. 2016. Annotated corpora and annotation tools. In M. Poesio, R. Stuckardt, and Y. Versley, editors, *Anaphora Resolution: Algorithms, Resources and Applications*, chapter 4. Springer.

Massimo Poesio and Renata Vieira. 1998. A corpus-based investigation of definite description use. *Computational Linguistics*, 24(2):183–216.

Sameer Pradhan, Xiaoqiang Luo, Marta Recasens, Eduard Hovy, Vincent Ng, and Michael Strube. 2014. Scoring coreference partitions of predicted mentions: A reference implementation. In *Proceedings of the 52nd Annual Meeting of the Association for Computational Linguistics (Volume 2: Short Papers)*, pages 30–35, Baltimore, Maryland. Association for Computational Linguistics.

Sameer Pradhan, Alessandro Moschitti, Nianwen Xue, Olga Uryupina, and Yuchen Zhang. 2012. CoNLL-2012 shared task: Modeling multilingual unrestricted coreference in OntoNotes. In *Proceedings of the Sixteenth Conference on Computational Natural Language Learning (CoNLL 2012)*, Jeju, Korea.

Sameer S. Pradhan, Lance Ramshaw, Ralph Weischedel, Jessica MacBride, and Linnea Micciulla. 2007. Unrestricted coreference: Indentifying entities and events in ontonotes. In *Proc. IEEE International Conference on Semantic Computing (ICSC)*, Irvine, CA.

Ellen F. Prince. 1981. Toward a taxonomy of given-new information. In P. Cole, editor, *Radical Pragmatics*, pages 223–256. Academic Press, New York.

Altaf Rahman and Vincent Ng. 2012. Resolving complex cases of definite pronouns: The Winograd schema challenge. In *Proceedings of the 2012 Joint Conference on Empirical Methods in Natural Language Processing and Computational Natural Language Learning*, pages 777–789, Jeju Island, Korea. Association for Computational Linguistics.

Marta Recasens and Ed Hovy. 2011. Blanc: Implementing the rand index for coreference evaluation. *Natural Language Engineering*.

Marta Recasens and M. Antònia Martí. 2010. AnCora-CO: Coreferentially annotated corpora for Spanish and Catalan. *Language Resources and Evaluation*, 44(4):315–345.

Keisuke Sakaguchi, Ronan Le Bras, Chandra Bhagavatula, and Yejin Choi. 2020. Winogrande: An adversarial winograd schema challenge at scale. *Proceedings of the AAAI Conference on Artificial Intelligence*, 34:8732–8740.

Andreas Stolcke, Klaus Ries, Noah Coccaro, Elizabeth Shriberg, Rebecca Bates, Daniel Jurafsky, Paul Taylor, Rachel Martin, Carol Van-Ess-Dykema, and Marie Meteer. 1997. Dialogue act modeling for automatic tagging and recognition of conversational speech. *Computational Linguistics*, 26(3):339–371.

Jack Urbanek, Angela Fan, Siddharth Karamcheti, Saachi Jain, Emily Dinan, Tim Rocktäschel, Douwe Kiela, Arthur Szlam, Samuel Humeau, and Jason Weston. 2019. Learning to speak and act in a fantasy text adventure game. ArXiv preprint arXiv:1903.03094.

Olga Uryupina, Ron Artstein, Antonella Bristot, Federica Cavicchio, Francesca Delogu, Kepa J. Rodriguez, and Massimo Poesio. 2020. Annotating a broad range of anaphoric phenomena, in a variety of genres: the ARRAU corpus. *Journal of Natural Language Engineering*.

Hardik Vala, Andrew Piper, and Derek Ruths. 2016. The more antecedents, the merrier: Resolving multiantecedent anaphors. In *Proceedings of the 54th Annual Meeting of the Association for Computational Linguistics (Volume 1: Long Papers)*, pages 2287–2296, Berlin, Germany. Association for Computational Linguistics.

Yannick Versley. 2008. Vagueness and referential ambiguity in a large-scale annotated corpus. *Research on Language and Computation*, 6:333–353.

Oriol Vinyals, Meire Fortunato, and Navdeep Jaitly. 2015. Pointer networks. *Advances in Neural Information Processing Systems*, 28:2692–2700.

Xuewei Wang, Weiyan Shi, Richard Kim, Yoojung Oh, Sijia Yang, Jingwen Zhang, and Zhou Yu. 2019. Persuasion for good: Towards a personalized persuasive dialogue system for social good. In *Proc. of ACL*.

Bonnie L. Webber. 1991. Structure and ostension in the interpretation of discourse deixis. *Language and Cognitive Processes*, 6(2):107–135.

Kellie Webster, Marta Recasens, Vera Axelrod, and Jason Baldridge. 2018. Mind the GAP: A balanced corpus of gendered ambiguous pronouns. *Transactions of the Association for Computational Linguistics*, 6:605–617.

Sam Wiseman, Alexander M. Rush, Stuart Shieber, and Jason Weston. 2015. Learning anaphoricity and antecedent ranking features for coreference resolution. In *Proceedings of the 53rd Annual Meeting of the Association for Computational Linguistics and the 7th International Joint Conference on Natural Language Processing (Volume 1: Long Papers)*, pages 1416–1426, Beijing, China. Association for Computational Linguistics.

Liyan Xu and Jinho D Choi. 2020. Revealing the myth of higher-order inference in coreference resolution. In *Proceedings of the 2020 Conference on Empirical Methods in Natural Language Processing (EMNLP)*, pages 8527–8533.

Juntao Yu, Bernd Bohnet, and Massimo Poesio. 2020a. Neural mention detection. In *Proceedings of the 12th Conference on Language Resources and Evaluation (LREC 2020)*.

Juntao Yu, Nafise Sadat Moosavi, Silviu Paun, and Massimo Poesio. 2020b. Free the plural: Unrestricted split-antecedent anaphora resolution. In *Proceedings of the 28th International Conference on Computational Linguistics*, pages 6113–6125, Barcelona, Spain (Online). International Committee on Computational Linguistics.

Juntao Yu, Nafise Sadat Moosavi, Silviu Paun, and Massimo Poesio. 2021. Stay together: A system for single and split-antecedent anaphora resolution. In *Proceedings of the 2021 Conference of the North American Chapter of the Association for Computational Linguistics: Human Language Technologies*. Association for Computational Linguistics.

Juntao Yu and Massimo Poesio. 2020. Multitask learning based neural bridging reference resolution. In *Proceedings of the 28th International Conference on Computational Linguistics*, pages 3534–3546, Barcelona, Spain (Online). International Committee on Computational Linguistics.

Amir Zeldes. 2017. The GUM corpus: Creating multilayer resources in the classroom. *Language Resources and Evaluation*, 51(3):581–612.

Ethan Zhou and Jinho D. Choi. 2018. They exist! introducing plural mentions to coreference resolution and entity linking. In *Proceedings of the 27th International Conference on Computational Linguistics*, pages 24–34, Santa Fe, New Mexico, USA. Association for Computational Linguistics.

Yilun Zhu, Sameer Pradhan, and Amir Zeldes. 2021. OntoGUM: Evaluating contextualized SOTA coreference resolution on 12 more genres. In *Proceedings of the 59th Annual Meeting of the Association for Computational Linguistics and the 11th International Joint Conference on Natural Language Processing (Volume 2: Short Papers)*, pages 461–467, Online. Association for Computational Linguistics.

Neural Anaphora Resolution in Dialogue

Hideo Kobayashi* and **Shengjie Li*** and **Vincent Ng**
Human Language Technology Research Institute
University of Texas at Dallas
Richardson, TX 75083-0688
{hideo,sxl180006,vince}@hlt.utdallas.edu

Abstract

We describe the systems that we developed for the three tracks of the CODI-CRAC 2021 shared task, namely entity coreference resolution, bridging resolution, and discourse deixis resolution. Our team ranked second for entity coreference, first for bridging resolution, and first for discourse deixis resolution.

1 Introduction

The CODI-CRAC 2021 shared task (Khosla et al., 2021), which focuses on anaphora resolution in dialogue, provides three tracks, namely entity coreference resolution, bridging resolution, and discourse deixis/abstract anaphora resolution. While the CRAC 2018 shared task (Poesio et al., 2018) provides the same three tracks, the two shared tasks differ by the genre they focus on: CRAC 2018 focuses primarily on text, whereas CODI-CRAC 2021 focuses exclusively on spoken dialogue.

Not only has entity coreference resolution been an active area of research in the NLP community in the past few decades, but recent years have seen considerable progress on entity coreference because of the development of span-based neural models (Lee et al., 2017, 2018). Compared to entity coreference, bridging resolution and discourse deixis resolution are much less studied, and hence they are arguably the more interesting tracks of this shared task. In particular, a relevant question is: can the successes of span-based models be extended from entity coreference to bridging resolution and discourse deixis resolution?

We participated in all three tracks of the shared task. For bridging and discourse deixis resolution, we submitted results based on both predicted mentions and gold mentions. Given the recent successes of span-based neural entity coreference models, which can learn task-specific representations of text spans, we use them as our starting point for all three tracks. Specifically:

- for entity coreference, we employ a pipeline architecture where we perform mention detection prior to coreference resolution. Our mention detection model is adapted from Xu and Choi's (2020) implementation of Lee et al.'s span-based model. For coreference resolution, we extend Xu and Choi's coreference model by (1) adding a sentence distance feature; (2) modifying the objective function used by the model so that it can learn to output singleton clusters; and (3) introducing non-coreference constraints for the dialogue domain.
- for discourse deixis resolution, we extend Xu and Choi's coreference model by (1) modifying the objective function so that it performs joint mention detection and discourse deixis resolution, and (2) classifying a span as a candidate anaphor or a candidate antecedent and only allowing candidate anaphors to be resolved to candidate antecedents.
- for bridging, we adopt a multi-pass sieve approach, where we use Yu and Poesio's (2020) multi-task learning (MTL) model, which jointly identifies bridging and coreference links, as one of the sieves and design a set of sieves that targets a particular kind of bridging links, namely same-head bridging links.

A brief overview of the approaches we adopted for the three tracks can be found in Table 1.

The rest of the paper is structured as follows. The next three sections describe our work for the three tracks, namely entity coreference (Section 2), discourse deixis (Section 3), and bridging (Section 4). Within each section, we describe our approach, our official results, and some quantitative analysis. We present our conclusions in Section 5.

*Equal contribution

Proceedings of the CODI-CRAC 2021 Shared Task on Anaphora, Bridging, and Discourse Deixis in Dialogue, pages 16–31
Punta Cana, Dominican Republic, November 10, 2021.

Entity Coreference Resolution	
Baseline	Xu and Choi's (2020) implementation of Lee et al.'s (2018) span-based model
Learning framework	A pipeline architecture consisting of a mention detection component and an entity coreference component. The coreference component extends the baseline by (1) adding a sentence distance feature; (2) modifying the objective so that it can output singleton clusters; and (3) enforcing dialogue-specific non-coreference constraints.
Markable identification	A mention detection model (adapted from Xu and Choi's coreference model) is trained to identify the entity mentions.
Training data	90% of the official training and dev sets
Development data	The remaining 10% of the official training and dev sets
Discourse Deixis Resolution	
Baseline	Xu and Choi's (2020) implementation of Lee et al.'s (2018) span-based model
Learning framework	Joint mention detection and coreference resolution enabled by modifying the objective function in Xu and Choi's model. For mention detection, each span is classified as a candidate anaphor, a candidate antecedent, or a non-mention. For deixis resolution, only candidate anaphors will be resolved, and they can only be resolved to candidate antecedents. The model developed for the Predicted setting differs from those developed for the Gold setting in terms of the heuristics used to determine which spans are candidate anaphors.
Markable identification	Obtained as part of joint mention detection and deixis resolution
Training data	Two setups: (1) use all official training and dev sets, leaving out the official dev set of the target domain; and (2) use 90% of the official training and dev sets.
Development data	Two setups: (1) use only the dev set for the target domain; and (2) use the remaining 10% of the official training and dev sets.
Bridging Resolution	
Baseline	Yu and Poesio's (2020) multi-task learning (MTL) model
Learning framework	A multi-pass sieve approach in which we use the MTL model as one of the sieves and design a set of learning-based sieves (trained using SVMs) that targets same-head bridging links. In the Gold setting, an anaphor detection model (adapted from the MTL model) is additionally trained to first identify the bridging anaphors from the gold mentions, and the resulting anaphors are then resolved by the sieves.
Markable identification	The MTL-based sieve learns markable boundaries whereas the SVM-based sieves use extracted NPs. In the gold setting, an anaphor detection model is also trained to identify bridging anaphors.
Training data	The MTL-based sieve is pretrained using ARRAU RST (train, dev, and test), Gnome, and Pear, and then fine-tuned using Trains 91, Trains 93, LIGHT (dev), AMI (dev), Persuasion (dev), and Switchboard (dev). The SVM-based sieves are trained using LIGHT (dev), AMI (dev), Persuasion (dev), and Switchboard (dev).
Development data	Trains 91, Trains 93, LIGHT (dev), AMI (dev), Persuasion (dev), and Switchboard (dev)

Table 1: Overview of the approaches we adopted for the three tracks.

2 Entity Coreference Resolution

To build our entity coreference system, we use as our baseline *coref-hoi*, which is Xu and Choi's (2020) coreference model. Below we first give an overview of coref-hoi and then describe our extensions to it.

2.1 Baseline: An Overview

Xu and Choi (2020) reimplement the end-to-end coreference model introduced by Lee et al. (2018). For each mention span x, the model learns a distribution $P(y)$ over possible antecedents $y \in \mathcal{Y}(x)$:

$$P(y) = \frac{e^{s(x,y)}}{\sum_{y' \in \mathcal{Y}(x)} e^{s(x,y')}}$$

where $s(x, y)$ is a pairwise score that incorporates three factors: (1) $s_m(x)$, a score that indicates how likely span x is a mention; (2) $s_m(y)$, a score that indicates how likely span y is a mention; and (3) $s_c(x, y)$, a score that indicates how likely spans x and y refer to the same entity:

$$\begin{aligned} s(x,y) &= s_m(x) + s_m(y) + s_c(x,y) \\ s_m(x) &= \texttt{FFNN}_m(g_x) \\ s_c(x,y) &= \texttt{FFNN}_c(g_x, g_y, \phi(x,y)) \end{aligned}$$

where g_x and g_y denote the span embeddings of x and y, $\texttt{FFNN}(\cdot)$ denotes a feedforward neural network, and $\phi(x, y)$ encodes the speaker information from the metadata as well as the segment distance between the two spans.[1]

Xu and Choi describe several higher-order inference (HOI) approaches that can be added to the basic end-to-end coreference model. We do not employ any HOI approaches because (1) Xu and Choi found that when using SpanBERT as the encoder, the impact of HOI is negative to marginal;

[1] Each document is split into independent segments with a maximum size of 512 tokens.

(2) in preliminary experiments, we found that better results could be achieved without HOI.

2.2 Approaches

Next, we describe two approaches to entity coreference resolution.

2.2.1 End-to-End Approach

We extend the aforementioned coref-hoi model with the following modifications.

Sentence distance We hypothesize that recency plays a role in resolution, so we add the sentence distance between two spans into $\phi(x, y)$ as another feature.

Type prediction Since the official scorer penalizes a mention e in the system output if e is not a referring entity mention, we follow our previous work (Lu and Ng, 2020) and extend the model so that it can predict the type of each span, where the type can be NULL (for non-entity spans), REFERRING (for referring entity mentions), or NON-REFERRING (for non-referring entity mentions), and subsequently remove from the output any spans that are predicted to be NULL or NON-REFERRING.

Type prediction proceeds as follows. For each span x, we pass its representation g_x to a FFNN, which outputs a vector ot_x of dimension 3. Each element $ot_x(t)$ of ot_x denotes the likelihood that span x belongs to type t. The span type t_x is then determined by the type with the highest score.

$$ot_x = \texttt{FFNN}_t(g_x)$$
$$t_x = \arg\max_t ot_x(t)$$

We compute the cross-entropy loss using ot_x. This type loss is then multiplied by a type loss coefficient and added to the loss function of coref-hoi.

Span constraint While span-based models typically impose length constraints on spans owing to computational tractability, we impose an additional constraint on spans based on our observation of the training and development data: a span cannot cover more than one speaker's utterances.

Resolution constraints We propose a consistency constraint on resolution that will be used in both training and inference. This constraint prevents two spans x and y that both start with a pronoun from being posited as coreferent if they are *conflicting*. More specifically, we check whether each of these spans belongs to one of the eight groups defined in Table 2, and if yes, then they cannot be coreferent if any of the following conditions is satisfied:

Group	Definition
1	span is or starts with: I, me, my, or mine
2	span is or starts with: you, your, or yours
3	span is or starts with: he, him, or his
4	span is or starts with: she or her
5	span is: their
6	span is: it or its
7	span is: here
8	span is: there

Table 2: The eight groups of spans on which the consistency constraints for entity coreference resolution are defined.

- Both spans (1) belong to the first four groups but are not in the same group and (2) have the same speaker.
- Both spans (1) belong to the first two groups and are in the same group and (2) have different speakers.

In addition, we impose two constraints on the resolution of *here* and *there*. Specifically, *here* cannot be coreferent with *my*, *your*, *his*, and *her* as well as a span that belongs to group 5, group 6 or group 8; and *there* cannot be coreferent with *my*, *your*, *his*, and *her*, as well as a span that belongs to group 5, group 6, or group 7. These conditions are derived based on our inspection of the training and development sets.

2.2.2 Pipeline Approach

In the end-to-end approach, type prediction is learned jointly with entity coreference resolution. In this subsection, we experiment with a *pipeline* approach where type prediction is performed prior to coreference resolution.

Step 1: Type prediction. The goal of this step is to identify the entity mentions (including both referring and non-referring mentions) from all the spans in the input text. Specifically, the model classifies each span as one of two types, NULL and ENTITY, where ENTITY covers both referring and non-referring mentions and NULL covers the remaining spans (i.e., the spans that do not correspond to entities). To perform this step, we train coref-hoi (with the extensions described in Section 2.2.1), but tune the type loss coefficient so that the model focuses on type prediction rather than coreference resolution.

Step 2: Coreference resolution. The goal of this step is to perform coreference resolution on all and only those spans that are classified as ENTITY in the first step. To perform this step, we train coref-hoi (with the extensions described in Section 2.2.1) on only the gold mentions in the input documents, tuning the type loss coefficient so that the model focuses on type prediction rather than coreference resolution.

2.3 Evaluation

We evaluate the pipeline approach and the end-to-end approach. In addition, to gain insights into the contribution of the constraints on performance, we evaluate a variant of the end-to-end approach without using the span and consistency constraints.

2.3.1 Training and Development Sets

We experiment with two different methods for partitioning the available annotated data into a training set and a development set.

`T1`: In the first method, we use all official training datasets and all official development sets other than the one to be evaluated on as our training data. The remaining official development data is then used for development. For example, when we train the model for evaluation on LIGHT_test, we use all official training data plus AMI_dev, Persuasion_dev, and Switchboard_dev as the training set, and use LIGHT_dev as the development set.

`T2`: In the second method, we merge all official training sets and all official development sets into one dataset. We then use 90% of this dataset for training and the remaining 10% for development.

2.3.2 Implementation Details

In all approaches we use $\text{SpanBERT}_{\text{Large}}$ as the encoder. Documents are split into independent segments with a maximum of 512 word pieces, and two segments from each document are used in training. We use different learning rates for BERT-parameters and task-parameters (1×10^{-5} and 3×10^{-4} respectively). Models are trained for 24 epochs with dropout rate 0.3. The type loss coefficient is found using grid search. See Appendix A for the optimal hyperparameters chosen for each approach.

For the end-to-end approach (and its "no constraint" variant), we use method `T1` to create the training and development sets. The model considers all spans that have a width of less than 70 *and* satisfy the span constraint mentioned in Section 2.2.1 (with the exception of the AMI dataset, where we set the maximum span width to 25 during inference because of memory limitations). To maintain computational tractability, the model selects for each document $0.4 \times \# \; of \; words \; in \; the \; document$ spans as top spans for further processing. Specifically, for each top span, the model selects 50 candidate antecedents for resolution purposes (with the exception of the AMI dataset, where we use only 12 candidate antecedents during inference because of memory limitations). The only parameter we tune is the type loss coefficient. Specifically, we search for the coefficient out of {0, 0.2, 0.4, 0.5, 0.6, 0.8, 1, 2}, and apply the model with the highest CoNLL score on the development set to the test sets.

For the pipeline approach, we use method `T2` to create the training and development sets. We set the parameters of the type prediction model to be the same as those used in the end-to-end approach. Specifically, it considers all spans with a width of less than 70 (with the exception of the AMI dataset, where we set the maximum span width to 25 during inference because of memory limitations), and selects $0.4 \times \# \; of \; words \; in \; the \; document$ spans as top spans for further processing. For each top span, the model selects 50 candidate antecedents for resolution purposes (with the exception of the AMI dataset, where we use only 12 candidate antecedents because of memory limitations). The only parameter we tune is the type loss coefficient. Specifically, we search for the coefficient out of {1, 2, 5, 10, 100, 200, 500}, and use the model with the highest entity mention recall on the development set to predict entity mentions in the test sets. Like in the type prediction model, the only parameter we tune in the coreference model is the type loss coefficient. Specifically, we search for the coefficient out of {0, 0.2, 0.4, 0.5, 0.6, 0.8, 1, 2}, and apply the model with the highest CoNLL score on the development set to the test sets.

2.3.3 Results and Discussion

Results of the three approaches (Pipeline, End-to-End and its "no constraint" variant) on the four test sets (LIGHT, AMI, Persuasion, and Switchboard) are shown in Table 3. Specifically, in the "F" columns we show the CoNLL score. To better understand the extent to which the singleton clusters and the non-singleton clusters contribute to overall performance, we report two additional scores. The "ns-F" columns show the CoNLL scores obtained

	LIGHT			AMI			Persuasion			Switchboard		
	F	ns. F	s-F	F	ns-F	s-F	F	ns-F	s-F	F	ns-F	s-F
End-to-End (no constraints)	74.8	55.7	31.5	60.1	43.3	28.0	70.4	51.3	32.2	68.3	51.9	29.1
End-to-End	76.3	57.6	31.5	58.2	43.2	26.1	72.6	54.6	31.8	66.3	51.1	28.2
Pipeline	79.6	60.2	32.9	57.4	42.9	25.2	77.5	56.5	35.3	72.6	53.7	32.5

Table 3: Entity coreference resolution: results of the three approaches on the test sets. For each approach, we show three scores: the unmodified CoNLL score (F), the CoNLL score obtained after removing all the singleton clusters from the system output (ns-F), and the CoNLL score obtained by keeping only the singleton clusters in the system output (s-F).

	MUC			B^3			$CEAF_e$			
	P	R	F	P	R	F	P	R	F	CoNLL
LIGHT	87.8	89.1	88.5	72.7	82.6	77.3	74.6	71.2	72.9	79.6
AMI	66.7	65.5	66.0	48.5	58.3	53.0	59.0	48.3	53.1	57.4
Persuasion	78.7	87.8	83.0	76.6	80.4	78.5	76.4	66.4	71.0	77.5
Switchboard	77.5	79.5	78.5	70.7	74.3	72.4	70.7	63.7	67.0	72.6

Table 4: Entity coreference resolution: official results on the test sets (obtained using the Pipeline approach).

	LIGHT			AMI			Persuasion			Switchboard		
	P	R	F	P	R	F	P	R	F	P	R	F
End-to-End (no constraints)	90.2	88.8	89.5	87.9	81.1	84.4	90.1	87.3	88.7	87.8	82.2	84.9
End-to-End	90.3	88.6	89.5	88.6	76.6	82.2	90.4	86.1	88.2	88.6	79.8	84.0
Pipeline	92.3	91.6	92.0	86.6	78.6	82.4	91.3	89.7	90.5	89.2	86.1	87.6

Table 5: Entity coreference resolution: mention extraction results on the test sets.

by removing the singleton clusters from the output prior to scoring, meaning that the scorers are applied to score only the non-singleton clusters. Similarly, the "s-F" columns show the CoNLL scores obtained by removing the non-singleton clusters from the output prior to scoring, effectively allowing the scorers to score only the singleton clusters.

As we can see, in terms of CoNLL F-score, on LIGHT and Persuasion, Pipeline outperforms the End-to-End, which in turn outperforms its "no constraint" counterpart. A closer look at these results reveals that Pipeline outperforms the other models w.r.t. the identification of both singleton and non-singleton clusters. On Switchboard, Pipeline still offers the best performance, but the use of constraints hurts performance: results on both singleton and non-singleton cluster identification deteriorate. Finally, on AMI we see a completely different trend: the "no constraint" variant offers the best performance while Pipeline performs the worst. While this is somewhat unexpected, recall that Pipeline is trained using setup `T2` while the other models are trained using setup `T1`. We hypothesize that (1) our constraints may not be as universally applicable as we expect, and (2) the distribution of the AMI test set is more similar to the development set in `T1` than that in `T2`, thus allowing better models to be selected.[2] Additional experiments are needed to determine the reason.

Our official test results, expressed in terms of MUC, B^3, and $CEAF_e$ precision (P), recall (R), and F-score (F), are shown in Table 4. While Pipeline underperforms the "no constraint" variant on the AMI test set, our official test set results are all obtained using the Pipeline approach. The reason is that the AMI test set was only released a few days prior to submission, and we did not have enough time to do a systematic comparison of the three models on the AMI test set.

2.3.4 Additional Analysis

Table 5 expresses mention detection results in terms of P, R, and F. Note that (1) these are results obtained on *referring* mentions only; and (2) we consider an entity mention correctly detected if it has an exact match with a gold referring mention in terms of boundary. Comparing the results in Tables 3 and 5, we can see that there is a perfect

[2]We did not have enough time prior to submission to obtain results of all three models using both `T1` and `T2`.

correlation between mention detection results and entity coreference results. These results corroborate results in previous shared tasks on coreference that mention detection plays a crucial role in entity coreference performance and that improving mention detection will likely lead to further improvements in coreference performance.

3 Discourse Deixis Resolution

We cast discourse deixis resolution as identity anaphora resolution. This allows us to continue to use the Xu and Choi (2020) entity coreference model as the baseline. The shared task divides the evaluation of discourse deixis resolution into two phases: (1) the Predicted phase, where a system needs to first identify all of the entity mentions that likely correspond to anaphors and antecedents, then perform discourse deixis resolution on the predicted mentions; and (2) the Gold phase, which is essentially the same as the Predicted phase except that the mentions corresponding to anaphors are to be extracted from the given gold mentions. Below we first describe the system we developed for the Predicted phase and then show how the system we used for the Gold phase differs from the one we used for the Predicted phase. As we will see shortly, our models for both phases perform joint mention extraction and discourse deixis resolution.

3.1 Predicted Phase

As mentioned above, we extend Xu and Choi's (2020) entity coreference model with the following additions, many of which are similar to those we used for entity coreference resolution.

Sentence distance We hypothesize that recency plays a role in resolution, so we add the sentence distance between two spans as a feature.

Type prediction Since the official scorer penalizes a mention e in the system output if e is neither a gold anaphor nor a gold antecedent, we extend the model so that it can predict the type of each span, where the possible types are NULL, ANAPHOR, or ANTECEDENT, and subsequently remove from the output any spans that are predicted to be NULL. For each span x, we predict its type as follows. First, we pass its representation g_x to a FFNN, which outputs a vector ot_x of length 3. Each element $ot_x(t)$ of ot_x denotes the likelihood that span x belongs to type t. The span type t_x is then determined by the type with the highest score.

$$ot_x = \texttt{FFNN}_t(g_x)$$
$$t_x = \arg\max_t ot_x(t)$$

We compute the cross-entropy loss using ot_x. This type loss is then multiplied by a type loss coefficient and added to the loss function of Xu and Choi's model.

Span constraint We enforce the same span constraint that we used for entity coreference, retaining spans in which at most one speaker is involved and whose width is less than 70.

Resolution constraint We enforce a hard constraint on resolution that will be used in both training and inference: only spans corresponding to candidate anaphors can be resolved, and only spans corresponding to candidate antecedents can be chosen as antecedents. We consider a span as a candidate anaphor if it ever appears as an anaphor in the training data, and anything else are considered candidate antecedents.[3]

3.2 Gold Phase

The system we developed for the Gold phase is the same as the one for the Predicted phase except that we modify the span constraint and the resolution constraint, as described below.

Span constraint We retain a span if it corresponds to consecutive sentences that involve only one speaker and is less than 150 words because it is likely to be a candidate antecedent.[4] We also retain a span if it is likely to be a anaphor. Here, we experiment with two heuristics for identifying likely anaphors. Heuristic `CA1` considers any span that corresponds to a gold mention as an anaphor, and Heuristic `CA2` considers any gold mention span that has appeared in the training data as an anaphor.

Resolution constraint We enforce a hard constraint on resolution that will be used in both training and inference: only spans classified in the type prediction step as ANAPHOR can be resolved, and only spans classified in the type prediction step as ANTECEDENT can be selected as antecedents.

[3]We could use the output of type prediction to determine whether a span should be considered as a candidate anaphor or a candidate antecedent, but we did not have time to consider this option during the Predicted phase. We did, however, experiment with this option during the Gold phase.

[4]We use a maximum span width of 150 in the Gold phase because the longest antecedent in the training set is at most 150 words. However, we only used a span width of 70 in the Predicted phase because of memory limitations.

	LIGHT			AMI			Persuasion			Switchboard		
	F	ns-F	s-F	F	ns-F	s-F	F	ns-F	s-F	F	ns-F	s-F
Predicted	**42.7**	47.0	2.2	**35.4**	37.9	2.6	**39.6**	42.1	1.0	**35.4**	39.1	2.0
Gold:T1,CA1,RC+	41.9	43.3	7.2	33.9	32.5	7.5	45.6	45.6	3.8	38.8	36.8	7.4
Gold:T1,CA2,RC+	39.8	40.2	7.3	35.3	34.0	6.4	46.9	47.3	3.2	**40.4**	36.6	9.5
Gold:T1,CA1,RC-	**43.4**	43.9	7.7	31.7	30.5	6.4	46.3	46.2	4.8	40.2	37.2	9.5
Gold:T2,CA1,RC+	38.4	39.8	6.6	**36.9**	35.2	8.4	51.7	53.0	3.0	39.6	36.8	9.4
Gold:T2,CA2,RC+	35.9	34.7	7.8	32.0	28.1	8.6	**52.1**	52.0	4.2	40.2	38.0	8.5
Gold:T2,CA1,RC-	41.6	43.3	6.2	34.7	32.8	5.7	51.2	52.1	3.2	37.9	34.7	8.2

Table 6: Discourse deixis resolution: results of different models on the test sets. For each model, we report three scores: the unmodified CoNLL score (F), the CoNLL score obtained after removing all the singleton clusters from the system output (ns-F), and the CoNLL score obtained by keeping only the singleton clusters in the system output (s-F). The boldfaced scores are our scores on the leaderboard.

3.3 Evaluation

We evaluate the models developed for both the Predicted phase and the Gold phase.

3.3.1 Implementation Details

For all models we use $\text{SpanBERT}_{\text{Large}}$ as the encoder. Documents are split into independent segments with a maximum of 512 word pieces, and two segments from each document are used in training. We use different learning rates for BERT-parameters and task-parameters (1×10^{-5} and 3×10^{-4} respectively). Models are trained for 24 epochs with dropout rate 0.3. The type loss coefficient is found using grid search on the test set. See Appendix A for the optimal hyperparameters chosen for each model.

For the Predicted phase, we use method `T1` to create the training and development sets. As in entity coreference, for efficiency reasons the model selects $0.4 \times \# \, of \; words \; in \; the \; document$ spans as top spans for further processing. For each top span, the model selects 50 candidate antecedents for resolution purposes (with the exception of the AMI dataset, where we use only 17 candidate antecedents during inference because of memory limitations).

For the Gold phase, we experiment with six variants. These variants differ along three dimensions: (1) whether `T1` or `T2` is used for partitioning the available annotated data into training and development sets; (2) whether `CA1` or `CA2` is used as the heuristic for identifying likely anaphors; and (3) whether the resolution constraint is used (`RC+`) or not used (`RC-`).

3.3.2 Results and Discussion

Table 6 shows the results of the model used in the Predicted phase as well as the six model variants used in the Gold phase on the test sets. Similar to Table 3, we report three scores for each model: the "F" columns show the CoNLL F-scores; the "ns-F" columns show the CoNLL F-scores obtained by removing the singleton clusters from the system output prior to scoring; and the "s-F" columns show the CoNLL F-scores obtained by removing the non-singleton clusters from the system output prior to scoring. Note that discourse deixis resolution is being viewed as a generalized case of event coreference resolution, and hence the scorer that is used to score entity coreference chains can be used to produce CoNLL F-scores for the output of a discourse deixis resolver.

Our official results for discourse deixis resolution are the boldfaced results in Table 6. Specifically, for the Predicted phase, we submitted the results corresponding to the highest CoNLL score in the first row, and for the Gold phase, we submitted the result of the model variant corresponding to the highest CoNLL score for each test set. The complete set of official results for both phases, which includes the scores obtained via each scorer, is shown in Table 7.

A few points deserve mention. First, while we opted to retain both singleton clusters and non-singleton clusters in the system output, removing the singleton clusters in the Predicted phase can substantially improve performance on all test sets. The reason could be attributed to the fact that singleton cluster identification results are very poor in the Predicted phase, but additional experiments are needed to determine the reason. In contrast, removing singleton clusters from the output in the Gold phase yields worse results in many cases. This could be attributed to the fact that single cluster identification is better in the Gold phase than the Predicted phase, but again additional experiments

	MUC			B^3			$CEAF_e$			
	P	R	F	P	R	F	P	R	F	CoNLL
	Predicted									
Light	44.6	31.2	36.8	56.2	37	44.6	55.3	40.5	46.7	42.7
AMI	45.5	21.2	28.9	52.4	29.5	37.8	44.9	35.1	39.4	35.4
Persuasion	45.5	20.3	28.1	64.9	30.2	41.2	61	41.8	49.6	39.6
Switchboard	35.2	21.3	26.5	52.3	30.4	38.5	50.5	34.9	41.3	35.4
	Gold									
Light	49.0	30.0	37.2	56.3	39.1	46.2	51.7	42.9	46.9	43.4
AMI	44.6	21.2	28.7	49.7	34.6	40.8	39.6	43.0	41.2	36.9
Persuasion	53.3	45.5	49.1	54.9	55.7	55.3	46.0	59.3	51.8	52.1
Switchboard	39.4	31.2	34.8	41.6	48.5	44.8	33.7	55.0	41.8	40.4

Table 7: Discourse deixis resolution: official results on the test sets.

		Light			AMI			Persuasion			Switchboard		
		P	R	F	P	R	F	P	R	F	P	R	F
Anaphor	Predicted	–	73.8	–	–	64.4	–	–	65.9	–	–	71.1	–
	Gold_Best	65.0	65.0	65.0	57.9	61.9	59.8	73.6	77.2	75.4	64.8	74.9	69.5
Antecedent	Predicted	–	27.7	–	–	20.5	–	–	21.2	–	–	21.5	–
	Gold_Best	59.7	33.0	42.5	49.5	32.3	39.1	52.4	58.9	55.5	38.2	52.4	44.2

Table 8: Discourse deixis resolution: mention extraction results on the test sets.

are needed. Second, while all model variants in the Gold phase outperform the model in the Predicted phase on Persuasion and Switchboard, the same is not true on LIGHT and AMI. Specifically, the best models in the Gold phase on these two test sets perform only slightly better than the model in the Predicted phase, and there are many model variants in the Gold phase that underperform the model in the Predicted phase. Finally, the best results for different test sets in the Gold phase are achieved by different model variants. In fact, varying just one of the three dimensions can already trigger non-trivial changes to model performance. Additional experiments are needed to determine the reason.

3.3.3 Additional Analysis

In Table 8, we report the mention extraction results of our officially best models for the Predicted phase and the Gold phase, including both the anaphor extraction results and the antecedent extraction results. Since the best results for different test sets in the Gold phase are achieved by different models, for ease of exposition we refer to them collectively as `Gold_Best`. As in entity coreference, we consider a mention correctly detected in discourse deixis resolution if and only if it has an exact match with a gold mention in terms of boundary.

Two points deserve mention. First, recall from Table 6 that while `Gold_Best` achieves better resolution results than `Predicted` on all four test sets, the differences are substantial on Persuasion and Switchboard but fairly small on LIGHT and AMI. The mention detection results in Table 8 can partially explain why. On Persuasion and Switchboard, `Gold_Best` outperforms `Predicted` for both anaphor detection and antecedent detection. However, on LIGHT and AMI, while `Gold_Best` outperforms `Predicted` for antecedent detection, the reverse is true for anaphor detection. The fact that `Gold_Best` does not consistently outperform `Predicted` for anaphor detection provides suggestive evidence that the Gold setting is not necessarily easier than the Predicted setting for discourse deixis resolution.

Second, `Gold_Best` substantially outperforms `Predicted` for antecedent detection on all four test sets. Two factors could account for this large difference: (1) the maximum span width of `Gold_Best` is a lot larger than that of `Predicted` (150 vs. 70), (2) the candidate antecedents of `Predicted` contain a lot of invalid spans (e.g., a span may start in the middle of a sentence and ends in the middle of another sentence), while the candidate antecedents of `Gold_Best` are restricted to be sentences.

To gain additional insights into the test sets and `Gold_Best`'s performances on them, we show in Table 9 (1) the top five most frequent anaphors in

LIGHT			AMI			Persuasion			Switchboard		
Anaphor	%	F	Anaphor	%	F	Anaphor	%	F	Anaphor	%	F
that	47.5	61.2	that	77.1	42.9	that	64.2	61.8	that	73.8	50.1
it	21.2	40.3	it	8.5	0.0	it	17.9	43.7	it	17.5	15.1
this	11.2	33.5	which	5.9	44.0	this	6.5	64.7	this	1.5	29.8
these terms	1.2	0.0	this	3.4	15.0	the same	3.3	26.1	which	1.1	41.7
more	1.2	0.0	similar effect	0.8	0.0	my research	0.8	0.0	that way	1.1	36.1

Table 9: Discourse deixis resolution: Gold_Best's CoNLL scores on the top five most frequently occurring anaphors.

each test set; (2) the percentage of anaphors that belong to each of the top five anaphors; and (3) `Gold_Best`'s performance on each top anaphor. To measure `Gold_Best`'s performance on each top anaphor, we retain all and only those clusters containing the anaphor in both the gold partition and the system partition and apply the scorer to the resulting partitions.

A few points deserve mention. First, for all test sets, more than 80% of the anaphors are one of the top five most frequently occurring anaphors. As can be seen, "that" and "it" are the most frequent anaphors in all test sets, followed by "this" and "which". As for resolution of the most frequent anaphors, the results for "that" are consistently among the best, and the same can be said for "which". However, the resolution results of "this" and "it" are comparatively less consistent across datasets. For example, the resolution of "it" appears to be much better on LIGHT and Persuasion than on AMI and Switchboard.

4 Bridging Resolution

The shared task divides the evaluation of bridging anaphora resolution into two phases: (1) the Predicted phase, where a system needs to first identify all of the entity mentions that likely correspond to anaphors and antecedents, then perform bridging resolution on the predicted mentions; and (2) the Gold phase, which is essentially the same as the Predicted phase except that bridging resolution is performed on the given gold mentions. Below we describe our approach and our official test results.

4.1 Approach

We employ a multi-pass sieve approach to bridging resolution. Our decision to employ a sieve-based approach is motivated in part by its successful application to bridging resolution in our previous work (Kobayashi and Ng, 2021), where we achieved state-of-the-art results by applying a rule-based sieve followed by a learning-based sieve.

The multi-pass sieve approach to entity coreference resolution, which was originally proposed by members of the Stanford NLP Group (Raghunathan et al., 2010), received a lot of attention in the coreference research community after their team won the CoNLL 2011 shared task on Unrestricted Coreference Resolution (Lee et al., 2011). Briefly, a *sieve* is composed of one or more heuristic rules. When applied to entity coreference resolution, each rule extracts a coreference relation between two mentions based on one or more conditions. For example, one rule in Stanford's discourse processing sieve posits two mentions as coreferent if they are both pronouns and are produced by the same speaker. Sieves are ordered by their precision, with the most precise sieve appearing first. To resolve a set of mentions in a document, the resolver makes multiple passes over them: in the i-th pass, it attempts to use only the rules in the i-th sieve to find an antecedent for each mention m_k. Specifically, when searching for an antecedent for m_k, its candidate antecedents are visited in an order determined by their positions in the associated parse tree (Haghighi and Klein, 2009). The partial clustering of the mentions created in the i-th pass is then passed to the $i+1$-th pass. Hence, later passes can exploit the information computed by previous passes, but a coreference link established earlier cannot be removed later.

Our sieve-based approach to bridging resolution differs from the conventional approach described above in two key aspects. First, rather than order the sieves by precision, we order them so that they collectively achieve the best performance on the test sets. Second, later sieves only attempt to resolve mentions that have not been resolved by earlier sieves (i.e., earlier decisions will not be overridden), but otherwise do not exploit the information computed by earlier sieves. Below we first present our sieves and then describe how we perform mention extraction.

4.1.1 Sieves

We employ five learning-based sieves, including one neural sieve and four "same head" sieves.

4.1.1.1 Neural Sieve

Our neural sieve uses Yu and Poesio's (2020) multi-task learning (MTL) based neural bridging resolver, which has achieved state-of-the-art results on standard evaluation corpora for bridging resolution.[5] Yu and Poesio presented two extensions to Kantor and Globerson's (2019) span-based neural entity coreference model. First, they provided gold mentions as input to the model, meaning that the model needs to learn the span representations but not the span boundaries. Second, they proposed to train the model to perform coreference and bridging in a MTL framework, where the span representation layer is shared by the two tasks so that information learned from one task can be utilized when learning the other task. Unlike feature-based approaches, where feature engineering plays a critical role in performance, this model employs only two features, the length of a mention and the mention-pair distance. To adapt the model to the dialogue domain, we have also added a feature that encodes the turn distance between mentions, where a turn is defined as a set of contiguous sentences by the same speaker.

In preliminary experiments with the MTL model, we found that resolution recall and precision can sometimes be fairly imbalanced. We hypothesize that having more balanced recall and precision numbers could result in better resolution F-score. To make recall-precision tradeoffs, we tune the *dummy score*, which is a mention-pair score assigned by the MTL model to the dummy candidate antecedent of a candidate anaphor and set to 0 by default. To understand why tuning the dummy score allows us to make resolution recall-precision tradeoffs, recall that the score reflects how likely the corresponding candidate antecedent will be chosen as the antecedent for the candidate anaphor under consideration. Hence, a higher dummy score makes it more likely for the anaphoric candidate to be resolved to the dummy antecedent, thereby potentially reducing recall and possibly improving precision. In contrast, a lower dummy score makes it less likely for the anaphoric candidate to be resolved to the dummy antecedent, thereby potentially reducing precision and improving recall.

4.1.1.2 Same-Head Sieves

Next, we design four sieves, all of which focus on establishing bridging links between two mentions that have the same head lemma. We therefore refer to them as *same-head* sieves. We focus on same-head sieves as opposed to different-head sieves because the former are arguably less challenging to design than the latter, especially in the Predicted setting where no gold mentions are given.

Each sieve operates by combining a *mention-pair model* (Soon et al., 2001; Ng and Cardie, 2002), which in our case is a binary classifier that determines whether two mentions having the same head are involved in a bridging relation, with a *closest-first single-link clustering* algorithm, which selects as the antecedent of an anaphoric candidate the closest preceding mention that is classified as its bridging antecedent. Motivated in part by the same-head bridging resolution rules developed by Rösiger (2018), we divide the same-head bridging links into four groups based on whether the anaphor, m_i, is singular or plural and whether the candidate antecedent, m_j, is singular or plural, and create one sieve for each group of bridging links. More specifically, the four sieves are: singular-singular (both mentions are singular), singular-plural (m_i is singular and m_j is plural), plural-singular (m_i is plural and m_j is singular), and plural-plural (both mentions are plural).

To train the mention-pair models, we use the SVM learner implemented in the SVM^{light} software package (Joachims, 1998). The training instances for a sieve include those that (1) correspond to same-head pairs and (2) match the singularity/plurality conditions on the anaphor and the candidate antecedents for the sieve under consideration. For instance, the training instances for the singular-singular sieve include only those training instances for which the mentions have the same head and are both singular. Positive training instances are created by pairing each anaphoric candidate with a gold antecedent or preceding mentions that are coreferent with the gold antecedent, following Yu and Poesio (2020). Negative training instances are created by pairing anaphoric mentions with preceding mentions that are not correct antecedents or by pairing non-anaphoric mentions with preced-

[5] We use their publicly available implementation from `https://github.com/juntaoy/dali-bridging`. All model parameters are set to the same values as in Yu and Poesio (2020) except for training, which will be described in Section 4.2.

ID	Features	Description	Motivation	Used by S-S	S-P	P-S	P-P
1	premodifiers' POS tags	the POS tag of the premodifier of m_i's head, if any, and the POS tag of the premodifier of m_j's head, if any; only three POS tags are considered: JJ, NN, VBN	presence of certain types of premodifiers may influence bridging decisions	✓	✓	✓	✓
2	speaker	whether the speakers of m_i and m_j are the same	may influence bridging decisions	✓	✓	✓	✓
3	turn distance	the turn distance between m_i and m_j binned into the following buckets: 1, 2, 3, 4, 5–7, 8–15, 16–31, 32–63, 64+	bridging link is less likely as distance increases	✓	✓	✓	✓
4	conflicting article pairs	features that encode the presence of select unordered pairs of articles possessed by m_i and m_j (see Table 11 for the list)	bridging link is more likely if the mentions possess any of these conflicting pairs	✓			
5	the-anaphor	whether m_i starts with "the"	could improve resolution precision			✓	
6	bare noun/article pairs	features that encode whether one mention is a bare noun (phrase) and the other possesses one of the select articles[6]	bridging link is more likely if any of these features is fired			✓	
7	dataset	the name of the dataset (e.g., AMI) in which m_i and m_j appears	could affect bridging decisions	✓		✓	

Table 10: Bridging resolution: features for training the four same-head sieves, namely, the singular-singular (S-S) sieve, the singular-plural (S-P) sieve, the plural-singular (P-S) sieve, and the plural-plural (P-P) sieve. Each feature encodes the candidate anaphor, m_i, and a candidate antecedent, m_j, or the relationship between them. The presence of a checkmark in row x and column y indicates that feature x is used to train sieve y.

ing mentions. We employ a *turn window* when generating training instances, meaning that training instances will be generated from two mentions only if the distance between them is within a certain number of turns. We treat the turn window as a tunable parameter. Test instances are created in the same manner as the training instances.

The four mention-pair models are trained using different features. Table 10 provides a description of these features, the motivation behind their design, as well as the features used to train each mention-pair model. We use Stanford CoreNLP (Manning et al., 2014) and spaCy (Honnibal et al., 2020) to extract the linguistic information needed to compute the features. A few features deserve mention. Feature 4, which is used by the singular-singular sieve, is a set of features encoding the presence of *conflicting* article pairs, which are manually identified via our inspection of the official development sets. Most conflicting pairs are composed of a definite article and an indefinite article, so the presence of a conflicting article pair makes the corresponding mentions less likely to be coreferent (because they differ in definiteness). At the same time, however, the presence of a conflicting pair makes the corresponding mentions more likely

the/a, the/the other, the/another, one/the, one/the other, an/another, that/their, the/your, my/your, an/the, that/next, the/next, my/a, the/your, the/my, your/my, my/this, a/your, the/some, this/next, a/our, such a/the, a/your, some/the, the/more, a/one, a/this, an/her, your/'s, an/[adj.] bare, a/[adj.] bare, [adj.] bare/the, any/[adj.] bare, some/[adj.] bare, this/[adj.] bare, our/[adj.] bare, my/[adj.] bare, some/[adj.] bare

Table 11: Conflicting article pairs. [adj.] bare means that a mention is a bare expression that is optionally premodified by an adjective.

to have a bridging relation. The same can be said for feature 6. Specifically, this group of features is applicable when one mention is a bare expression (which indicates genericity) and the other is a definite expression, and hence their presence makes it more likely for the two mentions to have a bridging relation.

4.1.2 Predicted vs. Gold Phases

The systems we developed for the Gold phase and the Predicted phase differ primarily in mention extraction. For the Predicted phase, the mentions used by the neural sieve and the same-head sieves are extracted differently. For the neural sieve, since Yu and Poesio's (2020) MTL model assumes as input the gold mentions in the input document, we modify their model to enable automatic learning of

[6]The select articles are: some, another, the, these, those, many, most, and all of the possessive personal pronouns.

span boundaries. For the same-head sieves, we use the noun phrases heuristically extracted from syntactic parse trees using Stanford CoreNLP (Manning et al., 2014). For the Gold phase, anaphors and their candidate antecedents are restricted to be gold mentions. More specifically, during training, we use the given gold mentions to train the neural sieve and the same-head sieves, and during inference, we only resolve those gold mentions that are predicted to be bridging anaphors. The model that predicts whether a gold mention is a bridging anaphor is trained by removing the FFNN layers for the bridging task and the coreference task from Yu and Poesio's (2020) MTL model and changing the loss function to sigmoid cross entropy, which is commonly used for binary classification tasks.

4.2 Evaluation

Next, we evaluate our sieve-based approach to bridging resolution.

4.2.1 Model Training and Parameter Tuning

In this subsection, we describe the data we use to (pre)train our models (i.e., the MTL model, the four SVM models, and the anaphor detection model) and the parameters we tune for these models.

The MTL model To train the MTL model, we first pre-train a model on the non-dialogue datasets, including ARRAU RST (train, dev, and test), Gnome, and Pear, and then fine-tune the resulting model on the dialogue datasets, including Trains 93 and the dev sets for Trains91, LIGHT, AMI, Persuasion, and Switchboard. Pre-training takes 15000 steps and fine-tuning takes an additional 7000 steps for both the Predicted and Gold settings.

The only parameter we tune for the MTL model is the dummy score, which we use to make precision-recall tradeoffs, as mentioned before. We tried dummy scores of 0, 0.5, 1.0, 1.5, and 2.0 and selected the score such that the neural sieve alone achieved the highest resolution F-score on the test sets.[7] Note that selecting the default dummy score (i.e., 0) is equivalent to not making any adjustment to the recall and precision scores produced by the MTL model.

The SVM models We train the SVM models using a linear kernel on the dev sets of LIGHT, AMI, Persuasion, and Switchboard. We tune two parameters. The first parameter is the regularization parameter C, which we search out of {1, 10, 100, 1000}. The second parameter is the turn window size. We consider window sizes from 2 to 10. Both parameters are tuned to maximize resolution F-score on the same data on which the models are trained.

Sieve ordering and removal Another parameter we tune involves sieve application. In particular, we need to determine (1) the order in which the sieves should be applied and (2) which SVM sieves should be retained/removed (we take the neural sieve as the basic sieve and do not consider removing it). The ordering that we select is the one that yields the highest resolution F-score on the test sets. Owing to time limitations, it is not feasible to exhaustively try all possible orderings, so we experiment with the following orderings. For the Predicted setting, we first determine whether we should apply all the SVM sieves before or after the neural sieve, then try to order the SVM sieves, and finally consider removing certain SVM sieves. For the Gold setting, we first experiment with as many ways of ordering the neural sieve and the SVM sieves as time permits, and then consider removing certain SVM sieves.

The anaphor detection model We pre-train and fine-tune the anaphor detection model in the same way as we pre-train and fine-tune the neural sieve. Pre-training takes 2000 steps and fine-tuning takes an additional 2000 steps. The only parameter we tune is the anaphoric fraction (AF), which we search out of {0.1, 0.2, 0.3, 0.4, 0.5, 0.6, 0.7, 0.8, 0.9}. Specifically, we select the AF that yields the highest resolution F-score on the test sets. Note that the tuning of AF is done after the sieves are selected and ordered.

Details of the selected hyperparameters can be found in Appendix A.

4.2.2 Results and Discussion

Table 12 shows the recognition and resolution results of our sieve-based approach to bridging resolution on the test sets. These are also our official results for the bridging track. For the Predicted setting, we achieve resolution F-scores of 13.3–21.9%. For the Gold setting, we achieve resolution F-scores of 19.6–31.4%. Note that these are entity-based F-scores, meaning that a bridging anaphor is considered correctly resolved as long as it is resolved to its antecedent or a preceding mention that is coreferent with its antecedent. As can be seen, the system performs better in the Gold setting with

[7] We could have tuned this parameter so that it maximized the resolution F-score achieved by the system rather than just the neural sieve, but could not do that due to time limitations.

		LIGHT			AMI			Persuasion			Switchboard		
		P	R	F	P	R	F	P	R	F	P	R	F
Predicted	Recognition	21.8	44.3	29.2	26.8	32.9	29.5	29.6	38.9	33.6	28.9	32.2	30.4
	Resolution	10.4	21.2	14.0	12.1	14.8	13.3	19.3	25.3	21.9	14.5	16.1	15.3
Gold	Recognition	34.7	40.7	37.5	37.0	42.2	39.4	43.0	52.1	47.1	37.7	50.9	43.3
	Resolution	18.3	21.4	19.7	18.4	21.0	19.6	28.7	34.7	31.4	18.4	24.8	21.1

Table 12: Bridging resolution: recognition and resolution results of our sieve-based approach on the test sets. These are also our official test set results.

respect to both recognition and resolution. These results are consistent with our intuition that the Gold setting is easier than the Predicted setting.

4.2.3 Additional Analysis

To gain additional insights into our approach, we perform two experiments. Since we did not store the parameters of the model that produced the official test results, we had to retrain the model to produce the results in these experiments. Hence, the performance numbers in these experiments may not be directly comparable to the official test results.

In the first experiment, we examine the contribution of each sieve to the overall performance of our approach. The recognition and resolution F-scores of this experiment are shown in Table 13. As can be seen, the optimal sieve ordering is determined to be the singular-plural sieve, followed by the plural-plural sieve, the plural-singular sieve, and MTL, and finally the singular-singular sieve. The sieve removal process begins after the optimal sieve ordering is determined. While sieve ordering is dataset-independent, sieve removal is performed in a dataset-dependent manner. As shown in the table, a checkmark appears next to a sieve if and only if the corresponding sieve is retained. For the most part, we can see that each sieve contributes positively to overall performance. Hence, these results demonstrate the usefulness of a sieve-based approach to bridging resolution.

In the second experiment, we examine the effects of (1) anaphor detection and (2) recall-precision balancing in the neural sieve on the overall performance of our approach by *ablating* one or both of these components/factors in our approach. Note that anaphor detection is applicable in the Gold setting only. The results of this experiment are shown in Table 14. For comparison purposes, we show the results achieved by MTL, the results of our approach (in "Ours") and the different ablated versions of our approach, including "Ours w/o AD" (our approach with anaphor detection ablated), "Ours w/o B" (our approach without recall-precision balancing), and "Ours w/o B&AD" (our approach with both of them ablated). As we can see, while the unablated version of our approach does not achieve the highest recognition F-score on all datasets, it does achieve the highest resolution F-score on all of them. A closer examination of the ablated results in the Gold setting reveals that the best resolution F-scores can sometimes be achieved without anaphor detection or recall-precision balancing, but applying them in combination yields the best result on all datasets.

5 Conclusions

We presented our systems we developed for the three tracks of the CODI-CRAC 2021 shared task, namely entity coreference resolution, discourse deixis resolution, and bridging resolution. Our team ranked second for entity coreference resolution, first for discourse deixis resolution, and first for bridging resolution. For entity coreference resolution, our analysis of our three approaches (Pipeline, End-to-End, as well as its "no constraint" variant) revealed that there is a perfect correlation between entity coreference performance and mention detection, suggesting that coreference performance can further be improved by improving mention detection. For discourse deixis resolution, our analysis revealed that (1) contrary to common wisdom, anaphor detection was not always easier in the Gold setting (where gold mentions were given) than the Predicted setting; and (2) substantial gains could be achieved simply by removing the singleton clusters from the output prior to scoring, especially in the Predicted setting. For bridging resolution, our results suggested that the Gold setting is easier than the Predicted setting, and our analysis showed that the sieves, anaphor detection, and recall-precision balancing all contributed positively to overall system performance. Finally, for a fur-

	LIGHT			AMI			Persuasion			Switchboard		
	Sieve	Recog	Resol	Sieve	Recog	Resol	Sieve	Recog	Resol	Sieve	Recog	Resol
						Predicted						
Sing-plur	✓	1.4	0.9	✓	3.3	1.5		–	–		–	–
+ Plur-plur	✓	2.2	1.3		–	–		–	–		–	–
+ Plur-sing		–	–		–	–		–	–		–	–
+ MTL	✓	27.9	13.2	✓	26.0	12.5	✓	33.9	21.0	✓	26.0	13.5
+ Sing-sing		–	–	✓	26.3	12.7	✓	34.7	21.2		–	–
						Gold						
Sing-plur	✓	1.4	1.0	✓	2.8	1.8	✓	3.4	2.0	✓	1.7	1.0
+ Plur-plur	✓	2.8	1.9		–	–		–	–		–	–
+ Plur-sing	✓	3.7	2.3	✓	6.0	3.3		–	–	✓	2.5	1.5
+ MTL	✓	38.2	21.4	✓	37.2	18.3	✓	47.7	32.5	✓	44.6	21.5
+ Sing-sing		–	–		–	–		–	–	✓	44.6	21.6

Table 13: Bridging resolution: recognition and resolution F-scores of our sieve-based approach on the test sets using the optimal sieve ordering and combination determined on development data. The models used in these experiments are (re)trained after the official submission, so these performance numbers may not be directly comparable to our official test set results.

		LIGHT			AMI			Persuasion			Switchboard		
		P	R	F	P	R	F	P	R	F	P	R	F
						Predicted							
Recognition	MTL	22.9	36.1	**28.0**	23.5	32.2	27.2	24.0	56.3	33.7	22.4	45.1	**29.9**
	Ours w/o B	22.5	36.9	27.9	23.5	33.0	**27.4**	23.8	57.6	33.7	22.4	45.1	**29.9**
	Ours	22.5	36.9	27.9	25.8	26.9	26.3	29.6	42.0	**34.7**	27.5	24.7	26.0
Resolution	MTL	10.7	16.9	13.1	10.0	13.7	11.6	14.1	33.0	19.8	9.8	19.7	13.0
	Ours w/o B	10.6	17.3	**13.2**	10.1	14.2	11.8	13.9	33.7	19.7	9.8	19.7	13.0
	Ours	10.6	17.3	**13.2**	12.4	13.0	**12.7**	18.1	25.7	**21.2**	14.2	12.8	**13.5**
						Gold							
Recognition	MTL	34.5	50.8	41.1	33.7	37.8	35.6	35.5	63.5	45.5	35.2	53.8	42.6
	Ours w/o B&AD	34.6	51.3	41.4	33.6	38.1	35.7	35.5	63.9	45.6	35.0	54.2	42.5
	Ours w/o B	35.9	49.2	**41.5**	38.0	36.3	**37.2**	36.7	62.5	46.2	39.0	52.1	**44.6**
	Ours w/o AD	39.7	37.1	38.4	33.6	38.1	35.7	41.4	54.9	47.2	35.0	54.2	42.5
	Ours	40.4	36.1	38.2	38.0	36.3	**37.2**	42.4	54.5	**47.7**	39.0	52.1	**44.6**
Resolution	MTL	16.7	24.6	19.9	16.4	18.3	17.3	23.3	41.7	29.9	16.9	25.8	20.4
	Ours w/o B&AD	17.2	25.5	20.6	16.6	18.8	17.6	23.3	42.0	30.0	16.9	26.2	20.6
	Ours w/o B	18.0	24.6	20.8	18.7	17.9	**18.3**	24.2	41.3	30.6	18.9	25.2	**21.6**
	Ours w/o AD	22.2	20.7	**21.4**	16.6	18.8	17.6	28.0	37.2	31.9	16.9	26.2	20.6
	Ours	22.6	20.2	**21.4**	18.7	17.9	**18.3**	28.9	37.2	**32.5**	18.9	25.2	**21.6**

Table 14: Bridging resolution: effect of anaphor detection and recall-precision balancing on the recognition and resolution performance of our sieve-based approach on the test sets. The models used in these experiments are (re)trained after the official submission, so these performance numbers may not be directly comparable to our official test set results.

ther analysis of our systems and other participating systems, we refer the reader to our cross-team analysis paper (Li et al., 2021), which also contains a discussion of the lessons we learned and our vision of how the field should move forward.

Acknowledgments

This work was supported in part by NSF Grant IIS-1528037. Any opinions, findings, conclusions or recommendations expressed in this paper are those of the authors and do not necessarily reflect the views or official policies, either expressed or implied, of the NSF.

References

Aria Haghighi and Dan Klein. 2009. Simple coreference resolution with rich syntactic and semantic features. In *Proceedings of the 2009 Conference on Empirical Methods in Natural Language Processing*, pages 1152–1161, Singapore. Association for Computational Linguistics.

Matthew Honnibal, Ines Montani, Sofie Van Landeghem, and Adriane Boyd. 2020. spaCy: Industrial-strength Natural Language Processing in Python. Zenodo.

Thorsten Joachims. 1998. Making large-scale support vector machine learning practical. In Bernhard Schölkopf, Christopher J. C. Burges, and Alexander J. Smola, editors, *Advances in Kernel Methods - Support Vector Learning*. MIT press, Cambridge, USA.

Ben Kantor and Amir Globerson. 2019. Coreference resolution with entity equalization. In *Proceedings of the 57th Annual Meeting of the Association for Computational Linguistics*, pages 673–677, Florence, Italy. Association for Computational Linguistics.

Sopan Khosla, Juntao Yu, Ramesh Manuvinakurike, Vincent Ng, Massimo Poesio, Michael Strube, and Carolyn Rosé. 2021. The CODI-CRAC 2021 shared task on anaphora, bridging, and discourse deixis in dialogue. In *Proceedings of the CODI-CRAC 2021 Shared Task on Anaphora, Bridging, and Discourse Deixis in Dialogue*. Association for Computational Linguistics.

Hideo Kobayashi and Vincent Ng. 2021. Bridging resolution: Making sense of the state of the art. In *Proceedings of the 2021 Conference of the North American Chapter of the Association for Computational Linguistics: Human Language Technologies*, pages 1652–1659, Online. Association for Computational Linguistics.

Heeyoung Lee, Yves Peirsman, Angel Chang, Nathanael Chambers, Mihai Surdeanu, and Dan Jurafsky. 2011. Stanford's multi-pass sieve coreference resolution system at the CoNLL-2011 shared task. In *Proceedings of the Fifteenth Conference on Computational Natural Language Learning: Shared Task*, pages 28–34, Portland, Oregon, USA. Association for Computational Linguistics.

Kenton Lee, Luheng He, Mike Lewis, and Luke Zettlemoyer. 2017. End-to-end neural coreference resolution. In *Proceedings of the 2017 Conference on Empirical Methods in Natural Language Processing*, pages 188–197, Copenhagen, Denmark. Association for Computational Linguistics.

Kenton Lee, Luheng He, and Luke Zettlemoyer. 2018. Higher-order coreference resolution with coarse-to-fine inference. In *Proceedings of the 2018 Conference of the North American Chapter of the Association for Computational Linguistics: Human Language Technologies, Volume 2 (Short Papers)*, pages 687–692, New Orleans, Louisiana. Association for Computational Linguistics.

Shengjie Li, Hideo Kobayashi, and Vincent Ng. 2021. The CODI-CRAC 2021 shared task on anaphora, bridging, and discourse deixis resolution in dialogue: A cross-team analysis. In *Proceedings of the CODI-CRAC 2021 Shared Task on Anaphora, Bridging, and Discourse Deixis in Dialogue*. Association for Computational Linguistics.

Jing Lu and Vincent Ng. 2020. Conundrums in entity coreference resolution: Making sense of the state of the art. In *Proceedings of the 2020 Conference on Empirical Methods in Natural Language Processing (EMNLP)*, pages 6620–6631, Online. Association for Computational Linguistics.

Christopher Manning, Mihai Surdeanu, John Bauer, Jenny Finkel, Steven Bethard, and David McClosky. 2014. The Stanford CoreNLP natural language processing toolkit. In *Proceedings of 52nd Annual Meeting of the Association for Computational Linguistics: System Demonstrations*, pages 55–60, Baltimore, Maryland. Association for Computational Linguistics.

Vincent Ng and Claire Cardie. 2002. Improving machine learning approaches to coreference resolution. In *Proceedings of the 40th Annual Meeting of the Association for Computational Linguistics*, pages 104–111, Philadelphia, Pennsylvania, USA. Association for Computational Linguistics.

Massimo Poesio, Yulia Grishina, Varada Kolhatkar, Nafise Moosavi, Ina Roesiger, Adam Roussel, Fabian Simonjetz, Alexandra Uma, Olga Uryupina, Juntao Yu, and Heike Zinsmeister. 2018. Anaphora resolution with the ARRAU corpus. In *Proceedings of the First Workshop on Computational Models of Reference, Anaphora and Coreference*, pages 11–22, New Orleans, Louisiana. Association for Computational Linguistics.

Karthik Raghunathan, Heeyoung Lee, Sudarshan Rangarajan, Nathanael Chambers, Mihai Surdeanu, Dan Jurafsky, and Christopher Manning. 2010. A multi-pass sieve for coreference resolution. In *Proceedings of the 2010 Conference on Empirical Methods in Natural Language Processing*, pages 492–501.

Ina Rösiger. 2018. Rule- and learning-based methods for bridging resolution in the ARRAU corpus. In *Proceedings of the First Workshop on Computational Models of Reference, Anaphora and Coreference*, pages 23–33.

Wee Meng Soon, Hwee Tou Ng, and Daniel Chung Yong Lim. 2001. A machine learning approach to coreference resolution of noun phrases. *Computational Linguistics*, 27(4):521–544.

Liyan Xu and Jinho D. Choi. 2020. Revealing the myth of higher-order inference in coreference resolution. In *Proceedings of the 2020 Conference on Empirical Methods in Natural Language Processing (EMNLP)*, pages 8527–8533, Online. Association for Computational Linguistics.

Juntao Yu and Massimo Poesio. 2020. Multitask learning-based neural bridging reference resolution. In *Proceedings of the 28th International Conference on Computational Linguistics*, pages 3534–3546, Barcelona, Spain (Online). International Committee on Computational Linguistics.

A Model Hyperparameters

Entity coreference:

- End-to-end (with and without constraints): the model is trained using a type loss coefficient of 0.2.
- Pipeline: the type prediction model uses a type loss coefficient of 500 and the coreference model uses a type loss coefficient of 0.2.

Discourse deixis:

- Predicted: for Persuasion, the type loss is 0.2; for other datasets, the type loss is 0.5.
- Gold:T1,CA1,RC+: for all datasets, the type loss is 0.2.
- Gold:T1,CA2,RC+: for Persuasion and AMI, the type loss is 0.2; for Light and Switchboard, the type loss is 0.5.
- Gold:T1,CA1,RC-: for all datasets, the type loss is 0.2.
- Gold:T2,CA1,RC+: for all datasets, the type loss is 0.2.
- Gold:T2,CA2,RC+: for Switchboard, the type loss is 0.2; for other datasets, type loss is 0.5.
- Gold:T2,CA2,RC-: for Persuasion, the type loss is 0.5; for other datasets, the type loss is 0.2.

Bridging:

- Neural sieve: For the Predicted setting, the selected dummy scores are: 0.0 for LIGHT, 0.5 for AMI, 2.0 for Persuasion, and 1.5 for Switchboard. For the Gold setting, the scores are: 1.0 for LIGHT, 0.0 for AMI, 1.0 for Persuasion, and 0.0 for Switchboard.

- SVM sieves: For the singular-singular sieve, the turn window sizes are 8 for the Predicted setting and 4 for the Gold setting. For each of the remaining sieves, the turn window size is the same for both settings, namely 10 for the singular-plural sieve, 5 for the plural-singular sieve, and 6 for the plural-plural sieve. The SVM regularization parameter is 100 for all SVM models.

- Optimal sieve ordering for each setting and the sieves selected for each dataset ("Lgt", "Prssn", and "Swbd" correspond to LIGHT, Persuasion, and Switchboard respectively):

	Lgt	AMI	Prssn	Swbd
	Predicted			
Sing-plur	✓	✓		
+ Plur-plur	✓			
+ Plur-sing				
+ MTL	✓	✓	✓	✓
+ Sing-sing		✓	✓	
	Gold			
Sing-plur	✓	✓	✓	✓
+ Plur-plur	✓			
+ Plur-sing	✓	✓		✓
+ MTL	✓	✓	✓	✓
+ Sing-sing				✓

- Anaphor detection model: The selected ratio is 0.4.

Anaphora Resolution in Dialogue: Description of the DFKI-TalkingRobots System for the CODI-CRAC 2021 Shared-Task

Tatiana Anikina, Cennet Oguz, Natalia Skachkova
Siyu Tao, Sharmila Upadhyaya, Ivana Kruijff-Korbayová
DFKI / Saarland Informatics Campus, Saarbrücken, Germany
ivana.kruijff@dfki.de

Abstract

We describe the system developed by the DFKI-TalkingRobots Team for the CODI-CRAC 2021 Shared-Task on anaphora resolution in dialogue. Our system consists of three subsystems: (1) the Workspace Coreference System (WCS) incrementally clusters mentions using semantic similarity based on embeddings combined with lexical feature heuristics; (2) the Mention-to-Mention (M2M) coreference resolution system pairs same entity mentions; (3) the Discourse Deixis Resolution (DDR) system employs a Siamese Network to detect discourse anaphor-antecedent pairs. WCS achieved F1-score of 55.6% averaged across the evaluation test sets, M2M 57.2% and DDR 21.5%, all on predicted mentions.

1 Introduction

This paper describes the anaphora resolution system developed by the DFKI-TalkingRobots Team for the *CODI-CRAC 2021 Shared-Task* (CCST)[1] (Khosla et al., 2021). Anaphora resolution (AR) is important for many natural language processing tasks, such as information extraction, summarization, question answering, etc. Most existing systems have been developed for AR in text and focus on coreference resolution. CCST was set up to address AR in dialogue, including not only coreference but also bridging and discourse deixis.

We were inspired to join CCST, although we did not have an existing AR system to start with. Initial small tests of publicly available pre-trained AR models from the AllenNLP and HuggingFace libraries on our dialogue data in the domain of disaster response team communication (Skachkova and Kruijff-Korbayová, 2020) yielded discouraging results. Participating in CCST was a way to kick start the development of an AR system of our own. Our long-term aim is to develop a domain-independent AR system to be used in several projects of the Talking Robots Group at DFKI[2], including for the interpretation of team communication in disaster response (Willms et al., 2019).

Track	AR	AR	DD
System	WCS Sec. 2.1	M2M Sec. 2.2	DDR Sec. 2.4
Setting	pred.	pred.	pred.
Baselines	–	–	–
Learning framework	workspace clustering	mention to mention pairing	heuristics Siamese Net
Markable identification	SpaCy	BiLSTM-CRF	SpaCy
Train. data	CCST	CCST	CCST
Dev. data	CCST	CCST	CCST

Table 1: Systems summary

Our system for the CCST is the first step in this direction, and should be considered work in progress. It consists of two independent AR subsystems: *Workspace Coreference Resolution System* (WCS, Sec. 2.1); *Mention-to-Mention Coreference Resolution System* (M2M, Sec. 2.2); and the *Discourse Deixis Resolution System* (DDR, Sec. 2.4).The subsystems were developed using the data provided for CCST and evaluated in the CCST tracks *Eval-AR* and *Eval-DD (Pred)*, respectively. See Tab. 1 for a summary.

Sec. 2 describes the subsystems one by one, including the respective approach, mention detection method and how we used the CCST data. We also highlight the differences between our approaches and recent related work in the respective subsections. In Sec. 3 we provide the results and error analysis for each subsystem. We conclude and point out future work in Sec. 4.

2 System description

2.1 Workspace Coreference System (WCS)

We designed and implemented a system for identity anaphora resolution based on the following

[1] URL: competitions.codalab.org/competitions/30312

[2] URL: dfki.de/mlt

Proceedings of the CODI-CRAC 2021 Shared Task on Anaphora, Bridging, and Discourse Deixis in Dialogue, pages 32–42
Punta Cana, Dominican Republic, November 10, 2021.

principles. First, our system processes the input incrementally to make the learning process resemble the way humans read and understand text and resolve coreference. Second, we restrict the number of possible coreference clusters considered at each step to only the salient candidates (i.e., those clusters that have been referred to recently in the conversation). Inspired by the clustering ideas outlined in Rahman and Ng (2011) our system creates clusters on-the-fly by comparing the current mention to the most recent members from each of the clusters available in the workspace.

We combined workspace-based clustering with a binary classification of referring expressions. Fig. 1 shows an overview of the whole system that considers one mention at each step and computes the probabilities for clustering this mention with other mentions available in the workspace.

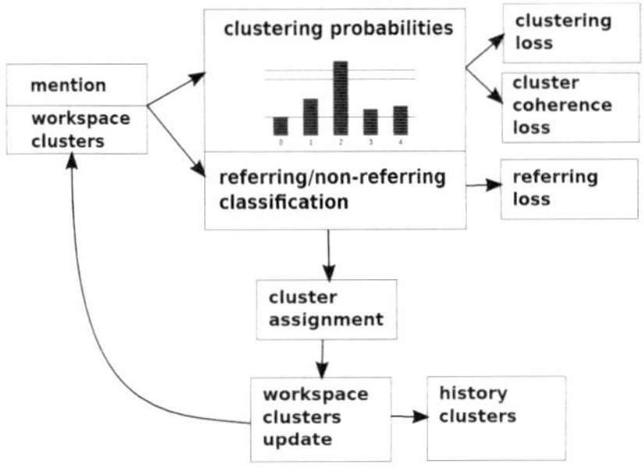

Figure 1: Workspace Coreference System Overview

Our implementation differs from other submissions to the Shared Task. Both winning models (lxucs and UTD_NLP) are based on the pairwise scoring of mentions and extend the coreference model from (Xu and Choi, 2020). The model submitted by KU_NLP is based on pointer networks whereas our system is more similar in spirit to the incremental approach introduced in (Xia et al., 2020). Similarly to their work we are building clusters of mentions incrementally and remove old mentions from the workspace if the corresponding clusters have not been updated for a long time.[3]

However, there are some important differences between our model and the work by Xia et al. (2020). For example, we do not use separate representations for clusters, but rather take the latest 5 mentions from each cluster and compute an average probability of assigning a new mention to the same cluster. Moreover, Xia et al. (2020) evict clusters based on their size and distance while our decision to remove a cluster from the workspace is based on the number of singletons that are allowed in the workspace as well as recency of the cluster updates. We also have substantial differences in the training procedure, e.g., rather than considering all correct antecedents, Xia et al. (2020) focus only on the most recent one while our system checks all antecedents, i.e., compares how many mentions in the assigned cluster are actually coreferent with the mention. We also update the parameters after each clustering decision and not once per document. Moreover, our model does not use SpanBERT embeddings or any other components pre-trained on coreference data[4] and is more focused on exploring different kinds of embeddings and how their combinations contribute to the coreference resolution.

2.1.1 Data

We used the data provided by the CCST organizers and split it into train and development set for WCS as follows. First, we extracted individual documents from each of the files (RST_DTreeBank, Gnome_Subset2, Pear_Stories, Trains_91, Trains_93, AMI_dev, LDC2021E05_Switchboard_3_dev, light_dev and Persuasion_dev). Then we randomly shuffled these documents to create a training set with 550 documents and a development set with 61 documents. We did not use any additional data for training/development. The system was tested on the CCST test set in the Eval-AR track.

2.1.2 SpaCy-based Mention Detection

We use SpaCy[5] to extract mention candidates (markables) for WCS. The candidates include all noun chunks detected by SpaCy (based on the *en_core_web_trf* model). We add all pronouns and adverbs like *'here'*, *'there'*, *'now'* and *'then'* because they are not recognized by SpaCy as noun phrases. We also check for each noun phrase whether it has a prepositional phrase or clause (based on the dependency relations *'prep'* and *'relcl'* in SpaCy) and extend the span if necessary.

After the release of the CCST annotated test set we checked the performance of our SpaCy-based approach by comparing the gold spans to those extracted by our system. We got the following

[3]The limit was set to 100 steps without updates in our experiments.

[4]Xia et al. (2020) used encoder weights that were already fine-tuned on the OntoNotes dataset and adopted both mention and pairwise scorers from (Joshi et al., 2020).

[5]https://spacy.io

micro-F1 scores: 72.4% on AMI, 85.6% on Light, 81.6% on Persuasion and 81.5% on Switchboard. These results show that the quality of the mention extraction significantly impacts the overall performance of the coreference resolution system. E.g., WCS had the lowest F1 score on AMI (43.93%) and the highest score on Light (67.28%), which is in line with the mention extraction performance.

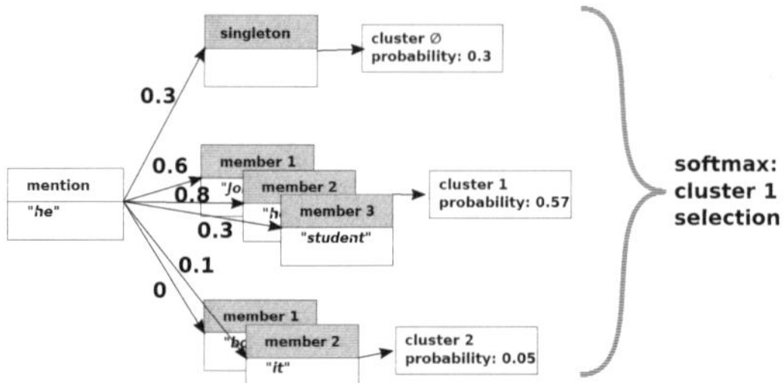

Figure 2: Workspace Clustering Example

2.1.3 WCS Input and Architecture

After extracting mentions we pre-process all sentences in the documents using BERT (pre-trained cased version) and extract various features for each mention, including the mention position within the document, the head lemma, head number,[6] animacy classification,[7] speaker embedding, BERT embedding (Devlin et al., 2018) of the mention's head, averaged BERT embedding for the span of the mention, Numberbatch concept embedding (Speer et al., 2017) for the head lemma, GloVe embedding (Pennington et al., 2014) for the head lemma, averaged GloVe span embedding and the masked language model (MLM) embedding for the mention. For the MLM embedding we use BERT (pre-trained cased base model) and take the current and the previous dialogue turns, mask the mention's head in the turn and ask the model to predict the top candidate for the masked token. We take the GloVe embedding of this candidate as the MLM embedding.

When processing a new mention we compare its representation to each of the workspace clusters. Note that the very first position in the workspace is always reserved for the singleton case. All embeddings for the singleton case have zero values but keep the same dimensions as the real cluster members. In order to compare a mention to the workspace clusters we took up to 5 latest members from each cluster and computed the probability for each member-mention pair. The individual pair-based probabilities were averaged to obtain the cluster-level probabilities as shown in Fig. 2.

When training the model we used the extracted features of different types and concatenated each mention feature with the corresponding member feature (e.g., mention speaker with the member speaker embedding) before passing them through the linear layers and activation functions to obtain the final embedding. A separate list of layers (a.k.a. channels) was used for each embedding type. We concatenated the output of different channels and passed it to the feed-forward network. We used ReLU as an activation function for most of the channels. ReLU was also used for the final decision (when combining the outputs of different channels). In parallel, we performed a binary referring expression classification using a network with two linear layers. This network helped the model to decide whether an input mention is referring or not. If it was classified as non-referring it was not clustered with any of the workspace clusters.

After obtaining a probability for each of the workspace clusters as shown in Fig. 2 we assign the mention to the most likely cluster. Then we add the new mention to the workspace clusters, either as a new member of some existing cluster or as a new singleton cluster. In each iteration the clusters in the workspace have to be re-arranged. If some clusters have not been updated for more than 100 steps they are removed from the workspace and stored in the history. Additionally, we limit the maximum number of singleton clusters in the workspace to 20. When deciding whether to put the cluster in the history or keep it in the workspace we sort all candidates by the recency of the last update.

We experimented with different kinds of embeddings and their combinations on a subset of the data. The details are presented in A.

2.1.4 WCS Training

In order to provide a learning signal for the network we combined three different loss functions. The first loss compares the gold clusters to the ones generated by the model (clustering loss). The second loss checks how heterogeneous are the mentions that appear in the same cluster (cluster coherence loss) and the third loss is a simple cross-entropy loss for the binary classification of referring/non-referring mentions (referring loss).

While training our model we used a teacher forcing ratio of 0.3 to enforce the correct clustering in

[6] We use SpaCy Lemmatization and number annotation.

[7] We trained a separate classifier for this using the CCST entity type annotations.

30% of all cases and make the network converge faster. We also checked the compatibility between the clusters based on the features typically used in coreference systems. These features include number and animacy compatibility and nesting. E.g., number compatibility guarantees that mentions in plural are not clustered together with the ones that are in singular and animacy compatibility prevents clustering animate and inanimate objects together. Nesting simply means that if some mention is within the NP represented by another mention these two should not be clustered together (e.g., *'a good student with a book'* and *'a book'*). These conditions were added in order to make the learning process easier by filtering out incompatible clusters at an early stage. However, since our animacy classification and number annotations were not perfect, the filtering stage could cause some mistakes in the later clustering. Additionally, we checked first person pronouns and speaker consistency. E.g., if the current cluster has a speaker A with the mention *'I'*, another mention *'I'* with a different speaker B cannot be put in the same cluster.

2.1.5 WCS Post-processing

At test time we used an additional constraint that all referential mentions that are third person pronouns such as *'it'* and *'they'* cannot form a new singleton cluster and must be clustered with one of the preceding workspace clusters. In order to score the workspace clusters for this task we ordered them by recency starting with the most recent ones and checked the mention-cluster compatibility as explained above (using animacy, number and nesting constraints). Among the compatible clusters we selected the one that had the highest probability according to the masked language model. For this we masked the current mention in the original sentence and checked one by one the likelihoods of mentions from different clusters to fill the position. These likelihoods were averaged for each cluster based on the 5 most recent members and finally the cluster with the highest likelihood was selected. We trained WCS for 5 epochs with a learning rate of 0.0001 and *Adam* as an optimizer.

2.2 Mention-to-Mention System (M2M)

Coreference resolution systems aim to find the mentions of the same entities which might be referred to by different expressions (e.g., synonyms, pronouns, etc.) or the same expressions according to their presented context in the document. This is challenging because changes in the context and mentions of the entities strongly affect the coreference resolution systems. Additionally, the same expressions might also refer to different entities in the real world. These noted points cause three different challenges that the M2M model aims to overcome. The first is pairing the same mentions of different entities because of the same context. The second is the problem with the different contexts of the same entities when they are referred to by the same expressions. The third one is the different mentions of the same entities in different contexts.

Most coreference resolution models have been adapted to rank the antecedents based on average embeddings (Lee et al., 2017, 2018) and contextualized embeddings (Joshi et al., 2019, 2020). Furthermore, Xu and Choi (2020) has adapted the model implementation from (Lee et al., 2018) and used the contextualized span embeddings (Joshi et al., 2020) to obtain the mention candidates through span enumeration and aggressive pruning. The M2M system combines the average and contextualized embeddings instead of using them alone, to avoid context variation of the same mentions and capture lexical similarities of different mentions. Therefore, the M2M system is designed with the aim of suppressing the context variations of different or the same entities. This simply means that the different mentions might be paired because their contexts are similar, and on the contrary, the same expressions might not be paired together because their context or tokens are different. Therefore, we aim first to investigate the effect of mention-mention matching, and then pooling them together with the paired entities into the same clusters. Therefore, the M2M system is designed to cluster the mentions which are paired with the common candidates.

Whereas the M2M implementation differs from the system of pointer network by KU_NLP, it is similar to the winning systems lxucs and UTD_NLP because it is designed to match the most similar entities with a pairwise comparison. M2M, however, forms clusters based on transitive closure over the mention-mention pairs, i.e., pairs which have a common mention are clustered together. Additionally, our mention representation method differs by the included distance vector.

2.2.1 Data

To train the M2M model we use the Light, Persuasion, and Switchboard data provided by the CCST organizers. All three datasets are used to train the

Pronoun and *Noun Models* (see below). For training the *Self Model* (see below) the Switchboard data is not used, because the speaker of the corresponding utterances is not given in the training data, only in test data. Therefore, only the Light and Persuasion data is used to train the *Self Model*.

2.2.2 Mention Detection with BiLSTM-CRF

We treat mention detection as a sequence tagging task, analogous to the common approach to Named Entity Recognition. Given an input sequence of tokens, our mention detection model extracts markable chunks by tagging the tokens in the IOB2 format, i.e., with the beginning of each chunk tagged B, any subsequent tokens in the chunk tagged I, and tokens not in any chunk tagged O.

We implemented a Bidirectional LSTM - Conditional Random Field (BiLSTM-CRF) Model, shown to be effective in sequence tagging (Huang et al., 2015). As the standard IOB2 format only annotates flat chunks, our model only predicts the markables with the widest scope in cases of nesting. We flattened the training data accordingly when converting it to the IOB2 format.

The architecture of the model is as follows: the input data (in IOB2 format) is first passed through an ELMo layer (Peters et al., 2018), where contextualized word representations (embeddings) were extracted for each word. The ELMo embeddings are then passed to the BiLSTM-CRF model. Finally, the CRF model predicts the tags for the input tokens. In a post-processing step, we used SpaCy (*en_core_web_trf*) to extract any nested noun chunks from the markables predicted by the model. Maximum sentence length was set to 50, and we used the *Adam* optimizer with a learning rate of 0.0005 and trained the model for 4 epochs.

The training and development sets are created as an 8:2 split of the documents in each CCST dataset. This was done to include sentences from all datasets and prevent bias towards one dataset. The label distribution is shown in Tab. 2.

Tag	# in data	F1 score
O	139,703	0.99
B	55,947	0.90
I	136,752	0.92

Table 2: BiLSTM-CRF : label distribution and F1-score on CCST train/development data

While our model achieves an overall F1 score of 0.98 on the development set, a breakdown of the score by label (Tab. 2) shows that the F1 score for B and I tags are significantly lower, at 0.92 and 0.90, respectively. This means that our current model is overly conservative in predicting the markable chunks, indicated by a large number of false negatives for the B and I tags. The false negatives result in incomplete markables being extracted and impact the performance of the downstream task.

2.3 M2M Training

We use contextualized word embeddings BERT and ELMo, and average word embeddings GloVe and Fasttext (Joulin et al., 2016). The individual utterances are considered as the input for the embedding systems to extract the vectors for the head and span of the mentions. In order to obtain the rich feature representation of the mentions, word embedding models are used under four different contributions: (1) the 10-*th* layer of BERT is used to obtain a significant local representation without global context of utterances; (2) ELMo is employed for positional encoding of full context of the utterances; (3) GloVe is applied to represent the external global context of each token; (4) Fasttext is utilized to extract the n-gram features of words. Because a mention can be represented with different language forms such as a span of multiple words, one word entity, pronoun, etc., we used different embeddings to obtain the vectors: only BERT is used for span representation, while a combination of BERT, ELMo, GloVe, and Fasttext is used for head representation of each mention.

Each mention is represented by using the word embedding methods with four different feature sets: (1) head embedding to represent similarities between the different mentions of the same entities; (2) span embeddings to represent the differences between similar mentions of the different entities; (3) the distance feature vector is obtained by using distance functions between the head embeddings of mentions to represent the similarities via a distance 7-*d* vector; (4) speaker embeddings by using the average embeddings.

Three different models are designed as part of the M2M system. The *Self Model* is built for personal pronouns with average embeddings of the speaker and head features of the mentions. The *Pronoun Model* is designed to pair the third person and place pronouns to the corresponding candidate by exploiting the head average embeddings of mentions. The *Noun Model* attempts to find the pairs of

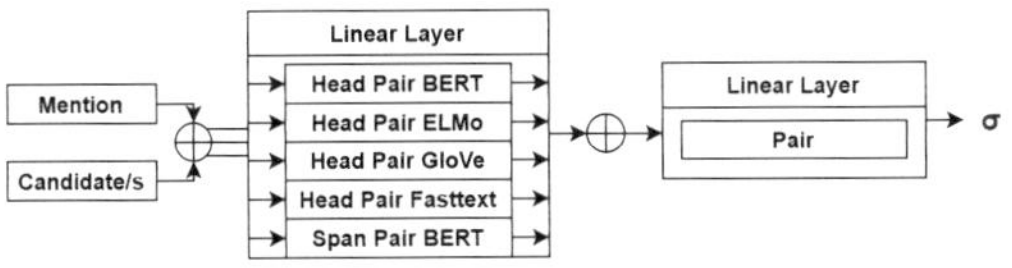

Figure 3: M2M Noun Model Architecture and Training

the mentions by using head and span embeddings with contextualized and average embeddings when they are noun phrases. Fig. 3 shows the Noun Model.

2.3.1 M2M Architecture and Training

The models are designed with linear layers with a ReLU activation function for the head, speaker and span features. Then the extracted vectors from embeddings are concatenated with a distance vector to train a linear layer with a ReLU activation function. Then a linear layer with a Sigmoid activation function is used for output probabilities.

The models are trained with the same hyper-parameters. The learning rate is defined as 0.0001 and the optimizer is *Adam*. For computing the loss, we specify *BCELoss* which is a criterion that measures the Binary Cross Entropy between the target and the output. Training is done for 30 epochs.

2.4 Discourse Deixis Resolution(DDR)

Webber (1991) defines discourse deixis as reference to a discourse entity such as a proposition, description, event, speech act, etc. The discourse entity is a part of the discourse model of the dialogue participant and is realized in a certain discourse segment, i.e. a chunk of a linguistic text, e.g., a sequence of clauses or utterances. The exact boundaries of discourse segments are often hard to define even for humans (Webber, 1991; Artstein and Poesio, 2006). In addition, the resolution of discourse deixis mentions requires cross-sentence information about rhetorical relations and focus/attention which is often not annotated. All this makes discourse deixis resolution a very challenging task.

There exist only a few frameworks focusing on the resolution of discourse deixis mentions. Most early works that we know of (e.g., Eckert and Strube (2000), Navarretta (2000), or Byron (2002)) are rule-based. They use hand-crafted rules to pick out anaphors, which are usually demonstrative pronouns. The right antecedent for each anaphor is found relying on candidates' dialogue act types. Early machine learning approaches are presented, e.g., by Strube and Müller (2003) and Müller (2008), who use many elaborate manually created feature vectors to represent markables, and train classifiers to predict whether an antecedent-anaphor pair is valid or not. Marasović et al. (2017) introduce a model that relies on a neural network (a Siamese Net) to rank potential antecedent candidates given an anaphor. The input for the network, i.e. sentences containing anaphors and antecedent candidates, is represented as feature vectors (embeddings) using bi-LSTM.

Works focusing on automatic identification of discourse deixis anaphors are also not many. An algorithm based on hand-crafted features to recognize discourse deictic *it*, *this* and *that* is suggested, e.g., by Müller (2008). Other works, e.g., by Eckert and Strube (2000), Kolhatkar et al. (2018), or Roussel et al. (2018) present analyses of anaphors with non-nominal antecedents and their properties, but no actual implementations.

Our approach combines machine learning and hand-crafted rules. The machine learning part is inspired by the mention-ranking model for abstract anaphora resolution by Marasović et al. (2017). Given a discourse deixis mention that needs to be resolved, the task is to choose the most suitable antecedent among several candidates. To do so, we train a scorer implemented as a Siamese Net with the goal to assign a higher score to true anaphor-antecedent pairs and lower scores to false ones. Our implementation of the Siamese Net is much simpler than that of Marasović et al. (2017) - instead of bi-LSTM we use BERT's [CLS] token to extract utterance embeddings, and our antecedent-anaphor score is defined as simple Euclidean distance between the two vectors produced by the Siamese Net. Identification of anaphors and the antecedent candidates is rule-based. We explain the details of our system below.

2.4.1 Data

The scorer is trained on all the CCST train and development data. Before that the light_dev file was used to work on the heuristic rules. We built our dataset as follows. For each utterance containing a discourse deixis anaphor (anchor utterance) we create a pair of examples (see Fig. 4) by replacing the anaphor with its true antecedent (a positive example) and with a false candidate (a negative example), which is usually the utterance before the true antecedent. The idea is to make the Siamese Net learn that the true antecedent fits semantically into the utterance containing the anaphor. In total

Anchor: *That* certainly scared the eternal daylights out of me !
Positive example: *I myself happened to look out from the kitchen and see his dangling legs in front of the window .* certainly scared the eternal daylights out of me !
Negative example: *He never experimented with flying contraptions again .* certainly scared the eternal daylights out of me !

Figure 4: Discourse deixis dataset instance

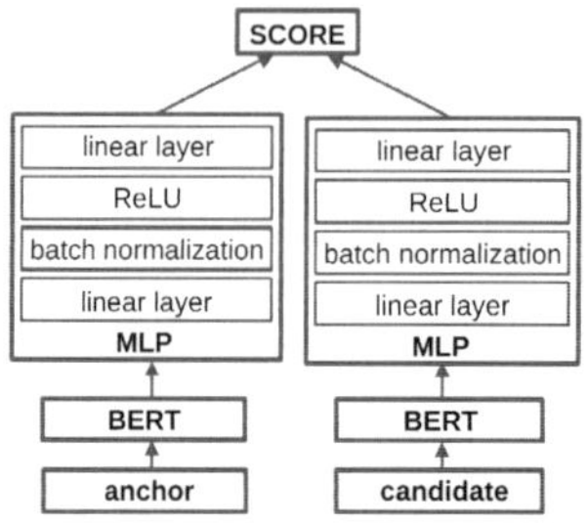

Figure 5: DDR scorer architecture

the dataset contains 5,171 examples.

2.4.2 Discourse Deixis Mention Detection

We do not assume that markables are given during testing, so it is our task to recognize and cluster them. For this we employ heuristic rules that are based on observations in the light_dev data.

First, we want to find discourse deixis mentions that need to be resolved. For now we focus only on demonstrative pronouns, which we detect using the SpaCy NLP pipeline (Honnibal et al., 2020). SpaCy does not distinguish between different types of non-personal pronouns, and labels them all with a DET tag. So, we consider all subtrees with a DET head linked to a parent node via *'dobj'*, *'pobj'*, *'nsubj'* or *'attr'* relations as discourse deixis markables that need to be resolved.

Next, we need to find the antecedents of the detected discourse deixis mentions and cluster the right mentions together. It should be noticed that, in most cases these clusters only include 2-3 mentions, and the antecedents can be found within the local context of several previous utterances. We assume that the antecedents are verbal phrases, clauses, or sequences of clauses (split antecedent cases).

For extracting the antecedent candidates we consider the current utterance containing the mention, and 3 previous ones. Each previous utterance, as well as their continuous sequences are viewed as possible (split) antecedents. Besides, we find all subtrees with VERB or AUX heads linked to the ROOT node via *'relcl'*, *'conj'*, *'ccomp'*, or *'advcl'* relations. We remove all overlapping candidates and candidates that occur after the mention to be resolved. In case of nested candidates, the longest one is chosen. We also apply the following simple heuristics to exclude unlikely candidates and improve the results. First, we limit the size of the clusters by two elements. Here we also consider cases of anaphors referring to split antecedents, which form their own singleton clusters. Second, we disregard all candidates that do not have verbal roots.

2.4.3 DDR Architecture and Training

The discourse deixis resolution system ranks the antecedent candidates using a scorer, sorts the scores in descending order and selects the top candidate. At this step we limit the output of the scorer to 5 candidates and re-sort them giving preference to the candidates closest to the anaphor, as usually the anaphor immediately follows its antecedent.

Being a Siamese Net, the scorer consists of two independent pipelines that have identical architectures. One pipeline is designed for the anchor, the other for an antecedent candidate. Each pipeline accepts input in the form of BERT input IDs, which are then fed into the $\text{BERT}_{\text{BASE}}$ model. We use the models' pooler output to represent each sequence, which is next processed by a simple multilayer perceptron (MLP) network containing two linear layers with a batch normalization and a ReLU activation function. Finally, the Euclidean distance between the feature representations produced by both MLP networks is calculated, and the pair with the smallest distance gets the biggest score. The scorer's architecture is shown in Fig. 5.

The scorer is trained for 12 epochs. We use adaptive learning rate starting with 3e-5, the *AdamW* optimizer and the *TripletMarginLoss* loss function.

3 Results and Error Analysis

3.1 Workspace Coreference System (WCS)

WCS achieved an average F1-score of 64.99% on Light, 43.93% on AMI, 59.93% on Persuasion and 53.55% on Switchboard. Although the results are lower than those of the top-performing systems, we believe that our approach presents a new way to treat coreference as an incremental clustering task and can be further improved by experimenting with different configurations of input and hyperparameters as well as more robust feature extraction.

We believe that our system should benefit from better animacy and number annotations because these are crucial for the decision on the mention-cluster compatibility as explained in Section 2.1. Using a better mention extraction model should further improve the scores. We also evaluated WCS using the gold mentions as input and obtained the following results: 73.24% on Light, 56.48% on AMI, 72.06% on Persuasion and 62.85% on Switchboard. The difference in scores shows that WCS gains up to 12% F-score on AMI and Persuasion, up to 9% on Switchboard and 6% on Light when it uses the correct mentions. We noticed that quite often markables extracted by SpaCy were incomplete and sometimes even missing. E.g., NPs such as *'my two year old'* and *'the whole time'* were not recognized as NPs by SpaCy and some parts of complex NPs such as *'the kind of things you're supposed to look for'* were missing. Nested NPs present another big challenge for SpaCy, e.g., *'case'* in *'the case material'* was not recognized as a markable. Our feature extraction process heavily relies on SpaCy because we use it together with some heuristics to find a head in each mention span and perform the lemmatization. For instance, in one case *'someones'* was selected as a head in *'someones free will'*, hence the incorrect embedding for *'someone'* instead of *'will'* was used for the clustering decision.

Some of the rules and heuristics we implemented for WCS do not apply in some cases. E.g., the AMI dataset proved to be especially challenging because the dialogues in AMI have several participants and there are references to objects that were not previously mentioned in the text. For instance, a third person pronoun *'it'* in *'do you wanna hold it'* does not have an antecedent in the preceding text because the object can be inferred from the physical context. But our algorithm requires to find an antecedent for each mention of *'it'* that is a referring expression, hence *'it'* ends up in the wrong cluster.

We plan to continue our experiments with WCS by improving the feature extraction process and applying WCS to different domains and genres.

3.2 Mention-to-Mention System (M2M)

The M2M system achieved F1-score of 61.26% on Light, 59.20% on Persuasion and 51.24% on Switchboard. Whereas *Self Model* shows high pairing performance, we observe that *Pronoun Model* struggles with lexical variation between pronouns and the corresponding nouns. We assume that the high performance of *Self Model* is based on the speaker invariant, i.e. two speakers occur in the data. For example, the model pairs the mentions *'I'* and *'my'* of a speaker always with the corresponding speaker. On the other hand, the delicate performance with the *Pronoun Model* is observed based on the high lexical variation: *'He'* needs to be paired with the *'father'* as well as *'his'*. However, the design of M2M is not able to handle more than one possible pair even though the correct pair count is more. The *Noun Model* is also affected by this problem.

To conclude, M2M performs effectively with the similar lexical features of mention-candidate pairs where the candidate variation is lower, e.g., personal pronouns of speakers. However, it struggles to pair the mentions when they are represented with different lexical features. At the same time, It suffers from the same mentions of different entities. In order to overcome the deficiencies of the M2M system, we expect that the clustering mechanism solves the lexical variation problem between mentions by obtaining one possible cluster instead of many possible candidate mentions.

3.3 Discourse Deixic Resolution (DDR)

The DDR system achieved F1-score 20.97% on the Light dataset, 17.43% on AMI, 23.76% on Persuation and 23.86% on Switchboard in the Eval-DD (Pred) track. The submitted system combines the scorer and four heuristic rules partially described in Sec. 2.4, namely limiting cluster size to two mentions, removing all non-verbal antecedent candidates, restricting the scorer's output to five candidates and re-scoring them by distance to the anaphor. For the error analysis we use fully annotated test data released after the competition ended. We perform discourse deixis mention detection as presented in Sec. 2.4.2, and check the performance of the system adding rules incrementally. These results are shown in Tab. 3. The first row of shows the F1 scores achieved by the scorer on the three fully annotated test sets. The next two rows present the scores for cases when the scorer is not forced to search for clusters larger than two mentions, and is applied after the removal of non-verbal candidates. The last four rows show the results after re-sorting the scorer's output by distance to the anaphor. N

Corpus	light	AMI	Persuasion
bare scorer	15.65	13.27	23.36
+ limiting cluster size	16.21	12.99	23.82
+ removing non-verbal	17.11	16.99	**26.48**
+ sort by dist. ($N = 3$)	21.38	17.36	26.06
+ sort by dist. ($N = 4$)	21.32	**17.62**	24.31
+ sort by dist. ($N = 5$)	**21.85**	17.16	23.60
+ sort by dist. ($N = 6$)	20.79	17.22	23.63

Table 3: DDR F1 scores on fully annotated test sets

stands for the number of candidates ranked by the scorer that we re-sort.

Without additional heuristic rules the performance of the scorer is really poor. We assume that the main reasons for this are as follows. First, our model does not possess any information about the semantics of separate tokens and utterances. The example in Fig. 4 illustrates the problem. Using only local context, it is impossible for the model to understand why *'seeing his dangling legs in front of the window'* is a better candidate for being scary than *'never experimenting with flying contraptions'*. BERT, which we use to get utterance representations, is not capable of providing such deep semantics. In the result, both positive and negative examples look legitimate for the model.

Second, the model also lacks information about the discourse structure and how different utterances relate to each other, and thus has difficulties recognizing split antecedents.

Next, our simple approach has a problem with both recall and precision. Recall is bad because mentions with determiner heads make up only 13%-35% (depending on the sub-corpus) of all discourse deixis mentions in the data. Precision is negatively affected by the fact that the DET tag in SpaCy is very general. As a result, we extract many false discourse deixis mentions, like relative pronoun *'that'* in *"I use it to clean the tower that I work in ."* or a determiner phrase *'some of these beautiful flowers'* which is a case of 'standard' anaphora.

Using heuristic rules mostly has a positive effect up to 5% on the test sets. However, not all of these rules work well with different dialogue data. Some sub-corpora contain a lot of fragments, many of which are rather short. As a result, the true antecedent may lie more than three utterances back. Some utterances are ungrammatical, and SpaCy makes mistakes parsing them, which leads to wrong candidate boundaries. Searching for antecedent candidates, we try to split complex and compound utterances. This often leads to rather cumbersome SpaCy-based rules that easily fail, because dialogue speech patterns are very diverse, so it is impossible to create an exhaustive set of rules to capture them. Our focus on verbal (split) antecedents may also lead to errors - we work with transcribed dialogue data, and antecedents are not necessarily verbal, they can also be represented by noun phrases like *'the inscriptions on the side of the fountain'*, prepositional phrases *'to Bath'*, adverbial phrases *'u : and back to Avon'*, etc. Finally, re-sorting the scorer's output by distance does not work for all types of dialogue data (see Tab. 3).

We plan to continue working on discourse deixis resolution, as our naive system offers some space for improvement. Recall and precision of discourse deixis mentions are first obvious aspects to work on. For this purpose current approaches to shell nouns resolution and event detection can be considered.

4 Conclusions and Outlook

We described the three anaphora resolution subsystems we developed from scratch for CCST using only the datasets provided by the CCST organizers. WCS is a coreference resolution approach that incrementally clusters mentions using semantic similarity based on embeddings combined with lexical feature heuristics. It employs SpaCy for markable detection. M2M is another coreference resolution approach which pairs the mentions for the same entities. For markable detection it uses our own BiLSTM-CRF model trained on the CCST data. WCS achieved F1-score of 55.6% averaged across the CCST evaluation test sets, using predicted markables; the M2M system achieved 57.2%. Finally, DDR employs a Siamese Network to distinguish true discourse anaphor-antecedent pairs. Its markable detection is also based on SpaCy. It has average F1-score 21.5% using predicted mentions.

Our models employ novel ideas, but are still in the early stages of development. CCST gave us a boost and we see many options for future work regarding both markable detection as well as the AR resolution models themselves. For example, we would like to improve the feature extraction for WCS; enhance M2M by clustering; combine WCS and M2M; and improve the detection of discourse deixis mentions that need to be resolved. We also plan to apply the systems on other datasets, which we are currently preparing.

References

Ron Artstein and Massimo Poesio. 2006. *Identifying reference to abstract objects in dialogue*. Universität Potsdam.

Donna Karen Byron. 2002. *Resolving pronominal reference to abstract entities*. University of Rochester.

Jacob Devlin, Ming-Wei Chang, Kenton Lee, and Kristina Toutanova. 2018. BERT: Pre-training of deep bidirectional transformers for language understanding. *arXiv preprint arXiv:1810.04805*.

Miriam Eckert and Michael Strube. 2000. Dialogue acts, synchronizing units, and anaphora resolution. *Journal of Semantics*, 17(1):51–89.

Matthew Honnibal, Ines Montani, Sofie Van Landeghem, and Adriane Boyd. 2020. SpaCy: Industrial-strength Natural Language Processing in Python.

Zhiheng Huang, Wei Xu, and Kai Yu. 2015. Bidirectional LSTM-CRF Models for Sequence Tagging.

Mandar Joshi, Danqi Chen, Yinhan Liu, Daniel S Weld, Luke Zettlemoyer, and Omer Levy. 2020. Spanbert: Improving pre-training by representing and predicting spans. *Transactions of the Association for Computational Linguistics*, 8:64–77.

Mandar Joshi, Omer Levy, Luke Zettlemoyer, and Daniel Weld. 2019. BERT for coreference resolution: Baselines and analysis. In *Proceedings of the 2019 Conference on Empirical Methods in Natural Language Processing and the 9th International Joint Conference on Natural Language Processing (EMNLP-IJCNLP)*, pages 5803–5808, Hong Kong, China. Association for Computational Linguistics.

Armand Joulin, Edouard Grave, Piotr Bojanowski, Matthijs Douze, Hérve Jégou, and Tomas Mikolov. 2016. FastText.zip: Compressing text classification models. *arXiv preprint arXiv:1612.03651*.

Sopan Khosla, Juntao Yu, Ramesh Manuvinakurike, Vincent NG, Massimo Poesio, Michael Strube, and Carolyn Rosé. 2021. The CODI-CRAC 2021 Shared Task on Anaphora, Bridging, and Discourse Deixis in Dialogue. In *Proceedings of the CODI-CRAC 2021 Shared Task on Anaphora, Bridging, and Discourse Deixis in Dialogue*. Association for Computational Linguistics.

Varada Kolhatkar, Adam Roussel, Stefanie Dipper, and Heike Zinsmeister. 2018. Anaphora with non-nominal antecedents in computational linguistics: A survey. *Computational Linguistics*, 44(3):547–612.

Kenton Lee, Luheng He, Mike Lewis, and Luke Zettlemoyer. 2017. End-to-end neural coreference resolution. In *Proceedings of the 2017 Conference on Empirical Methods in Natural Language Processing*, pages 188–197, Copenhagen, Denmark. ACL.

Kenton Lee, Luheng He, and Luke Zettlemoyer. 2018. Higher-order coreference resolution with coarse-to-fine inference. In *Proceedings of the 2018 Conference of the North American Chapter of the Association for Computational Linguistics: Human Language Technologies, Volume 2 (Short Papers)*, pages 687–692, New Orleans, Louisiana. ACL.

Ana Marasović, Leo Born, Juri Opitz, and Anette Frank. 2017. A mention-ranking model for abstract anaphora resolution. *arXiv preprint arXiv:1706.02256*.

Mark-Christoph Müller. 2008. *Fully automatic resolution of'it','this', and'that'in unrestricted multi-party dialog*. Ph.D. thesis, Universität Tübingen.

Costanza Navarretta. 2000. Abstract anaphora resolution in danish. In *1st SIGdial Workshop on Discourse and Dialogue*, pages 56–65.

Jeffrey Pennington, Richard Socher, and Christopher D Manning. 2014. Glove: Global vectors for word representation. In *Proceedings of the 2014 conference on empirical methods in natural language processing (EMNLP)*, pages 1532–1543.

Matthew E. Peters, Mark Neumann, Mohit Iyyer, Matt Gardner, Christopher Clark, Kenton Lee, and Luke Zettlemoyer. 2018. Deep contextualized word representations. *CoRR*, abs/1802.05365.

Altaf Rahman and Vincent Ng. 2011. Narrowing the modeling gap: A cluster-ranking approach to coreference resolution. *J. Artif. Intell. Res.*, 40:469–521.

Adam Roussel, Stefanie Dipper, Sarah Jablotschkin, and Heike Zinsmeister. 2018. Towards the automatic resolution of anaphora with non-nominal antecedents: Insights from annotation.

Natalia Skachkova and Ivana Kruijff-Korbayová. 2020. Reference in team communication for robot-assisted disaster response: An initial analysis. In *Proceedings of the 3rd Workshop on Computational Models of Reference, Anaphora and Coreference. Workshop on Computational Models of Reference, Anaphora and Coreference (CRAC-2020), befindet sich COLING'2020, December 12, Virtual, Spain*. Association for Computational Linguistics.

Robyn Speer, Joshua Chin, and Catherine Havasi. 2017. ConceptNet 5.5: An Open Multilingual Graph of General Knowledge. In *Proceedings of the Thirty-First AAAI Conference on Artificial Intelligence*, AAAI'17, page 4444–4451. AAAI Press.

Michael Strube and Christoph Müller. 2003. A machine learning approach to pronoun resolution in spoken dialogue. In *Proceedings of the 41st Annual Meeting of the Association for Computational Linguistics*, pages 168–175.

Bonnie Lynn Webber. 1991. Structure and ostension in the interpretation of discourse deixis. *Language and Cognitive processes*, 6(2):107–135.

Christian Willms, Constantin Houy, Jana-Rebecca Rehse, Peter Fettke, and Ivana Kruijff-Korbayová. 2019. Team communication processing and process analytics for supporting robot-assisted emergency response. In *IEEE SSRR*.

Patrick Xia, João Sedoc, and Benjamin Van Durme. 2020. Incremental neural coreference resolution in constant memory. In *Proceedings of the 2020 Conference on Empirical Methods in Natural Language Processing, EMNLP 2020, Online, November 16-20, 2020*, pages 8617–8624.

Liyan Xu and Jinho D. Choi. 2020. Revealing the myth of higher-order inference in coreference resolution. In *Proceedings of the 2020 Conference on Empirical Methods in Natural Language Processing (EMNLP)*, pages 8527–8533. ACL.

Acknowledgements

The authors are supported by the German Ministry of Education and Research (BMBF): T. Anikina and I. Kruijff-Korbayová in project CORA4NLP (grant Nr. 01IW20010); C. Oguz in IMPRESS (grant Nr. 01IS20076) and N. Skachkova in A-DRZ (grant No. I3N14856).

A Appendix: WCS Embeddings

We experimented with using different kinds of embeddings and their combinations for the WCS subsystem on a subset of the data. We used RST_DTreeBank_dev, Switchboard_3_dev and Persuasion_dev files for training and evaluated performance on the light_dev data. In total, we used 50 documents for training and 20 for testing. Unlike other participants (lxucs and UTD_NLP) we did not use SpanBERT embeddings, but we explored GloVe, BERT, Numberbatch, masked LM embeddings as well as separate embeddings for speaker, position and distance between mentions.

Embeddings:	1	2	3	4	5	6	7	8	9	10
GloVe head	+	-	+	-	-	-	+	-	+	+
GloVe span	-	+	+	-	-	-	+	-	+	+
BERT head	-	-	-	+	-	+	+	+	+	+
BERT span	-	-	-	-	+	+	+	+	+	+
Numberbatch	-	-	-	-	-	-	-	+	+	+
Masked LM	-	-	-	-	-	-	-	-	+	+
Distance	-	-	-	-	-	-	-	-	+	+
Speaker	-	-	-	-	-	-	-	-	+	+
Position	-	-	-	-	-	-	-	-	-	+
CoNLL score:	65.09	62.79	66.28	64.82	66.43	66.59	66.96	68.08	68.13	70.09

Table 4: Average CoNLL scores for different combinations of embeddings in WCS

Table 4 shows some of the results. GloVe head embedding works better than GloVe span embedding (experiments 1 and 2); the difference in CoNLL score is 2.3% (65.09% vs. 62.79%). Combined head and span embeddings (3) further improve the performance by 1.2%. Interestingly, the trend is different for BERT: BERT head (4) achieves 64.82% and BERT span (5) 66.43%. Note that in our case BERT span refers to an average over all BERT embeddings of the tokens within the mention span (this is different from SpanBERT). We observe a very small increase in performance when BERT span is combined with BERT head (6), 66.59% CoNLL score; BERT and Glove combined together (7) achieve 66.96%. We also found that WCS performs better when we add Numberbatch embeddings, e.g., BERT with Numberbatch (8) has 68.08% CoNLL score. We found that the combination of GloVe, BERT, Numberbatch, Masked LM, distance and speaker embeddings (9) gives us 68.13% on the test data. Furthermore, when the position embedding is added (10) the score increases to 70.09 that indicates that the positions of mentions within the document[8] play a very important role in resolving coreference.

Although we tested various combinations of embeddings, our experiments were limited to a subset of the data (we used only 50 documents for training). Another limitation of our approach is that we defined the dimensionality of each embedding separately, i.e., when passing an embedding through several linear layers we defined the output dimensionality independently for each embedding type. It would be interesting to see how interactions between different embeddings affect the dimensionality. For example, it might be that 100 dimensions work well for GloVe when it is used alone but when it is combined with BERT the dimensionality should be increased (or decreased) to achieve better performance. We would also like to test whether ablation studies show similar trends with different types of data (e.g., dialogue vs. non-dialogue, different genres) and perform a proper statistical analysis of the results. We see our present results as a starting point of an investigation of interactions between the embedding types in dialogue, to determine what embeddings work best in which case and what dimensionality they should have.

[8]Position embedding for each mention is computed as a start position divided by the total number of tokens in the document. When computing a score for clustering we concatenate both referent and antecedent positions and then pass them through a linear layer that increases the dimensionality of embedding to 200.

The Pipeline Model for Resolution of Anaphoric Reference and Resolution of Entity Reference

Hongjin Kim[*], Damrin Kim[*], Harksoo Kim
Konkuk University / Seoul, South Korea
{jin3430, ekafls33, nlpdrkim}@konkuk.ac.kr

Abstract

The objective of anaphora resolution in dialogue shared-task is to go above and beyond the simple cases of coreference resolution in written text on which NLP has mostly focused so far, which arguably overestimate the performance of current SOTA models. The anaphora resolution in dialogue shared-task consists of three subtasks; subtask1, resolution of anaphoric identity and non-referring expression identification, subtask2, resolution of bridging references, and subtask3, resolution of discourse deixis/abstract anaphora. In this paper, we propose the pipelined model (i.e., a resolution of anaphoric identity and a resolution of bridging references) for the subtask1 and the subtask2. In the subtask1, our model detects mention via the parentheses prediction. Then, we create mention representation using the token representation constituting the mention. Mention representation is fed to the coreference resolution model for clustering. In the subtask2, our model resolves bridging references via a MRC framework. We construct a query for each entity with *"What is related of ENTITY?"*. The input of our model is query and documents(i.e., all utterances of dialogue). Then, our model predicts entity span that is answer for a query.

1 Introduction

Coreference Resolution (CR) is a task which identifying and clustering mentions referring to the same entity in text. Multiple benchmark datasets of CR have been developed in recent years, However, most of these corpora only focus on identity coreference resolution and neglect relations like discourse deixis or bridging anaphora. The goal of the anaphora resolution in dialogue shared-task is to go above and beyond the simple cases of coreference resolution in these datasets (Khosla et al., 2021). This shared-task consists of three subtasks; subtask1 for resolution of anaphoric identity and non-referring expression identification, subtask2 for identifying references to entities related to already introduced entities, and subtask3 for resolution of discourse deixis/abstract anaphora. The dataset consists conversations, so it might has grammatical error. To deal with this dataset, we need to perform speaker grounding of pronouns and focus on long-distance conversation structure. In this paper, we propose the pipelined model for the subtask1 and the subtask2 (i.e., a resolution of anaphoric identity and a resolution of bridging references).

[*]equal contribution

2 Task Description

Track	AR	BR	
		Pred	**Gold**
System	Sec. 3.1	Sec. 3.2	
Setting	Pred	Pred	Gold
Baselines	-	-	
Learning framework	Pointer Net.	MRC	
Markable identification	Sec. 3.1.1	Sec. 3.1.1	
Train. data	STD	QUOREF, STD	
Dev. data	STD	STD	

Table 1: System summary

In the subtask1, our goal is to identify coreference chains which consist more cases of including split antecedent and singleton. We propose two

Proceedings of the CODI-CRAC 2021 Shared Task on Anaphora, Bridging, and Discourse Deixis in Dialogue, pages 43–47
Punta Cana, Dominican Republic, November 10, 2021. ©2021 Association for Computational Linguistics

models for the subtask1, First is the mention detection model and second is the coreference resoultion model. Our mention detection model identifies mention via the parentheses prediction. Then, based on the prediction of mention detection model, we create the mention representation using the token representation constituting the mention. Finally, mention representation is fed to the coreference resolution model for clustering. In the subtask2, our goal is to identify associative anaphoric references (i.e., references to entities related to already introduced entities). Inspired by Li et al. (2019), we propose a machine reading comprehension (MRC) framework for the subtask2. Given a question, MRC models predict answer spans from a context. Following this framework, we transformed the subtask2 to a QA task: each bridging pair $P(e_i, e_j)$ can be reconstructed as a question $q(x)$ and a answer y. We constructed the question to *"What is related of x?"*. The input of our bridging reference model is a question and the document(i.e., all utterances of the dialogue). Then, our model extracts the related entity(y) span that is an answer for the question. Our MRC model is pre-trained using QUOREF Dasigi et al. (2019) dataset. Our systems were developed using the shared-task datasets (STD) and evaluated in the tracks Eval-AR, Eval-Br(Pred) and Eval-Br(Gold), respectivly. See Table 1 for a summary.

3 Key Components of Our Model

3.1 Subtask1

3.1.1 Mention Detection

In mention detection, we perform mention detection via parentheses prediction for the token of each utterance. All mentions in the dataset is indicated in parentheses and some of these are the nested mentions. Since some of mentions are nested, traditional sequence labeling is not fit for the mention detection. For example, In *"((Health) and (education))"*, it can be expressed to [B-I-I(*Health and education*), B-O-O(*Health*), O-O-B(*education*)] by the BIO tag. To address this issue, we propose a method to predict the opening parentheses and the closing parentheses independently. Firstly we need to transform the tagging-style of the dataset. For the opening parentheses, *"((Health) and (education))"* can be tagged to ["((", "O", "("]. For the closing parentheses, it can be tagged to [")", "O", "))"].

We adopt pre-trained ELECTRA-large model Clark et al. (2020) as a backbone. Given an each utterance, $U = \{u_1, u_2, ..., u_n\}$, where n denotes the number of tokens, ELECTRA receives the input tokens and outputs the context token representation $E = \{E_1, E_2, ..., E_n\}$. For the parentheses prediction layer, we adopt the label attention network (LAN) Cui and Zhang (2019). The context token representation E is used as input to the parentheses prediction layer which is consists the opening parentheses prediction and the closing parentheses prediction. The parentheses prediction layer calculates the association of the token representation with the opening and closing parenthesis embedding vectors, the opening and closing parenthesis predictions are performed independently. More detail, the token representation E is fed to BILSTM as follows:

$$\begin{aligned} \overleftrightarrow{h}_i^1 &= \text{LSTM}(E_i, \overleftrightarrow{h}_{i-1}^1) \\ \overleftrightarrow{H}^1 &= \{\overleftrightarrow{h}_1^1, \overleftrightarrow{h}_2^1, ..., \overleftrightarrow{h}_n^1\} \end{aligned} \quad (1)$$

For the label attention, the scaled dot-product attention produces an attention matrix α consisting of a potential label distribution for each token. We define $Q = \overleftrightarrow{H}^1, K = V = Emb_k$, where k denotes the number of the parentheses. In embedding vector, two embedding vector tables are randomly initialized. One is the opening parentheses embedding and another is the closing parentheses embedding. Opening and closing parenthesis embedding are used in opening and closing parenthesis predictions, respectively. In other words, Emb_k can be Emb_k^{open} or Emb_k^{close}. The label attention vector is calculated as follows:

$$\begin{aligned} A^1(C_i) &= attention(Q, K, V) = \alpha V \\ \alpha &= softmax(\frac{Q * K^T}{\sqrt{d_h}}) \end{aligned} \quad (2)$$

Then, we concatenate the hidden states of BILSTM $\overleftrightarrow{H}^1$ and the label attention vector $A^1(C_i)$ to represent $H^1 = [\overleftrightarrow{H}^1; A^1(C_i)]$. H^1 is fed to subsequent BILSTM as follows:

$$\begin{aligned} \overleftrightarrow{h}_i^2 &= \text{LSTM}(H^1, \overleftrightarrow{h}_{i-1}^2) \\ \overleftrightarrow{H}^2 &= \{\overleftrightarrow{h}_1^2, \overleftrightarrow{h}_2^2, ..., \overleftrightarrow{h}_n^2\} \end{aligned} \quad (3)$$

Finally, the parentheses of each token is predicted based on the attention scores as follows:

$$\begin{aligned} A^2(C_i) &= softmax(\frac{Q * K^T}{\sqrt{d_h}}) \\ \hat{y}_i^{opening} &= argmax(A^2(C_i^{opening})) \\ \hat{y}_i^{closing} &= argmax(A^2(C_i^{closing})) \end{aligned} \quad (4)$$

We define $Q = \overleftrightarrow{H}^2, K = Emb_k$. It trains to minimize the cross-entropy between the predicted parenthesis and the correct parenthesis as follows:

$$loss_{opening} = -\sum_i \hat{y}_i^{opening} \log {y^{opening}}_i$$
$$loss_{closing} = -\sum_i \hat{y}_i^{closing} \log {y^{closing}}_i$$
$$loss_{total} = 0.5 * loss_{opening} + 0.5 * loss_{closing} \tag{5}$$

However, the parenthesis prediction layer may predict the number of opening and closing parentheses differently. In this case, we extract mentions based on the number of opening parentheses without using any post-processing.

3.1.2 Coreference Resolution

In coreference resolution, we create the mention representation using the token representation constituting the mention as follows:

$$M_i = \frac{1}{N-k+1} \sum_k^N \overleftrightarrow{h}_k^1 \tag{6}$$

$\overleftrightarrow{h}_k^1$ is the contextual token representation in the Equation 1. Then, the mention representations $M = \{M_1, M_2, ...M_l\}$, where l denotes the number of mentions, are fed to coreference model. We also use ELECTRA which is fine-tuned in the mention detection model. To resolve coreference, all mentions in the document need to be fed to system. However, due to the restriction of the input length, all mentions can not be fed to model at once. Therefore, we segment according to the maximum input length. Using the pointer network Vinyals et al. (2015), our model is trained to point to the mention that is referencing the closest distance. For example, if three mentions (M_i, M_j, M_k) are in the same cluster, our model is trained that (M_i, M_j, M_k) points to $(M_j, M_k, root)$, respectively (assume $i < j < k$ and mentions are sorted by the order of appearance). In case of the singleton, Our model is trained that the singleton points to itself. In the pointer network, the self-attention mechanism is used to point the mention that is referencing as follows:

$$A(M_i) = \frac{M * M}{\sqrt{d_h}}$$
$$\hat{y}_i^{coref} = argmax(softmax(A(M_i))) \tag{7}$$

For clustering, we need to post-process the prediction of our model. Since our model is trained to predict to the closest reference, we merge the cluster sequentially. If M_i points to M_j, we merge these mentions as $[M_i, M_j]$ and if M_j points to the next mention, it will be merged sequentially. If M_i points to M_i (i.e., singleton), we create the new cluster $[M_i]$. We only use this post-processing method without any other methods.

3.2 Subtask2

In the bridging references, we propose a MRC framework. We adopt pre-trained RoBERTa-large model Liu et al. (2019) as a backbone. In our MRC model, when given a query *"What is related of x"*, each token representation in document that is the output of the RoBERTa-large model is fed into a fully connected layer for predicting a starting position and an ending position of the related entity span. Since our MRC model answers for a query, it is important to decide which word to substitute for x in a query. The MRC model can be confused by the pronouns in a query, since a document might have many pronouns of the same word. We assume that the first mention (i.e., the earliest appeared mention) is not a pronoun but an ANCHOR. To avoid x being replaced by a pronoun, we substitute x with the first mention in each cluster that is result of the subtask1. The cluster $C = \{c_1, c_2, ...c_n\}$, where n denotes the number of clusters, is the result of our coreference resolution model. The mention $M_{i,1}$ in each cluster $c_i = \{M_{i,1}, M_{i,2}, ..., M_{i,j}\}$ is used as "x". j denotes the number of mentions in each cluster. For example, If the mention $M_{i,1}$ references $M_{k,1}$, a query is "what is related of $M_{i,1}$?" and our system predicts the span of $M_{k,1}$. The input of our model is a query and the document (i.e., all utterances) as *"[CLS] query [SEP] utterance$_1$ [SEP] utterance$_2$ [SEP] , ... , SEP]"*. The training objective function is the log-likelihood of the correct span.

4 Experiments

4.1 Experiments on Mention Detection

For mention detection, we evaluate our model on datasets of the anaphora resolution in dialogue shared-task. In dev-phase, For example, when we evaluate *light* dataset, we train the rest of datasets except *light*. Same manner is used for evaluating other datasets. In test-phase, we train all of the dev datasets. We use precision, recall and F1 socres for

Datasets	Precision	Recall	F1-score
light	94.09	91.25	92.67
AMI	69.29	54.04	85.55
Persuasion	93.89	91.19	92.54
Switchboard	89.46	86.76	88.11
ARRAU	84.98	93.74	89.36

Table 2: Results on mention detection for dev datasets.

Datasets	Precision	Recall	F1-score
light	95.36	93.00	94.18
AMI	92.12	89.64	90.88
Persuasion	92.91	92.95	92.93
Switchboard	92.70	89.43	91.07

Table 3: Results on mention detection for test datasets.

mention detection evaluation. As shown in Table 3, our mention detection model shows 94.18% F1 scores in the light dataset. 90.88 in the AMI dataset, 92.93 in the Persuasion dataset, and 91.07 in the Switchboard dataset.

4.2 Experiments on Coreference Resolution

		Light	AMI	Persuasion	Switchboard	ARRAU
	P	87.6	70.7	80.8	80.7	81.6
MUC	R	70.8	44.6	72.0	67.4	65.9
	F1	78.2	54.7	76.1	73.4	73.0
	P	65.0	63.7	66.1	64.5	67.5
Bcub	R	55.0	43.3	67.7	60.6	53.2
	F1	59.6	51.6	66.9	62.5	59.5
	P	53.0	41.9	61.7	54.0	36.3
CEAFe	R	78.1	70.1	75.4	75.5	75.9
	F1	63.1	52.4	67.9	62.9	49.1
CoNLL		67.0	52.9	70.3	66.31	60.5

Table 4: Results on coreference resolution for dev datasets.

Table 4 and Table 5 shows the results of the scores of MUC Vilain et al. (1995), B-cubed Bagga and Baldwin (1998), CEAF Luo (2005), and the averaged CoNLL score Pradhan et al. (2014). As shown in Table 5, our model shows 69.1% in the light, 57.5% in the AMI, 71.0% in the Persuasion and 65.6% in the Switchboard respectively. Our model achieved the overall average score 65.9% (ranked at top 3 in subtask1) of all datasets.

4.3 Experiments on Bridging Reference

In test-phase of bridging reference, there are two phases depending on whether the gold mention is given. When the gold mention is given in Eval-Br(Gold) phase, but in Eval-Br(Pred), we need to extract the mentions. In Eval-Br(Pred) phase, we

		Light	AMI	Persuasion	Switchboard
	P	89.3	69.0	76.5	80.9
MUC	R	76.1	53.5	78.4	66.7
	F1	82.1	60.3	77.3	73.1
	P	64.9	63.6	65.6	66.2
Bcub	R	56.1	49.8	72.6	58.7
	F1	60.2	55.9	68.9	62.2
	P	55.7	46.5	61.9	52.0
CEAFe	R	78.4	72.4	73.1	75.8
	F1	65.1	56.6	67.0	61.7
CoNLL		69.1	57.59	71.0	65.67

Table 5: Results on coreference resolution for test datasets.

		Light	AMI	Persuasion	Switchboard
	P	28.7	32.3	20.9	29.7
AR	R	54.6	38.3	60.4	43.4
	F1	37.7	35.0	31.0	35.2
	P	7.2	7.1	6.5	6.8
FBM	R	14.9	9.1	20.1	10.7
	F1	9.7	8.0	9.8	8.3
	P	10.2	9.4	8.2	9.2
FBE	R	19.5	11.2	23.9	13.5
	F1	13.4	10.2	12.3	10.9

Table 6: Results on bridging reference in Eval-Br(Pred) phase.

use our mention detection model and coreference resolution model. In Eval-Br(Gold) phase, we only use our coference resolution model. In other words, we use the result of in the subtask1. For evaluating bridging reference, we use precision, recall and f1-score of AR, FBM and FBE. AR is anaphora recognation, FBM is full bridging at mention level and FBE is full bridging at entity level. Table 6 shows the results of the Eval-Br(Pred) phase. In FBE scores, recall is significantly higher than precision. One possible reason is that our bridging reference MRC model can not classfy no-answerable query. Even if a no-answerable query is given to our model, it is inevitable to predict answer span since our model does not train to classify whether a query is answerable. Table 7 shows the results of the Eval-Br(Gold) phase. In FBE scores, precision is significantly improved compare with the Eval-Br(Pred) phase. It suggests that the correct mention detection is effective for coreference resolution and bridging reference. Our model achieved the overall average score 11.76% (ranked at top 2) and 17.27% (ranked at top 2) in Eval-Br(Pred) and Eval-Br(Gold) respectively.

		Light	AMI	Persuasion	Switchboard
AR	P	38.1	41.9	31.2	41.1
	R	34.6	30.8	53.1	30.9
	F1	36.3	35.5	39.3	35.3
FBM	P	11.9	12.9	11.7	14.9
	R	12.2	10.9	22.5	13.1
	F1	12.0	11.8	15.4	14.0
FBE	P	17.5	18.0	14.9	21.3
	R	15.9	13.2	25.3	16.0
	F1	16.6	15.3	18.7	18.3

Table 7: Results on bridging reference in Eval-Br(Gold) phase.

5 Conclusion

We proposed the pipeline model for resolution of anaphoric reference and resolution of entity reference. Our resolution of anaphoric reference model consists of mention detection model and coreference resolution model. Mention detection model extracts mentions via the parentheses prediction. Based on the result of mention detection model, the mention representation is created and then is fed to the coreference resolution model. Our coreference resolution model points to the closest mention using pointer network, and then merges mentions in same cluster sequentially. In subtask1, Our model achieved 65.9% the overall average score of all datasets (ranked at top 3). Our resolution of entity reference model utilizes a MRC framework. Given a query for related entity, our model predicts the related entity span. Our model achieved the overall average score 11.76% (ranked at top 2) and 17.26% (ranked at top 2) in Eval-Br(Pred) and Eval-Br(Gold) respectively.

Acknowledgements

This work was supported by Institute of Information communications Technology Planning Evaluation (IITP) grant funded by the Korea government (MSIT) (No.2020-0-00368, A Neural-Symbolic Model for Knowledge Acquisition and Inference Techniques). Also, This work was supported by the National Research Foundation of Korea (NRF) grant funded by the Korea government (MSIT) (No. 2020R1F1A1069737).

References

Amit Bagga and Breck Baldwin. 1998. Algorithms for scoring coreference chains. In *The first international conference on language resources and evaluation workshop on linguistics coreference*, volume 1, pages 563–566. Citeseer.

Kevin Clark, Minh-Thang Luong, Quoc V Le, and Christopher D Manning. 2020. Electra: Pre-training text encoders as discriminators rather than generators. *arXiv preprint arXiv:2003.10555*.

Leyang Cui and Yue Zhang. 2019. Hierarchically-refined label attention network for sequence labeling. In *Proceedings of the 2019 Conference on Empirical Methods in Natural Language Processing and the 9th International Joint Conference on Natural Language Processing (EMNLP-IJCNLP)*, pages 4115–4128.

Pradeep Dasigi, Nelson F Liu, Ana Marasović, Noah A Smith, and Matt Gardner. 2019. Quoref: A reading comprehension dataset with questions requiring coreferential reasoning. *arXiv preprint arXiv:1908.05803*.

Sopan Khosla, Yu Juntao, Manuvinakurike Ramesh, Ng Vincent, Poesio Massimo, Strube Michael, and Rosé Carolyn. 2021. The codi-crac 2021 shared task on anaphora, bridging, and discourse deixis in dialogue. In *Proceedings of the CODI-CRAC 2021 Shared Task on Anaphora, Bridging, and Discourse Deixis in Dialogue, Association for Computational Linguistics*.

Xiaoya Li, Fan Yin, Zijun Sun, Xiayu Li, Arianna Yuan, Duo Chai, Mingxin Zhou, and Jiwei Li. 2019. Entity-relation extraction as multi-turn question answering. *arXiv preprint arXiv:1905.05529*.

Yinhan Liu, Myle Ott, Naman Goyal, Jingfei Du, Mandar Joshi, Danqi Chen, Omer Levy, Mike Lewis, Luke Zettlemoyer, and Veselin Stoyanov. 2019. Roberta: A robustly optimized bert pretraining approach. *arXiv preprint arXiv:1907.11692*.

Xiaoqiang Luo. 2005. On coreference resolution performance metrics. In *Proceedings of Human Language Technology Conference and Conference on Empirical Methods in Natural Language Processing*, pages 25–32.

Sameer Pradhan, Xiaoqiang Luo, Marta Recasens, Eduard Hovy, Vincent Ng, and Michael Strube. 2014. Scoring coreference partitions of predicted mentions: A reference implementation. In *Proceedings of the conference. Association for Computational Linguistics. Meeting*, volume 2014, page 30. NIH Public Access.

Marc Vilain, John D Burger, John Aberdeen, Dennis Connolly, and Lynette Hirschman. 1995. A model-theoretic coreference scoring scheme. In *Sixth Message Understanding Conference (MUC-6): Proceedings of a Conference Held in Columbia, Maryland, November 6-8, 1995*.

Oriol Vinyals, Meire Fortunato, and Navdeep Jaitly. 2015. Pointer networks. *arXiv preprint arXiv:1506.03134*.

An End-to-End Approach for Full Bridging Resolution

Joseph Renner, Priyansh Trivedi, Gaurav Maheshwari, Rémi Gilleron, Pascal Denis
Magnet, INRIA Lille, France
{joseph.renner, priyansh.trivedi, gaurav.maheshwari,
remi.gilleron, pascal.denis}@inria.fr

Abstract

In this article, we describe our submission to the CODI-CRAC 2021 Shared Task on Anaphora Resolution in Dialogues – Track BR (Gold)[1]. We demonstrate the performance of an end-to-end transformer-based higher-order coreference model finetuned for the task of *full bridging*. We find that while our approach is not effective at modeling the complexities of the task, it performs well on bridging resolution, suggesting a need for investigations into a robust anaphor identification model for future improvements.

1 Introduction

Anaphora is a discourse level phenomenon wherein a linguistic entity (referred to as **anaphor**) is associated with some other linguistic entity (referred to as an antecedent) within a document (Tognini-Bonelli, 2001). Broadly, the phenomenon is divided into coreference and bridging anaphora depending on whether the anaphoric references are linked to associated antecedents with an identical (*is-a*), or a non-identical ($\neg$ *is-a*) relation, respectively. Following is an example of bridging anaphora – the focus of this article:

> Starbucks has a new take on the unicorn cappuccino. **One employee** accidentally leaked a picture of the secret new drink.

Here, the noun phrase "*One employee*" (bridging anaphor) is anaphorically linked to the antecedent – "*Starbucks*". In this instance, bridging anaphor can be thought of as an expression with an implicit argument, i.e., *one employee (of Starbucks)* (Rösiger et al., 2018).

The task of *full bridging* is that of identifying anaphors from a given set of linguistic entities in the document and linking them with their non-identical associated antecedent. This task is arguably more difficult and relatively understudied than that of entity coreference resolution – which involves identifying coreferent linguistic entities. This difficulty can be seen from the fact that Bridging anaphors are less likely to conform to syntactic or surface clues (Kobayashi and Ng, 2020), and the low inter-annotator agreement for bridging annotations (Markert et al., 2012). Hindrances to rapid progress on the task, however, also include lack of ample gold labeled data (Rösiger, 2018; Hou, 2020), and standardised evaluation schemes (Kobayashi and Ng, 2020). The CODI-CRAC 2021 shared task (Khosla et al., 2021) is thus a welcome addition to the existing set of datasets in the field as it provides a consistent benchmark across multiple gold-annotated datasets.

However, unlike the task variant that the majority of existing approaches tackle, the shared task also includes identification of the bridging anaphors as a part of the task. That is, most existing approaches (Lassalle and Denis, 2011; Hou et al., 2013; Hou, 2018a,b) assume the anaphor (here, "*one employee*") to be given, and are limited to selecting the correct antecedent for this phrase, amongst a predefined list of linguistic entities. The identification of anaphors compounds the difficulty of the task, owing to, amongst other things, the number of markables (linguistic entities) in a document (See Table 1), and low recall of anaphoric noun phrases in existing datasets (Rösiger et al., 2018).

That said, coreference resolution is a more complex task in terms of the decisions to be taken for correct predictions. Coreference chains are variadic, whereas relations representing bridging anaphors are binary. Further, contemporary approaches treat mention detection as a part of the task. The neural architectures thus proposed for

[1]Task home page - https://competitions.codalab.org/competitions/30312

Proceedings of the CODI-CRAC 2021 Shared Task on Anaphora, Bridging, and Discourse Deixis in Dialogue, pages 48–54
Punta Cana, Dominican Republic, November 10, 2021. ©2021 Association for Computational Linguistics

coreference resolution are often more expressive than the task of full bridging (with gold markables) requires. Based on this observation, we aim to find whether the aforementioned neural architectures can be adapted for solving a linguistically complex but simpler (in the above stated terms) task of full bridging. To that end, we experiment with the *independent* variant of the transformer based higher-order coreference model (Joshi et al., 2019).

We empirically find that the approach is inadequate in solving the task, and posit that the currently available amount of gold-labeled data is insufficient for this family of approaches. This suggests a need for more data, or the use of external information in solving the full bridging task when using this family of approaches. However, we observe that when tasked with only the resolution of bridging anaphors (i.e., the anaphoric markables are provided as a part of the task), this approach performs significantly better, suggesting that a two-step identification and resolution approach might be beneficial for the task.

2 Task Description

In this section, we introduce domain specific terms used throughout the article, and formalise the different variants of tasks corresponding to identification and association of bridging anaphors. We use the nomenclature used in (Rösiger et al., 2018).

Markables: A set of linguistic entities in a document of which anaphors and antecedents are both subsets.

Bridging Anaphor: A markable whose interpretation depends upon an antecedent, or more generally, which is implicitly linked to an antecedent with a non-identity relation. We refer to them as simply *anaphors* in the rest of this article.

Antecedent: The markable which is related to the anaphor with an implicit non-identity relation.

2.1 Task Variants

There are two primary variants of the task, defined as follows:

- **Bridging Resolution**: Given a document, and bridging anaphor markables, the task is that of finding the associated antecedent corresponding to each given bridging anaphors, from one of the markables preceding it.
- **Full Bridging**: Given a document, identify the bridging anaphors and find their associated antecedent from one of the markables preceding it.

If the markables are provided alongwith the corpus annotations, we call them **gold** markables. Otherwise, the approaches solving the task are expected to predict these markables. We refer to the latter as **predicted** markables.

The *CODI-CRAC 2021 Shared-Task: Anaphora Resolution in Dialogues* - Track BR (Gold) that we target is thus that of **Full Bridging with Gold Markables**[2].

3 Approach

3.1 Full Bridging with Higher-Order coreference model

Our full bridging system is based on the independent version (Joshi et al., 2019) of the higher-order coreference resolution model described in (Lee et al., 2018). As their model is designed for the coreference resolution with **predicted** markables, we adapt it for the full bridging task with gold markables. In this sub-section, we provide a brief overview of our augmented model and the associated problem formulation.

Following the footsteps of (Lee et al., 2018), we formulate the problem as selecting an antecedent y_i, from the set $\gamma(i)$, for each markable m_i in the document. The set includes a dummy antecedent ϵ and all the markables in the document before m_i, that is $\gamma(i) = \{\epsilon, m_1, ..., m_{i-1}\}$. A non-dummy assignment represents an anaphor-antecedent link between m_i and y_i, while a dummy assignment means that the markable has no antecedent in the document i.e., the markable is not a bridging anaphor.

For each markable m_i, the model learns a distribution $P(y_i)$ over all the previous markable set $\gamma(i)$:

$$P(y_i) = \frac{e^{s(m_i, y_i)}}{\sum_{y' \in \gamma(i)} e^{s(m_i, y')}} \quad (1)$$

The s(x,y) is the scoring function consisting of three parts defined as:

$$s(x, y) = s_m(x) + s_m(y) + s_p(x, y) \quad (2)$$

$$s_m(x) = \text{FFNN}_m(\mathbf{x}) \quad (3)$$

$$s_p(x, y) = \text{FFNN}_p(\mathbf{x}, \mathbf{y}, \phi(x, y)) \quad (4)$$

[2]For the purposes of further analysis, we also consider **Bridging Resolution with Gold Markables** over provided train sets.

Here $\mathbf{x}$ and $\mathbf{y}$ are the encoded representation of the two markables. These encodings are obtained by concatenating the transformer's output at the start and end of the span along with the attention vector computed over the output representation of the tokens in the span. $\phi(x, y)$ refers to the hand crafted features (the genre indicating the dataset to which this document belongs , speaker-ids, length of the two markables, and the number of tokens between them), while FFNN_m and FFNN_p represents feed forward network.

Recall that the approach in (Lee et al., 2018) is factored into a two-staged beam search. The first stage is responsible for predicting markables: a beam of up to M potential markables is computed based on the spans with the highest markable scores $s_m(x)$ out of all possible text spans, up to a certain width, in a document. In the second stage, the pairwise scores $s_p(x, y)$ are then only computed between the top markables, in a coarse-to-fine manner. Since we have access to the **gold** markables, we repurpose the markable scorer $s_m(x)$ to score markables as possible antecedents or anaphors. The number of markables can be large in documents, thus the beam search is necessary to keep memory costs down, otherwise the pairwise scoring would not be feasible.

We refer interested readers to (Lee et al., 2018) for a more detailed explanation of the model, including the coarse-to-fine pairwise scorer. The model is trained by the marginal log-likelihood of the possible correct antecedents. We further add a binary cross entropy based supervision over the outputs of the markable scorer $s_m(i)$, labeling markables as 0 if its neither an antecedent or an anaphor, and 1 if it is either of the two.

3.2 Bridging Resolution with Higher-Order coreference model

We adapt the model explained above to also solve the Bridging Resolution task (See Sec. 2.1). That is, since the set of anaphor markables is given, we do not intend for the model to identity anaphors, as well as resolve their antecedents, but only do the latter. This allows simplifications to the model and training setting: first, we can pass each anaphor, together with the document (up to the end of the anaphor sentence), into the model at a time, predicting one antecedent for the input anaphor given the relevant part of the document, instead of passing the entire document into the model and predicting all the anaphors and their antecedents at the same time.

This change in setting considerably alleviates memory constraints, since the pairwise scorer $s_p(x, y)$ is only computed between the one given anaphor and the possible antecedent markables, as opposed to an *n by n* pairwise scorer in the full bridging setting. This eliminates the need for both the mention scorer $s_m(x)$ and the coarse part of the coarse to fine pairwise scorer, leaving just the higher order, "fine" pairwise scorer described in (Lee et al., 2018). Also, this allows the use of a cross entropy loss over all possible antecedents (excluding the dummy class, as we know each labeled anaphor has an antecedent) for each anaphor. Finally, we remove the auxiliary supervision over the markable scorer outputs, as the scorer is no longer used.

4 Experiments

In this first experiment, we perform **full bridging** (with gold mentions) over the provided datasets (Sec. 4.1).

4.1 Datasets

The shared task is comprised of conversational documents from four domains, annotated with bridging anaphors using the Universal Anaphora format (Poesio et al., 1999). The five domains are:
Switchboard: A subset of the Switchboard Dialog Act Corpus (Godfrey et al., 1992), this dataset consists of transcribed phone conversations between two participants about varied topics including child care, recycling and news media. We filter out transcribed speech disfluencies (such as "emm", "ahh", "uh", etc) based on a hand-crafted list of bi-grams as a pre-processing step.
Light: Light is a collection of "character driven, human-human crowdworker interaction involving action, emotes and dialogue" (Urbanek et al., 2019) in the context of a fantasy text adventure game.
Persuasion: A collection of crowdsourced online conversations where a persuader tries to convince the persuadee to donate to a charity were introduced in (Wang et al., 2019). An annotated subset of these conversations are a part of this shared task.
AMI: Some of the transcripts of multi-speaker office meetings (Carletta, 2006) were annotated with bridging anaphors. Generally, these conversations are the longest of the four.

In all four cases, the test set is held out but

Dataset	Anaphors	Documents	Avg. Words	Avg. Markables	Avg. Words Between
Switchboard	603	11	1362 ± 339	366 ± 100	131 ± 228
Light	381	20	575 ± 79	194 ± 28	71 ± 100
Persuasion	245	21	474 ± 98	131 ± 30	41 ± 28
AMI	851	7	4820 ± 2258	1276 ± 595	197 ± 560
Trains-91	67	15	956 ± 691	190 ± 132	99 ± 165
Trains-93	610	94	726 ± 408	148 ± 83	66 ± 100

Table 1: Some statistics about the train sets of the datasets used in the shared task. From left to right, we report (i) the number of *anaphors* across all documents, (ii) number of documents, (iii) avg. length of each document, (iv) avg. number of markables in a document, and, (v) avg. number of tokens between an anaphor and its antecedent.

documents from the train set are annotated with markables, bridging anaphors and their antecedents. Apart from these, annotated instances from Trains-1993 (Allen, James and Heeman, Peter A., 1995), and Trains-1991 (Gross et al., 1993) Spoken Dialog Corpus, a subset of the ARRAU corpus (Uryupina et al., 2020) were used for training the models as well. Table 1 contains further statistics on the train set of these datasets.

4.2 Experimental Setup

We use Entity-F1 (Pradhan et al., 2012) as our metric for this experiment. We initialize our model, as outlined in Sec. 3.1 with a transformer based encoder with `bert-base-uncased` weights (Devlin et al., 2019) provided on the HuggingFace Model Hub (Wolf et al., 2020), and freeze it before subsequent fine-tuning. We use a two layer network with its hidden dimension and dropouts specified below, and a ReLU activation in the feed forward layers indicated in Eqn. 4.

During training, we set the batch size as 1, vary the hidden dimension of feed forward subnetworks between $\{256, 512\}$, and their dropout between $\{0.0, 0.3, 0.5\}$. We also experiment with multiple class weights for auxiliary supervision over the mention scorer's outputs, to compensate for the imbalance between anaphoric and non-anaphoric markables. We vary the inclusion of hand-crafted features (see $\phi(x, y)$ in Eq. 4 and the description of hand crafted features in Sec. 3.1) as a part of the grid search.

This experiment also represents our submission to the shared task. Corresponding to each of the aforementioned datasets, we submit a separate model. The hyperparameters for these models are found by running a 5-fold cross validation based grid search where, in each fold, the models are trained on 80% of instances of the corresponding dataset, and 100% of train instances of the remaining datasets[3], and is evaluated on the held out instances from the corresponding dataset. Once the hyperparameters are fixed corresponding to a dataset, we retrain the model from scratch on all training instances of all datasets for up to 20 epochs. The performance of the approach can be found in Table 2.

4.3 Results

We find that our end-to-end approach performs sub-optimally on all four datasets. Upon closer inspection, this performance is indicative of the challenge arisen by the amount of markables in a document. For instance, a document in Persuasion (F1: 16.28) contains only 134 markables on average, whereas a document in AMI (F1: 6.00) contains 1381 markables. This alludes to an inverse correlation between the average number of markables in document of a dataset and the entity F1 score on it. Also, the "Avg. words between" column in Table 1 indicates that anaphors and antecedents lie closer to each other in Persuasion when compared to other datasets. We hypothesise that this correlation, modeled as a part of hand-crafted features is actively exploited by our approach to increase a higher relative performance on the task.

Moreover, full bridging can be thought of as a combination of anaphor identification and bridging resolution. In order to ascertain whether our approach falters disproportionately on either of the two tasks, we perform a subsequent bridging resolution experiment over the train sets of these datasets (as they contain identified anaphors).

4.4 Bridging Resolution

We make the changes to the model and training procedure as outlined in Sec. 3.2. We keep the

[3] Including Trains-91 and Trains-93 datasets

Test Set	Ent F1	Track	Setting	Baselines	Learning Framework	Markable Identification Model	Training Set	Development Set
Switchboard	7.79	Bridging	Gold	-	-	-	All_{train}	5CV_{dev}
Light	9.35	Bridging	Gold	-	-	-	All_{train}	5CV_{dev}
Persuasion	16.28	Bridging	Gold	-	-	-	All_{train}	5CV_{dev}
AMI	6.00	Bridging	Gold	-	-	-	All_{train}	5CV_{dev}

Table 2: Results, and settings of our submission to the shared task as detailed in Sec. 4.2. As mentioned, we use the Entity-F1 metric to report the performance. All_{train} refers to the collection of all instances from the training set of the datasets mentioned in Sec. 4.1, and 5CV_{dev} refer to the *development* subsets, as they occur in each fold of the aforementioned 5-fold cross-validation based grid search in Sec. 4.2.

Approach	Switchboard Acc	Light Acc	Persuasion Acc	AMI Acc
Random	3.96	6.8	6.94	7.29
Skip-Gram	21.44	25.21	36.33	18.10
Unnamed	34.00	33.08	55.51	31.02

Table 3: Results of the experiment outlined in Sec. 4.4.

same hyperparameters (and grid search based hyperparameter search) as above, and train one model to make the predictions. However, unlike before, this experiment is performed in a 5-fold cross validation setup. Specifically, in each fold, we treat 20% of instances from each dataset as the test set. Another 10% are reserved for hyperparameter optimisation, and the remaining 70% of the instances are used for training the model. The performance reported in Table 3 is averaged over the five folds.

4.4.1 Baselines

We also report the performance of two baselines, outlined below.

Random: We select one of the markables at random which appears either in the first sentence of the document, or up to two sentences behind the anaphor. This sentence based strategy seemed to perform better than the one used in (Rösiger et al., 2018; Poesio et al., 2004).

Skip-Gram: We take the mean of pretrained Skip-Gram (Mikolov et al., 2013) embeddings of every token in a markable to create its vector representation. Then, using the cosine distance as a measure of anaphora, we select the antecedent which lies closest to the anaphor.

4.4.2 Results

We find that while the task is far from solved, our approach is significantly better at bridging resolution, compared to full bridging. That is, our model is unable to perform anaphor identification with a reasonable accuracy leading to a much worse performance on the full bridging task. Interestingly, the performance gap between the random and skip-gram baseline suggests that anaphor and antecedent markables often lie close in the vector spaces in a non-trivial amount of cases.

Across different datasets, we observe a similar trend as in the previous experiment. Our approach (as well as the skip-gram baseline) achieve its highest score on Persuasion, followed by Switchboard, Light and AMI. The performance gap between AMI and the next best approach is not as stark here (-9.3% here; -23% in Exp. 1). This can be explained by observing the random baseline. Its performance suggests that the sentences around the anaphor in AMI conversations have the least amount of markables to choose from, thereby making the task slightly easier.

5 Conclusion

In this work, we experiment with a higher-order coreference model based end-to-end approach for the full bridging task over conversational documents. We find that it is unable to model the task's complexities, however, its performance on bridging resolution is significantly better. This suggests a different approach to anaphor detection is needed, whether it be a stand alone anaphor detection model or a more guided adaptation of the higher-order coreference model (Joshi et al., 2019) that better suits the bridging task. We leave investigations along this line for the future. We also aim to experiment with approaches that can prime a model towards conversational documents, such as including the SpanBERT (Joshi et al., 2020) pretraining objective as a pre-finetuning step.

References

Allen, James and Heeman, Peter A. 1995. Trains spoken dialog corpus.

Jean Carletta. 2006. Announcing the ami meeting corpus. *The ELRA Newsletter*, 11(1):3–5.

Jacob Devlin, Ming-Wei Chang, Kenton Lee, and Kristina Toutanova. 2019. BERT: pre-training of deep bidirectional transformers for language understanding. In *Proceedings of the 2019 Conference of the North American Chapter of the Association for Computational Linguistics: Human Language Technologies, NAACL-HLT 2019, Minneapolis, MN, USA, June 2-7, 2019, Volume 1 (Long and Short Papers)*, pages 4171–4186. Association for Computational Linguistics.

John J. Godfrey, Edward Holliman, and Jane McDaniel. 1992. SWITCHBOARD: telephone speech corpus for research and development. In *1992 IEEE International Conference on Acoustics, Speech, and Signal Processing, ICASSP '92, San Francisco, California, USA, March 23-26, 1992*, pages 517–520. IEEE Computer Society.

Derek Gross, James Allen, and David Traum. 1993. The trains 91 dialogues.

Yufang Hou. 2018a. A deterministic algorithm for bridging anaphora resolution. In *Proceedings of the 2018 Conference on Empirical Methods in Natural Language Processing, Brussels, Belgium, October 31 - November 4, 2018*, pages 1938–1948. Association for Computational Linguistics.

Yufang Hou. 2018b. Enhanced word representations for bridging anaphora resolution. In *Proceedings of the 2018 Conference of the North American Chapter of the Association for Computational Linguistics: Human Language Technologies, NAACL-HLT, New Orleans, Louisiana, USA, June 1-6, 2018, Volume 2 (Short Papers)*, pages 1–7. Association for Computational Linguistics.

Yufang Hou. 2020. Bridging anaphora resolution as question answering. In *Proceedings of the 58th Annual Meeting of the Association for Computational Linguistics, ACL 2020, Online, July 5-10, 2020*, pages 1428–1438. Association for Computational Linguistics.

Yufang Hou, Katja Markert, and Michael Strube. 2013. Global inference for bridging anaphora resolution. In *Proceedings of the 2013 Conference of the North American Chapter of the Association for Computational Linguistics: Human Language Technologies*, pages 907–917.

Mandar Joshi, Danqi Chen, Yinhan Liu, Daniel S. Weld, Luke Zettlemoyer, and Omer Levy. 2020. Spanbert: Improving pre-training by representing and predicting spans. *Trans. Assoc. Comput. Linguistics*, 8:64–77.

Mandar Joshi, Omer Levy, Luke Zettlemoyer, and Daniel S. Weld. 2019. BERT for coreference resolution: Baselines and analysis. In *Proceedings of the 2019 Conference on Empirical Methods in Natural Language Processing and the 9th International Joint Conference on Natural Language Processing, EMNLP-IJCNLP 2019, Hong Kong, China, November 3-7, 2019*, pages 5802–5807. Association for Computational Linguistics.

Sopan Khosla, Juntao Yu, Ramesh Manuvinakurike, Vincent Ng, Massimo Poesio, Michael Strube, and Carolyn Rosé. 2021. The codi-crac 2021 shared task on anaphora, bridging, and discourse deixis in dialogue. In *Proceedings of the CODI-CRAC 2021 Shared Task on Anaphora, Bridging, and Discourse Deixis in Dialogue, Association for Computational Linguistics*.

Hideo Kobayashi and Vincent Ng. 2020. Bridging resolution: A survey of the state of the art. In *Proceedings of the 28th International Conference on Computational Linguistics, COLING 2020, Barcelona, Spain (Online), December 8-13, 2020*, pages 3708–3721. International Committee on Computational Linguistics.

Emmanuel Lassalle and Pascal Denis. 2011. Leveraging different meronym discovery methods for bridging resolution in french. In *Anaphora Processing and Applications - 8th Discourse Anaphora and Anaphor Resolution Colloquium, DAARC 2011, Faro, Portugal, October 6-7, 2011. Revised Selected Papers*, volume 7099 of *Lecture Notes in Computer Science*, pages 35–46. Springer.

Kenton Lee, Luheng He, and Luke Zettlemoyer. 2018. Higher-order coreference resolution with coarse-to-fine inference. In *Proceedings of the 2018 Conference of the North American Chapter of the Association for Computational Linguistics: Human Language Technologies, Volume 2 (Short Papers)*, pages 687–692, New Orleans, Louisiana. Association for Computational Linguistics.

Katja Markert, Yufang Hou, and Michael Strube. 2012. Collective classification for fine-grained information status. In *The 50th Annual Meeting of the Association for Computational Linguistics, Proceedings of the Conference, July 8-14, 2012, Jeju Island, Korea - Volume 1: Long Papers*, pages 795–804. The Association for Computer Linguistics.

Tomás Mikolov, Kai Chen, Greg Corrado, and Jeffrey Dean. 2013. Efficient estimation of word representations in vector space. In *1st International Conference on Learning Representations, ICLR 2013, Scottsdale, Arizona, USA, May 2-4, 2013, Workshop Track Proceedings*.

Massimo Poesio, Florence Bruneseaux, and Laurent Romary. 1999. The mate meta-scheme for coreference in dialogues in multiple languages. In *ACL'99 Workshop Towards Standards and Tools for Discourse Tagging*, pages 65–74.

Massimo Poesio, Rahul Mehta, Axel Maroudas, and Janet Hitzeman. 2004. Learning to resolve bridging references. In *Proceedings of the 42nd Annual Meeting of the Association for Computational Linguistics,*

21-26 July, 2004, Barcelona, Spain, pages 143–150. ACL.

Sameer Pradhan, Alessandro Moschitti, and Nianwen Xue, editors. 2012. *Joint Conference on Empirical Methods in Natural Language Processing and Computational Natural Language Learning - Proceedings of the Shared Task: Modeling Multilingual Unrestricted Coreference in OntoNotes, EMNLP-CoNLL 2012, July 13, 2012, Jeju Island, Korea*. ACL.

Ina Rösiger. 2018. BASHI: A corpus of wall street journal articles annotated with bridging links. In *Proceedings of the Eleventh International Conference on Language Resources and Evaluation, LREC 2018, Miyazaki, Japan, May 7-12, 2018*. European Language Resources Association (ELRA).

Ina Rösiger, Arndt Riester, and Jonas Kuhn. 2018. Bridging resolution: Task definition, corpus resources and rule-based experiments. In *Proceedings of the 27th International Conference on Computational Linguistics, COLING 2018, Santa Fe, New Mexico, USA, August 20-26, 2018*, pages 3516–3528. Association for Computational Linguistics.

Elena Tognini-Bonelli. 2001. *Corpus linguistics at work*, volume 6. John Benjamins Publishing.

Jack Urbanek, Angela Fan, Siddharth Karamcheti, Saachi Jain, Samuel Humeau, Emily Dinan, Tim Rocktäschel, Douwe Kiela, Arthur Szlam, and Jason Weston. 2019. Learning to speak and act in a fantasy text adventure game. In *Proceedings of the 2019 Conference on Empirical Methods in Natural Language Processing and the 9th International Joint Conference on Natural Language Processing, EMNLP-IJCNLP 2019, Hong Kong, China, November 3-7, 2019*, pages 673–683. Association for Computational Linguistics.

Olga Uryupina, Ron Artstein, Antonella Bristot, Federica Cavicchio, Francesca Delogu, Kepa Joseba Rodríguez, and Massimo Poesio. 2020. Annotating a broad range of anaphoric phenomena, in a variety of genres: the ARRAU corpus. *Nat. Lang. Eng.*, 26(1):95–128.

Xuewei Wang, Weiyan Shi, Richard Kim, Yoojung Oh, Sijia Yang, Jingwen Zhang, and Zhou Yu. 2019. Persuasion for good: Towards a personalized persuasive dialogue system for social good. In *Proceedings of the 57th Conference of the Association for Computational Linguistics, ACL 2019, Florence, Italy, July 28- August 2, 2019, Volume 1: Long Papers*, pages 5635–5649. Association for Computational Linguistics.

Thomas Wolf, Lysandre Debut, Victor Sanh, Julien Chaumond, Clement Delangue, Anthony Moi, Pierric Cistac, Tim Rault, Rémi Louf, Morgan Funtowicz, Joe Davison, Sam Shleifer, Patrick von Platen, Clara Ma, Yacine Jernite, Julien Plu, Canwen Xu, Teven Le Scao, Sylvain Gugger, Mariama Drame, Quentin Lhoest, and Alexander M. Rush. 2020. Transformers: State-of-the-art natural language processing. In *Proceedings of the 2020 Conference on Empirical Methods in Natural Language Processing: System Demonstrations*, pages 38–45, Online. Association for Computational Linguistics.

Adapted End-to-End Coreference Resolution System for Anaphoric Identities in Dialogues

Liyan Xu
Computer Science
Emory University, Atlanta, GA
liyan.xu@emory.edu

Jinho D. Choi
Computer Science
Emory University, Atlanta, GA
jinho.choi@emory.edu

Abstract

We present an effective system adapted from the end-to-end neural coreference resolution model, targeting on the task of anaphora resolution in dialogues. Three aspects are specifically addressed in our approach, including the support of singletons, encoding speakers and turns throughout dialogue interactions, and knowledge transfer utilizing existing resources. Despite the simplicity of our adaptation strategies, they are shown to bring significant impact to the final performance, with up to 27 F1 improvement over the baseline. Our final system ranks the 1st place on the leaderboard of the anaphora resolution track in the CRAC 2021 shared task, and achieves the best evaluation results on all four datasets.

1 Introduction

Coreference resolution of anaphoric identities (a.k.a. anaphora resolution) is a long-studied Natural Language Processing (NLP) task, and is still considered one of the unsolved problems, as it demands deep semantic understanding as well as world knowledge. Although there is a significant performance boost recently by the neural decoders (Lee et al., 2017, 2018) and deep contextualized encoders such as BERT and SpanBERT (Joshi et al., 2019, 2020), the majority of the experiments are based on *OntoNotes* (Pradhan et al., 2012) from the CoNLL 2012 shared task, which may overestimate the model performance due to two perspectives: the lack of support for harder cases such as singletons and split-antecedents, and the lack of focus on real-world dialogues. In this work, we target on the task of anaphora resolution in the CRAC 2021 shared task (Khosla et al., 2021) that addresses both perspectives, and present an effective coreference resolution system that is adapted from the recent end-to-end coreference model.

All datasets in the CRAC 2021 shared task are in the Universal Anaphora format. For simplicity, we refer to it as the UA format, and refer to the annotation scheme of the CoNLL 2012 shared task as the CoNLL format. The UA format is an extension of the CoNLL format, and further supports bridging references and discourse deixis. For anaphora resolution, the UA format differs from the CoNLL format on three aspects: the support of singletons, split-antecedents, and non-referring expressions (excluded from the current evaluation). Our approach specifically addresses the singleton problem (Section 3.1), which is shown to be a critical component under the UA setting that brings 17-22 F1 improvement on all datasets (Section 5.2). Few recent work has studied the split-antecedent problem (Zhou and Choi, 2018), and we leave the split-antecedents as future work.

In addition to singletons, our approach also emphasizes on the speaker encoding (Section 3.3) and knowledge transfer (Section 3.4) to address the dialogue-domain perspective. Especially, we use a simple strategy of speaker-augmented encoding that captures the speaker interaction and dialogue-turn information, utilizing the strong Transformers encoder. It has been shown by the previous study that conversational metadata such as speakers can be significant for coreference resolution on dialogue documents (Luo et al., 2009), and we do see 2-3 F1 improvement on three datasets by simply applying the speaker encoding strategy (Section 5.3).

Knowledge transfer from other existing resources is also shown to be important in our approach. Two different strategies are experimented, and the domain-adaptation strategy is able to bring large improvement, boosting 8 F1 for *LIGHT* and 6 F1 on *PSUA* (Table 3).

Our final system ranks the 1st place on the leaderboard of the anaphora resolution track in the CRAC 2021 shared task, and achieves the best evaluation results on all four datasets, with 63.96 F1 for *AMI*, 80.33 F1 for *LIGHT*, 78.41 F1 for *PSUA*, 74.49 F1 for *SWBD* (Section 5.1). A brief summary of our final submission is shown in Table 4.

Proceedings of the CODI-CRAC 2021 Shared Task on Anaphora, Bridging, and Discourse Deixis in Dialogue, pages 55–62
Punta Cana, Dominican Republic, November 10, 2021.

2 Related Work

Pretrained Transformers encoders have been successfully adopted by recent coreference resolution models and shown significant improvement (Joshi et al., 2019, 2020). We also adopt the Transformers encoder in our approach because of its superior performance. For the neural decoder, there have been two popular directions from recent work. One is mention-ranking-based, where the model predicts only one antecedent for each mention without focusing on the cluster structure (Wiseman et al., 2015; Lee et al., 2017; Wu et al., 2020). The other is cluster-based, where the model maintains the predicted clusters and performs cluster merging (Clark and Manning, 2015, 2016; Xia et al., 2020; Yu et al., 2020). We adopt the mention-ranking framework in our approach because of its simplicity as well as its state-of-the-art decoding performance.

3 Approach

3.1 Mention-Ranking (`MR`)

Our baseline model `MR` adopts the mention-ranking strategy, and follows the architecture of the end-to-end neural coreference resolution model (Lee et al., 2017, 2018) with a Transformer encoder (Joshi et al., 2019, 2020). Given a document with T tokens, the model first enumerates all valid spans, and scores every span for being a likely mention, denoted by the mention score s_m. The model then greedily selects top λT spans by s_m as mention candidates that may appear in the final coreference clusters. Let $\mathcal{X} = (x_1, \ldots, x_{\lambda T})$ be the list of all mention candidates in the document, ordered by their appearance. For each mention candidate $x_i \in \mathcal{X}$, the model selects a single coreferent antecedent from all its preceding mention candidates, denoted by $\mathcal{Y}_i = (\epsilon, x_1, \ldots, x_{i-1})$, with ϵ being a "dummy" antecedent that may be selected when x_i is not anaphoric (no antecedents).

The antecedent selection is performed by the pairwise scoring process between the current mention candidate x_i and each of its preceding candidate $y \in \mathcal{Y}_i$. The final pairwise score $s(x_i, y)$ consists of three scores: how likely each candidate being a mention, measured by the mention score s_m; and how likely they refer to the same entity, measured by the antecedent score s_a. The final score $s(x_i, y)$ can be denoted as follows:

$$s(x_i, y) = s_m(x_i) + s_m(y) + s_a(x_i, y, \phi(x_i, y))$$

Both s_m and s_a are computed by the FeedForward Neural Network (FFNN), and $\phi(x_i, y)$ represents additional meta features. Unlike previous work, we do not include the specific genre as a feature; instead, we simply use a binary feature on whether the document is dialogue-based or article-based, since dialogues can exhibit quite different traits from written articles (Aktaş and Stede, 2020). We also adopt a speaker feature that indicates whether two candidates are from the same speaker, or whether the speaker information is not available, which is important for written articles or two-party dialogues. In Section 3.3, we further adapt more speaker encoding to benefit multi-speaker dialogues and the personal pronoun issue.

For inference, the selected antecedent is the preceding candidate with the most pairwise score, denoted by $\text{argmax}_{y' \in \mathcal{Y}_i} s(x_i, y')$. For training, the marginal log-likelihood of all gold antecedents $\hat{\mathcal{Y}}_i \subseteq \mathcal{Y}_i$ for each $x_i \in \mathcal{X}$ is optimized, denoted by the loss $\mathcal{L}_c$:

$$P(y) = \frac{e^{s(x_i, y)}}{\sum_{y' \in \mathcal{Y}_i} e^{s(x_i, y')}} \quad (1)$$

$$\mathcal{L}_c = -\log \prod_{x_i \in \mathcal{X}} \sum_{\hat{y} \in \hat{\mathcal{Y}}_i} P(\hat{y}) \quad (2)$$

3.2 Singleton Recognition (`SR`)

As the UA format does support singletons, `MR` would fail to predict those singleton clusters, since the antecedent selection can only generate clusters with at least one pair of mentions. Several previous work has addressed the singleton problem from different perspectives (Yu et al., 2020; Zaporojets et al., 2021). Our `SR` model is built upon `MR` and further recognizes singletons based on the simple strategy as follows: we make use of the mention score s_m in the antecedent selection process, and create a singleton cluster for any candidates with $s_m > 0$ that have not yet found any antecedents, which poses an additional requirement on the mention score, such that only valid mentions should have $s_m > 0$. Let $\Psi^+ \subseteq \mathcal{X}$ be the set of gold mention candidates, and $\Psi^- = \mathcal{X} \setminus \Psi^+$ be the set of other mention candidates. We optimize the mention score with the binary cross-entropy loss $\mathcal{L}_m$

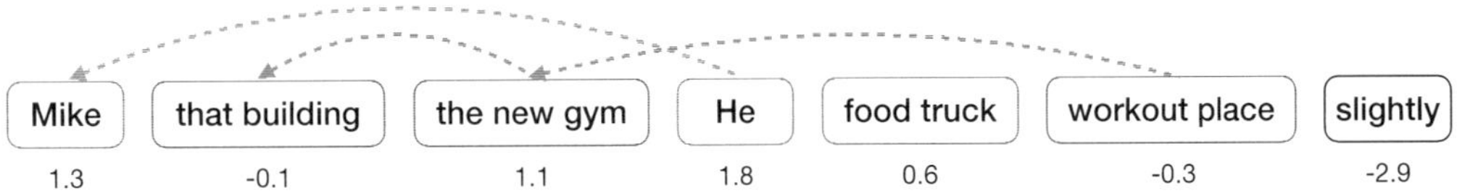

Figure 1: Example of the new antecedent selection process that support singletons (Section 3.2). Each arrow indicates the selected antecedent (the dummy antecedent is excluded), and the mention score s_m is shown below each mention. Mentions of the same predicted clusters are marked in the same color. Although no antecedent is selected for "food truck", it will still be assigned as a singleton cluster because of $s_m = 0.6 > 0$. "that building" and "workout place" are still assigned to the corresponding cluster even though their $s_m < 0$, to allow some slacks on the mention score prediction. "slightly" will not be assigned to any clusters.

and joinly train with the coreference loss $\mathcal{L}_c$:

$$\mathcal{L}_m = - \sum_{x_i \in \Psi^+} \log \sigma(s_m(x_i)) - \sum_{x_j \in \Psi^-} \log(1 - \sigma(s_m(x_j))) \quad (3)$$

$$\mathcal{L} = \mathcal{L}_c + \alpha_m \cdot \mathcal{L}_m \quad (4)$$

σ is the sigmoid function, and α_m is a hyperparameter. $\mathcal{L}$ is the final loss composed of two tasks. In practice, we also perform negative sampling on Ψ^- dynamically, so that Ψ^+ and Ψ^- are of similar sizes ($|\Psi^+| \approx |\Psi^-|$), to alleviate the negative effects from the skewed class distribution.

In the new selection process, we still regard the selected non-dummy antecedent y to be valid by $y = \text{argmax}_{y' \in \mathcal{Y}_i} s(x_i, y')$, even though the mention score of either candidate can be negative ($s_m(x_i) < 0$ or $s_m(y) < 0$). This is to allow certain slacks on the mention score prediction which could help with the mention recall. Figure 1 shows three different cases of the predicted clusters by the SR model.

3.3 Speaker Encoding (SE)

Our SE model is further adapted upon SR model and aims to strengthen the speaker encoding for each candidate representation. As we are targeting on the coreference resolution in dialogues, encoding speaker interactions becomes more critical, especially for the correct understanding of the speaker-grounded personal pronouns that are more frequent in dialogues than other non-dialogue genres (Aktaş and Stede, 2020).

The speaker feature introduced in Section 3.1 provides shallow distinction on whether two mentions are from the same speaker. However, the speaker interactions across dialogue turns are not presented in the document encoding; therefore, the representation of each candidate has no awareness on the speaker interactions at all. To provide deeper knowledge on the interactions, we adopt a simple but effective strategy that is similar to some other work in speaker encoding (Le et al., 2019; Wu et al., 2020): a special speaker token is prepended to each sentence, and we feed the new speaker-augmented document to the encoder directly.

Table 1 shows an example on this speaker augmentation. Each speaker is indexed by the order of the first appearance in the dialogue. All the special speaker tokens are added to the tokenizer vocabulary, and will be picked up in the tokenization and encoding process. Therefore, all encoded candidate representation in the SE model is conditioned on the entire speaker interactions, and automatically learns to fuse the information of speakers and turns in the training process.

John: Do you know Mike? Mary: He is my best friend! Paul: I like him too! Mary: We should meet together!
[SPK1] Do you know Mike ? **[SPK2]** He is my best friend ! **[SPK3]** I like him too ! **[SPK2]** We should meet together !

Table 1: Example for the speaker-augmented encoding. A special speaker token is assigned to each speaker and prepended to each corresponding sentence.

3.4 Knowledge Transfer

We also emphasize on the knowledge transfer in this task, as the training resources of dialogue corpora annotated in the UA format are limit and expensive to obtain, while there already exist larger-scale training corpora for other domains in different annotation schemes, e.g. the *OntoNotes* dataset in the CoNLL format that mainly consists of non-dialogue genres. For clarity, we denote the provided data annotated in the UA format as *UAD*, and other existing data in non-UA format as *OD*. We investigate two common ways to make use of *OD* in the training for SE, denoted as follows:

- $\texttt{SE}^{+M}$: **M**ix *OD* and *UAD* together as a larger dataset, regarding *OD* as data augmentation that provides more knowledge.
- $\texttt{SE}^{+P}$: **P**retrain the model on *OD* first, then further train the model on *UAD* only, regarding training on *UAD* as domain adaptation.

Above two choices are plausible in our approach, because we only use data in the CoNLL format for *OD*, which is still largely similar to the UA format, despite the difference on the singletons, non-referring expressions, and split-antecedents.

Similarly, we denote the model as $\texttt{SR}^{+M/P}$ if the SR model is used instead of SE.

4 Experiments

4.1 Datasets

For data in the UA format (*UAD*), we use the ARRAU corpus (Poesio et al., 2018) from the CRAC 2018/2021 shared task. Four sub-corpora are used as the training set for *UAD*, namely *TRAINS-93*, *PEAR*, *RST*, *GNOME*. One sub-corpus named *TRAINS-91* is used as one of the development (dev) set. In addition, four other corpora from the CRAC 2021 shared task are also used as the development set as well as the final test set, namely *AMI*, *LIGHT*, *Persuasion for Good* (*PSUA*), *Switchboard* (*SWBD*). All above datasets are of the dialogue domain except for *RST* and *GNOME*. Table 2 shows the detailed statistics of all *UAD* datasets. Note that certain datasets do not provide speaker information, therefore their averaged numbers of speakers per document are shown as 0.

For non-UA format data (*OD*), we use two datasets in the CoNLL format: *OntoNotes* (*ON*) (Pradhan et al., 2012) and *BOLT* (Li et al., 2016). *OntoNotes* consists of documents in six genres, where only two genres "Telephone Conversation" and "Broadcast Conversation" are of the dialogue domain; we use the same provided train/dev/test split for *OntoNotes*. *BOLT* has the same annotation scheme as *OntoNotes* and consists of documents from discussion forums, instant messages and telephone conversations. We perform a random 80/10/10 split for the train/dev/test set of *BOLT*. Detailed statistics of both datasets are shown in the bottom of Table 2.

	#D	#M	#C	#S
TRAINS-93	98	12148	4523	0.0
PEAR	20	3401	1168	0.0
RST	413	62409	38724	0.0
GNOME	5	5499	2598	0.0
TRAINS-91	16	2501	828	0.0
AMI (DEV)	7	7441	3120	4.0
LIGHT (DEV)	20	3448	1357	2.0
PSUA (DEV)	21	2437	1273	2.0
SWBD (DEV)	11	3421	1771	0.0
AMI (TST)	3	4139	1883	4.0
LIGHT (TST)	21	3501	1359	2.0
PSUA (TST)	28	3446	1857	2.0
SWBD (TST)	22	7847	3897	2.0
ON (TRN)	2802	155558	35142	0.6
ON (DEV)	343	19155	4545	0.8
ON (TST)	348	19764	4532	0.8
BOLT (TRN)	1110	58146	12854	2.5
BOLT (DEV)	137	8029	1649	2.5
BOLT (TST)	137	7599	1610	2.5

Table 2: Statistics for all datasets (Section 4.1), excluding non-referring expressions. *UAD* datasets are shown in the upper part, and *OD* datasets shown in the bottom part. TRN/DEV/TST: the train/dev/test split. `#D`: total number of documents; `#M`: total number of mentions; `#C`: total number of clusters; `#S`: averaged number of speakers per document (excluding unknown speakers).

4.2 Preprocessing

We only perform one trivial preprocessing step specific to the training set of *UAD* datasets: remove all non-referring expressions and regard them as non-mentions, as they will not be counted in the final evaluation (Section 5). In addition, our current approach does not consider split-antecedents, which we will leave as future work.

4.3 Implementation

Our system is based on the PyTorch implementation of the end-to-end coreference resolution model from Xu and Choi (2020), and we follow the similar hyperparameter settings. Specifically, $\text{SpanBERT}_{\text{Large}}$ (Joshi et al., 2020) is used as the Transformers encoder with maximum sequence length of 512. Long documents are split into multiple sequences, and each sequence is encoded by $\text{SpanBERT}_{\text{Large}}$ independently, as suggested by (Joshi et al., 2019). During training, we limit the maximum sequences to be 3 due to the GPU memory constraints, and a long document will be truncated into multiple documents if it exceeds the maximum sequences.

Hyperparameters For all datasets, nested mentions are always enabled. We set the $\lambda = 0.5$ and maximum span width to be 30 in the span enumer-

	AMI				*LIGHT*			
	MUC	B^3	$CEAF_{\phi_4}$	Avg F1	MUC	B^3	$CEAF_{\phi_4}$	Avg F1
MR	46.06	31.28	17.87	31.73	79.47	48.61	24.06	50.71
SR	54.66	53.32	53.64	53.87	79.12	63.34	65.59	69.35
SR^{+P}	50.08	52.63	52.60	51.77	86.39	74.68	**69.57**	76.88
SE	57.01	53.91	53.65	54.86	77.38	63.91	65.46	68.92
SE^{+M}	**59.36**	48.49	40.05	49.30	86.92	68.49	41.66	65.69
SE^{+P}	56.93	**55.27**	**53.92**	**55.37**	**87.23**	**74.91**	68.86	**77.00**
SE^{+P}+DEV	70.70	61.37	59.81	63.96	90.03	79.19	71.77	80.33

(a) Evaluation results on the test set of *AMI* and *LIGHT*.

	PSUA				*SWBD*			
	MUC	B^3	$CEAF_{\phi_4}$	Avg F1	MUC	B^3	$CEAF_{\phi_4}$	Avg F1
MR	75.15	50.80	21.78	49.24	72.70	46.65	22.54	47.30
SR	73.36	67.97	64.15	68.49	73.92	62.38	58.01	64.77
SR^{+P}	78.96	73.83	65.27	72.69	75.30	65.16	57.69	66.05
SE	72.99	68.56	64.37	68.64	74.47	63.32	58.77	65.52
SE^{+M}	81.63	65.82	44.83	64.10	76.54	61.43	43.97	60.65
SE^{+P}	**82.19**	**76.50**	**67.46**	**75.38**	**77.56**	**67.56**	**59.36**	**68.16**
SE^{+P}+DEV	84.04	79.57	71.63	78.41	80.63	74.39	68.45	74.49

(b) Evaluation results on the test set of *Persuasion for Good* (*PSUA*) and *Switchboard* (*SWBD*).

Table 3: Evaluation results on the test set of four datasets (Section 4.1). The macro-averaged F1 of MUC, B^3, and $CEAF_{\phi_4}$ is the main evaluation metric. Section 3 describes the details of all listed approaches. SE^{+P}+DEV is the setting of our final submission to the CRAC 2021 shared task, where all available development sets are also added in the training process for SE^{+P} (Section 5.1).

Track	Resolution of anaphoric identities
Setting	Predicted mentions
Baseline	MR (§3.1). The end-to-end coreference resolution model with the SpanBERT encoder (Joshi et al., 2020; Xu and Choi, 2020) is used as the baseline.
Approach	SE^{+P}+DEV (§3.4). The final model is built upon baseline with three key adaptations: 1) An updated antecedent selection process is used to support singletons, with an additional optimization on the mention scores. 2) Speaker-augmentation strategy is used to encode the speakers and dialogue-turns. 3) Knowledge transfer is employed that pretrains the model on CoNLL datasets, then further trains on the UA datasets as a domain adaptation step. The final submission includes the dev data into training.
Train Data	*TRAINS-93, PEAR, RST, GNOME, ON, BOLT* (§4.1)
Dev Data	*TRAINS-91, AMI, LIGHT, PSUA, SWBD, ON, BOLT* (§4.1)

Table 4: Summary of our final submission to the CRAC 2021 shared task. Train/Dev Data: all datasets we use for the training set and development set.

ation stage, and limit the maximum antecedents to be 50 in the pair scoring process. Adam optimizer is used for the optimization, with the weight decay rate of 10^{-2} and gradient clipping norm of 1. We employ the learning rate of 1×10^{-5} for Transformers parameters, and 3×10^{-4} for task parameters. $\alpha_m = 0.1$ is used for Eq (4). In particular, we do not apply any higher-order inferences, as their benefits are shown trivial (Xu and Choi, 2020).

Training When training *UAD* or *OD* alone, we concatenate and mix all its corresponding corpora together as the training data. For SE^{+M}, we concatenate and mix all available training corpora together regardless of *UAD* or *OD*. All experiments are conducted on a Nvidia A100 GPU. 20 training epochs are used for all the settings, and the training takes around 1-2 hours for *UAD* and 3-4 hours for *OD*.

In particular, development sets are not added to the training data, except for our final submission to the shared task, where the best-performed model has been identified, then we train the final model with the same setting but adding all development sets in the training (Section 5.1).

5 Results and Analysis

The Universal Anaphora Scorer[1] is used in the official evaluation process. For the task of anaphora resolution, the main evaluation metric is the averaged F1 score of MUC, B^3 and $CEAF_{\phi_4}$, same as the CoNLL 2012 shared task. Singletons and split-antecedents are included in the evaluation, while non-referring expressions are excluded.

5.1 Results

Table 3 shows the evaluation results on the test set of four datasets using different approaches. Among all approaches without adding the dev sets into training, $\texttt{SE}^{+P}$ achieves the best results on all four datasets. Another $\texttt{SE}^{+P}$ model is then trained with adding the dev sets as our final submission, dentoed by $\texttt{SE}^{+P}$+DEV, which further yields the best results, and ranks the 1st place at the "anaphoric identity" track in the CRAC 2021 shared task.

Final Submission Table 4 lists the summary of our final submission to the shared task.

5.2 Analysis: Singleton Recognition

One of the main differences between the UA and CoNLL format is that UA supports singletons, as UA annotates all noun phrases. The left side of Table 6 shows the total number and percentage of the singleton clusters on the test set of four datasets. Singletons are indeed prevalent, and all four datasets have at least 73% of their gold clusters as singletons. Therefore, recognizing singletons can become critical for coreference resolution on the UA formatted data.

Comparing MR and SR in Table 3, it is clear that singleton recognition plays a pivotal role in the final performance, with SR outperforming MR by a huge margin of 17-22 Avg F1 on all four datasets. To further examine the performance of SR, we collect the precision/recall of the predicted mentions by different models, as well as the precision/recall of predicted singletons over gold singletons, as shown in Table 5. Compared with MR, all models that support singletons receive huge gains on the mention recall with 26-36% improvement, with relatively small 5-10% degradation on the mention precision.

	Mentions			*Singletons*		
	P	R	F	P	R	F
MR	**90.3**	40.6	56.1	-	-	-
SR	84.7	76.4	80.3	44.7	54.8	49.2
$\texttt{SR}^{+P}$	83.1	74.3	78.5	42.8	54.0	47.8
SE	83.4	77.7	80.4	43.1	**55.9**	48.7
$\texttt{SE}^{+M}$	81.5	69.5	75.0	29.8	35.7	32.5
$\texttt{SE}^{+P}$	84.1	**77.9**	**80.9**	**45.8**	53.5	**49.4**

(a) Statistics on the test set of *AMI*.

	Mentions			*Singletons*		
	P	R	F	P	R	F
MR	**97.1**	60.0	74.2	-	-	-
SR	87.7	86.8	87.2	56.3	72.1	63.2
$\texttt{SR}^{+P}$	90.1	89.4	89.7	**65.1**	68.3	**66.6**
SE	87.6	86.3	87.0	55.0	**73.6**	62.9
$\texttt{SE}^{+M}$	91.4	71.7	80.3	43.1	23.9	30.8
$\texttt{SE}^{+P}$	90.0	**89.6**	**89.8**	62.1	68.4	65.1

(b) Statistics on the test set of *LIGHT*.

	Mentions			*Singletons*		
	P	R	F	P	R	F
MR	**94.9**	56.8	71.1	-	-	-
SR	89.5	85.4	87.4	66.2	55.4	60.3
$\texttt{SR}^{+P}$	91.8	86.4	89.0	74.3	51.5	60.8
SE	88.8	86.0	87.4	64.6	**57.2**	60.7
$\texttt{SE}^{+M}$	90.5	69.9	78.9	53.6	26.0	35.1
$\texttt{SE}^{+P}$	91.9	**87.4**	**89.6**	**74.8**	54.4	**63.0**

(c) Statistics on the test set of *Persuasion for Good* (*PSUA*).

	Mentions			*Singletons*		
	P	R	F	P	R	F
MR	**92.0**	54.0	68.1	-	-	-
SR	85.7	80.1	82.8	54.0	51.8	52.9
$\texttt{SR}^{+P}$	86.3	80.3	83.2	52.9	50.5	51.7
SE	85.0	80.6	82.7	53.3	**54.0**	**53.7**
$\texttt{SE}^{+M}$	86.3	68.9	76.6	39.2	31.7	35.1
$\texttt{SE}^{+P}$	87.4	**81.0**	**84.1**	**56.9**	50.5	53.5

(d) Statistics on the test set of *Switchboard* (*SWBD*).

Table 5: Statistics of different approaches on the test set of four datasets. The left side shows the Precision/Recall/F1 (P/R/F) of the predicted mentions over gold mentions, and the right side shows the predicted singletons over gold singletons.

[1]https://github.com/juntaoy/universal-anaphora-scorer

	#AC	#SC	#AM	#PM
AMI	1883	1383 (73.5%)	4139	1566 (37.8%)
LIGHT	1359	1024 (75.4%)	3501	1676 (**47.9%**)
PSUA	1857	1525 (**82.1%**)	3446	1464 (42.5%)
SWBD	3897	2968 (76.2%)	7847	3746 (47.7%)

Table 6: Statistics on the test set of all four datasets. `#AC`: total number of all clusters. `#SC`: total number of singleton clusters, with the corresponding percentage indicated inside parentheses. `#AM`: total number of all mentions. `#PM`: total number of personal pronoun mentions, with the percentage inside parentheses. All statistics exclude non-referring expressions.

More interestingly, most `SR`/`SE`-related models are able to recover the majority of gold singletons on all four datasets, up to 73% recall on *LIGHT*, demonstrating the effectiveness of the mention score optimization in Eq (3) and the new antecedent selection process. Nevertheless, the best F1 for singletons is still below 67 out of four datasets, suggesting that resolving singletons alone can be a challenging aspect already.

5.3 Analysis: Speaker Encoding

Despite the simple strategy of speaker-augmented encoding described in Section 3.3, $\texttt{SE}^{+P}$ shows decent improvement over its counterpart $\texttt{SR}^{+P}$, with 2-3% enhancement on Avg F1 on all datasets, except for *LIGHT* that has only trivial improvement, confirming that stronger speaker encoding is indeed important for the dialogue domain.

Meanwhile, `SE` does not show advantages over `SR` due to the fact that the current training corpora of all ARRAU datasets do not provide the speakers (Table 2); consequently, neither models could learn to use the speaker information, resulting in similar performance. This on the other side also demonstrates the significance of knowledge transfer that utilizes other existing resources.

5.4 Analysis: Knowledge Transfer

Comparing the two knowledge transfer strategies, the pretraining paradigm $\texttt{SE}^{+P}$ performs significantly better than the mixing paradigm $\texttt{SE}^{+M}$. In fact, while the pretraining brings improvement over `SE`, the mixing paradigm even performs worse than without knowledge transfer, likely because of the domain mismatch and the annotation format mismatch, showing that the pretraining strategy should always be preferred in this case.

The impact of the pretraining on OD can be dataset-specific, as shown by Table 3. $\texttt{SE}^{+P}$ is able to boost performance upon `SE` by a good margin on *AMI*/*SWBD* with 0.5/2.6 F1 respectively, while *LIGHT*/*PSUA* can benefit significantly, with 6.7/8.1 F1 improvement. Encouraged by the results, we suggest to further explore the utilization of existing resources as a future direction.

6 Conclusion

In this work, we present an adapted end-to-end coreference resolution system for anaphoric identities in dialogues, specifically addressing three aspects: the support for singletons, stronger speaker and turn encoding through the dialogue interactions, as well as the knowledge transfer utilizing other existing resources. Our final system achieves the best results on all four datasets on the leaderboard of the CRAC 2021 shared task, and further analysis is performed to show the effectiveness of our proposed adaptation strategies.

References

Berfin Aktaş and Manfred Stede. 2020. Variation in coreference strategies across genres and production media. In *Proceedings of the 28th International Conference on Computational Linguistics*, pages 5774–5785, Barcelona, Spain (Online). International Committee on Computational Linguistics.

Kevin Clark and Christopher D. Manning. 2015. Entity-centric coreference resolution with model stacking. In *Proceedings of the 53rd Annual Meeting of the Association for Computational Linguistics and the 7th International Joint Conference on Natural Language Processing (Volume 1: Long Papers)*, pages 1405–1415, Beijing, China. Association for Computational Linguistics.

Kevin Clark and Christopher D. Manning. 2016. Improving coreference resolution by learning entity-level distributed representations. In *Proceedings of the 54th Annual Meeting of the Association for Computational Linguistics (Volume 1: Long Papers)*, pages 643–653, Berlin, Germany. Association for Computational Linguistics.

Mandar Joshi, Danqi Chen, Yinhan Liu, Daniel S. Weld, Luke Zettlemoyer, and Omer Levy. 2020. Spanbert: Improving pre-training by representing and predicting spans. *Transactions of the Association for Computational Linguistics*, 8:64–77.

Mandar Joshi, Omer Levy, Luke Zettlemoyer, and Daniel Weld. 2019. BERT for coreference resolution: Baselines and analysis. In *Proceedings of the 2019 Conference on Empirical Methods in Natural Language Processing and the 9th International Joint Conference on Natural Language Processing*

(EMNLP-IJCNLP), pages 5803–5808, Hong Kong, China. Association for Computational Linguistics.

Sopan Khosla, Juntao Yu, Ramesh Manuvinakurike, Vincent Ng, Massimo Poesio, Michael Strube, and Carolyn Rosé. 2021. The codi-crac 2021 shared task on anaphora, bridging, and discourse deixis in dialogue. In *Proceedings of the CODI-CRAC 2021 Shared Task on Anaphora, Bridging, and Discourse Deixis in Dialogue*. Association for Computational Linguistics.

Ran Le, Wenpeng Hu, Mingyue Shang, Zhenjun You, Lidong Bing, Dongyan Zhao, and Rui Yan. 2019. Who is speaking to whom? learning to identify utterance addressee in multi-party conversations. In *Proceedings of the 2019 Conference on Empirical Methods in Natural Language Processing and the 9th International Joint Conference on Natural Language Processing (EMNLP-IJCNLP)*, pages 1909–1919, Hong Kong, China. Association for Computational Linguistics.

Kenton Lee, Luheng He, Mike Lewis, and Luke Zettlemoyer. 2017. End-to-end neural coreference resolution. In *Proceedings of the 2017 Conference on Empirical Methods in Natural Language Processing*, pages 188–197, Copenhagen, Denmark. Association for Computational Linguistics.

Kenton Lee, Luheng He, and Luke Zettlemoyer. 2018. Higher-order coreference resolution with coarse-to-fine inference. In *Proceedings of the 2018 Conference of the North American Chapter of the Association for Computational Linguistics: Human Language Technologies, Volume 2 (Short Papers)*, pages 687–692, New Orleans, Louisiana. Association for Computational Linguistics.

Xuansong Li, Martha Palmer, Nianwen Xue, Lance Ramshaw, Mohamed Maamouri, Ann Bies, Kathryn Conger, Stephen Grimes, and Stephanie Strassel. 2016. Large multi-lingual, multi-level and multi-genre annotation corpus. In *Proceedings of the Tenth International Conference on Language Resources and Evaluation (LREC'16)*, pages 906–913, Portorož, Slovenia. European Language Resources Association (ELRA).

Xiaoqiang Luo, Radu Florian, and Todd Ward. 2009. Improving coreference resolution by using conversational metadata. In *Proceedings of Human Language Technologies: The 2009 Annual Conference of the North American Chapter of the Association for Computational Linguistics, Companion Volume: Short Papers*, pages 201–204, Boulder, Colorado. Association for Computational Linguistics.

Massimo Poesio, Yulia Grishina, Varada Kolhatkar, Nafise Moosavi, Ina Roesiger, Adam Roussel, Fabian Simonjetz, Alexandra Uma, Olga Uryupina, Juntao Yu, and Heike Zinsmeister. 2018. Anaphora resolution with the ARRAU corpus. In *Proceedings of the First Workshop on Computational Models of Reference, Anaphora and Coreference*, pages 11–22, New Orleans, Louisiana. Association for Computational Linguistics.

Sameer Pradhan, Alessandro Moschitti, Nianwen Xue, Olga Uryupina, and Yuchen Zhang. 2012. CoNLL-2012 shared task: Modeling multilingual unrestricted coreference in OntoNotes. In *Joint Conference on EMNLP and CoNLL - Shared Task*, pages 1–40, Jeju Island, Korea. Association for Computational Linguistics.

Sam Wiseman, Alexander M. Rush, Stuart Shieber, and Jason Weston. 2015. Learning anaphoricity and antecedent ranking features for coreference resolution. In *Proceedings of the 53rd Annual Meeting of the Association for Computational Linguistics and the 7th International Joint Conference on Natural Language Processing (Volume 1: Long Papers)*, pages 1416–1426, Beijing, China. Association for Computational Linguistics.

Wei Wu, Fei Wang, Arianna Yuan, Fei Wu, and Jiwei Li. 2020. CorefQA: Coreference resolution as query-based span prediction. In *Proceedings of the 58th Annual Meeting of the Association for Computational Linguistics*, pages 6953–6963, Online. Association for Computational Linguistics.

Patrick Xia, João Sedoc, and Benjamin Van Durme. 2020. Incremental neural coreference resolution in constant memory. In *Proceedings of the 2020 Conference on Empirical Methods in Natural Language Processing (EMNLP)*, pages 8617–8624, Online. Association for Computational Linguistics.

Liyan Xu and Jinho D. Choi. 2020. Revealing the myth of higher-order inference in coreference resolution. In *Proceedings of the 2020 Conference on Empirical Methods in Natural Language Processing (EMNLP)*, pages 8527–8533, Online. Association for Computational Linguistics.

Juntao Yu, Alexandra Uma, and Massimo Poesio. 2020. A cluster ranking model for full anaphora resolution. In *Proceedings of The 12th Language Resources and Evaluation Conference*, pages 11–20, Marseille, France. European Language Resources Association.

Klim Zaporojets, Johannes Deleu, Chris Develder, and Thomas Demeester. 2021. Dwie: An entity-centric dataset for multi-task document-level information extraction. *Information Processing & Management*, 58(4):102563.

Ethan Zhou and Jinho D. Choi. 2018. They exist! introducing plural mentions to coreference resolution and entity linking. In *Proceedings of the 27th International Conference on Computational Linguistics*, pages 24–34, Santa Fe, New Mexico, USA. Association for Computational Linguistics.

Anaphora Resolution in Dialogue: Cross-Team Analysis of the DFKI-TalkingRobots Team Submissions for the CODI-CRAC 2021 Shared-Task

Natalia Skachkova, Cennet Oguz, Tatiana Anikina,
Siyu Tao, Sharmila Upadhyaya, Ivana Kruijff-Korbayová
DFKI / Saarland Informatics Campus, Saarbrücken, Germany
ivana.kruijff@dfki.de

Abstract

We compare our team's systems to others submitted for the CODI-CRAC 2021 Shared-Task on anaphora resolution in dialogue. We analyse the architectures and performance, report some problematic cases in gold annotations, and suggest possible improvements of the systems, their evaluation, data annotation, and the organization of the shared task.

1 Introduction

The goal of this paper is to compare the results obtained by the anaphora resolution systems developed by the DFKI-TalkingRobots Team for the *CODI-CRAC 2021 Shared-Task* (CCST) (Khosla et al., 2021) to the results of the other systems in CCST.[1] We submitted two systems for the anaphora resolution task (AR), and one system for discourse deixis resolution (DD). Table 1 shows their main characteristics, for detailed descriptions see Anikina et al. (2021).

Track	AR	AR	DD
System	WCS	M2M	DDR
Setting	pred.	pred.	pred.
Baselines	–	–	–
Learning framework	workspace clustering	mention to mention pairing	heuristics Siamese Net
Markable identification	SpaCy	BiLSTM-CRF	SpaCy
Train. data	CCST	CCST	CCST
Dev. data	CCST	CCST	CCST

Table 1: WCS, M2M and DDR systems summary

2 Workspace Coreference System (WCS)

2.1 System Overview

First we discuss our Worspace Coreference System (WCS) for standard anaphora resolution, which we implemented from scratch for the CCST AR Track. WCS employs a clustering approach explained in (Anikina et al., 2021). WCS differs from other models that participated in the competition in several ways. Both winner models (UTD and lxucs) are based on the implementation described in (Xu and Choi, 2020) that is an adaptation of the end-to-end c2f-coref model introduced by (Lee et al., 2018). The model which achieved the third best result (KU_NLP) uses pointer networks and models pairwise relations between mentions. Unlike these models WCS compares each mention to the clusters available in the workspace and decides whether it should be assigned to one of the existing clusters or initiates a new cluster. Also, WCS did not use any additional data for training and relied only on the annotations provided by the CCST organizers.

WCS achieved an average F1-score of 64.99% on the Light data, 43.93% on AMI, 59.93% on Persuasion and 53.55% on Switchboard. When evaluated on the gold mentions, WCS showed the following results: 73.24% F-score on Light, 56.48% on AMI, 72.06% on Persuasion and 62.85% on Switchboard. Having gold mentions as input gives an improvement of up to 12% on AMI and Persuasion, up to 9% on Switchboard and 6% on Light.

WCS ranked number four on the leaderboard. We see this as an encouraging result for the first prototype of this coreference system.

2.2 Performance Analysis

We analyzed the precision and recall tables provided by the CCST organizers and compared the outputs of different systems. In general, personal pronouns were confused most frequently by all models. For example, in the AMI corpus (*we*, *we*) pairs were annotated incorrectly most of the time, followed by (*I*, *I*) and (*I*, *you*) wrong pairings. On average, there were 5,608 incorrectly resolved pairs of *'we'* pronouns and 3,252 incorrect pairings of *'I'*

[1] URL: competitions.codalab.org/competitions/30312

Proceedings of the CODI-CRAC 2021 Shared Task on Anaphora, Bridging, and Discourse Deixis in Dialogue, pages 63–70
Punta Cana, Dominican Republic, November 10, 2021.

in the AMI test set.[2] This indicates that the methods used by the systems to handle speaker information and switching leave room for improvement.

For example, we noticed that UTD clustered several first person pronouns (*we*, *we*) that were very far apart in the document and not necessarily coreferent. On the contrary, WCS avoided clustering such unrelated pronouns at the expense of missing some cases of long-distance coreference. Our system was unable to annotate these cases because WCS looks only at the recent and salient workspace clusters when making a clustering decision.

In general, WCS avoided clustering *'we'* and *'they'* if they were uttered by the same speaker while the output of other systems includes such pairings. To encode speaker information WCS uses a randomly generated embedding of fixed dimensionality, concatenated with other mention features to create input for the clustering network. However, the random nature of such speaker embeddings might result in some instability during training. We believe that the speaker augmentation approach implemented in the lxucs model suits the coreference task better because it handles speaker information in a more uniform way by prepending a special token to each utterance in dialogue.

Merged tokens such as *'Ill'* posed another challenge. E.g., the AMI test set had 16 *'Ill'* pronouns and WCS was unable to handle them properly because it requires more strict tokenization and uses special features for personal pronouns. Although markables extracted by other models were often more flexible and not dependent on the SpaCy output, they were also incorrect in quite a few cases. For example, we believe that UTD_NLP could achieve even better results by filtering markables since some pairs annotated by them as coreferent included phrases such as *'gon na'* (paired with *'I'*) or *'D _'* (paired with *'it'*).

WCS did not mix up *'we'* and *'well'* or *'were'* and *'we'* and did not annotate different occurrences of *'two'* as coreferent (this was a problem for both UTD and lxucs). However, WCS suffered from the wrong head matching. Especially, when there was an overlap between the two spans WCS tended to cluster both mentions together. For example, *'we'* was clustered with a long noun phrase that contained the same pronoun: *'a power supply which* ***we*** *d probably get its probably gon na be the battery'*. Also, noun phrase extraction of WCS that was based on the SpaCy chunking module contributed to some errors, e.g., phrases like *'Yeah i'* and *'Great and you'* were considered as valid markables by WCS.

WCS often fails to recognize coreference between concrete and metaphoric expressions: *'the royal dog'/'you'* or *'poor soul'/'you'*. In some cases WCS puts too much emphasis on the head features and in other cases it suffers from the hard constrains introduced by filters at the post-processing stage (especially number and animacy filters). Gold annotations include mentions of the same entity that may differ in number, e.g., in the following pair of sentences: *"Well, then you will be interested to know that the* ***STC*** *website is already pledging to help these kids out!"* and *"Have you ever been on* ***their*** *website?"* *'STC'* is coreferent with *'their'* but the number feature is not the same, hence these two mentions were not clustered by WCS.

Some errors were common among all systems. For instance, partial NP- or head-overlap was often treated as an indication of coreference. Phrases like *'speech* ***recognition****'* and *'sound* ***recognition****'* were considered coreferent by 4 out of 5 systems. Deictic expressions such as *'here'*, *'a week'* or *'today'* were also annotated as coreferent by most systems even when they referred to different entities.

Other hard cases include coreference between contextually related mentions (e.g., *'your pay for this task'* and *'the whole thing'*, or *'this sword'* and *'your gift to us, the soldiers'*). Some abbreviations were also not resolved correctly by the participating systems: *'R_S_I'* and *'repetitive strain injury'*. Moreover, anaphoric cases that require additional inference to establish coreference were missing in the system outputs (e.g., *'the remote control'* and *'the product'*, or *'here'* and *'Texas'*).

Our observations suggest that the span errors and wrong clustering of personal pronouns are among the most frequent errors that are common for all participating systems. We observed that WCS makes less extra mention mistakes compared to other systems while it has more missing mentions in the output. This can be explained by the fact that the workspace in WCS has a limited size and if some mentions refer to the same entity but are very far apart in the document they are not clustered by WCS (e.g., in the Switchboard data there were occurrences of entity *'capital punishment'* separated by more than 380 tokens).

[2]This number represents the total number of wrong pairings divided by the number of participating systems.

2.3 Observations on Gold Annotations

We found some unclear and problematic cases in the gold annotation. For instance, *'although the temple is full , no one is speaking and all you can hear are muted scuffling feet'* and *'I'* were marked as the same entity in the Light data (episode_8093). Another example comes from the Persuasion test set that has two different entity IDs for *'I'* and *'Tommy'* in the sentence *"I m Tommy, by the way"* (Persuasion, 20180826-180314-10). We would expect these mentions to have the same entity IDs because both can be used to refer to the same entity interchangeably. Besides, there were some valid markables missing in the gold annotation, e.g. *'my university'* did not have a markable/entity annotation in *"And when I cant give monetarily donate food, my time, and go to blood drives on **my university**"* (Persuasion, 20180826-180314-24).

2.4 Outlook

We would like to perform an error-driven analysis as described in (Kummerfeld and Klein, 2013) to gain more insight in the types of mistakes made by different systems (e.g., missing vs. extra entities or divided vs. conflated entities). Kummerfeld and Klein (2013) implemented a tool for automated evaluation of different types of mistakes but it does not handle the CONLLUA format and, importantly, requires syntactic parse in the gold annotation. Since we do not have this information in the gold data we cannot perform a fine-grained analysis at this time.

As for the performance of WCS, we would like to improve it based on the analysis results and experiment with different features and embeddings. In particular, we are interested in trying out SpanBERT embeddings (Joshi et al., 2020) that were used by the winner models and combine WCS with the M2M system that was also implemented by the DFKI-TalkingRobots team (cf. Section 3).

The analysis revealed that the recall of our model was impaired by the hard animacy and number constraints. Hence, we would like to model these constraints differently, i.e., not as binary filters but as additional features provided as input to the clustering model. Another interesting venue to explore is contextual knowledge, because for each markable that needs to be resolved we need to identify relevant context that goes beyond the utterance and this context should be used for further inference. For example, coreference between such pairs as *'a child in the US'* and *'a child in need'* (Persuasion, 20180826-044626) proved difficult to resolve without reasoning over broader context since both NPs start with an indefinite article and have different PPs modifying the head noun. In fact, none of the participating systems annotated this pair correctly.

More work needs to be done on the dialogue-specific issues, especially personal pronouns and temporal/spatial deixis such as *'today'* and *'here'*. Our analysis showed that all systems had difficulties with such cases and a rule-based approach is not sufficient to handle them. Perhaps deictic mentions could be detected and resolved using a different module within the coreference system.

Finally, we would like to further investigate different ways of representing mentions and clusters in dialogue and apply our model to other data, e.g., dialogues from the emergency response domain (Kruijff-Korbayová et al., 2015). Some of the contextual reference challenges observed in these dialogues are discussed in (Skachkova and Kruijff-Korbayová, 2020).

3 Mention-to-Mention System (M2M)

3.1 System Overview

Our second submission to the AR track was the Mention-to-Mention (M2M), cf. system (Anikina et al., 2021). M2M differs from the other participating systems in that it resolves anaphora in a pair-wise fashion: For each mention, M2M performs a similarity comparison with all preceding mentions and pairs the current mention with the most similar preceding one (or none). After processing all mentions in a document M2M creates clusters based on transitive closure over the mention-mention pairs, i.e., pairs which have a common mention are clustered together. To compute similarity, M2M uses the head, speaker, and span features of mentions as well as a distance vector generated with several distance functions, namely minkowski, euclidean, manhattan, chebyshev, cityblock, and braycurtis.

M2M consists of three different models. The *Self Model* is built for personal pronouns with average embeddings of the speaker and head features of the mentions. The *Pronoun Model* is designed to pair third person and place pronouns to the corresponding candidate by exploiting the head average embeddings of mentions. The *Noun Model* attempts to pair mentions by using head and span embeddings with contextualized and average embeddings when they are noun phrases. All three models are implemented with linear layers with a ReLU activation function to use the pair of mention's head, speaker, and span features. The extracted features from the linear layers are passed to a sigmoid function for obtaining output probabilities.

The candidate mentions for M2M were extracted using a BiLSTM-CRF sequence tagging model with an ELMo embedding layer. The model is trained using the data provided by the CCST organizers. The data were preprocessed into IOB2 format, which means that, in cases of nested markables, only the markable with the widest scope is used in training. Consequently, we use SpaCy (*en_core_web_trf* model) to extract all noun chunks as nested markables in a post-processing step. See (Anikina et al., 2021) for more details.

3.2 Performance Analysis

We first evaluate the performance of the BiLSTM-CRF model in extracting the candidate mentions. We observe that the system predicts many more candidate mentions than are in the gold annotations, which implies a high false positive rate. This is indeed further confirmed in our analysis, as we note poor precision scores across the four test sets (25.8% on Light, 23.7% on Persuasion, 23.5% on Switchboard, and 23.1% on AMI).

Although the high false positive rates are not ideal and preclude meaningful manual inspection of the results, they are not wholly unexpected, as our model was meant to extract as many markable candidates as possible, with the possibility of false positives taken into account in further procesteps. Thus, the recall is perhaps the better metric for our purposes and indeed we observe better recall scores than precision across the board (48.7% on Light, 47.3% on Persuasion, 56.9% on Switchboard, and 54.7% on AMI). Nevertheless, as the mention extraction has a lot of room for improvement, we expect that the M2M system will perform better if evaluated on the gold mentions instead.

The M2M system achieved F1-score of 61.26% on Light, 59.20% on Persuasion and 51.24% on Switchboard. Since only one model of each team is included in the CCST Official Ranking document provided by the organizers, we do not have details for a performance comparison of M2M against the other systems. An analysis of M2M's predictions against the gold annotations reveals that the *Self Model* shows high performance. Thus, the utilized distance vector of the speaker names increases the similarity of the mentions even though the pronouns for the entities are changing, e.g., *'I'* - *'you'*. On the other hand, the performance of both *Pronoun* and *Noun Model* decreases, because of the lexical difference between an anaphor mention and a candidate antecedent mention, e.g. *'he'* and *'father'*, and *'father'* and *'Paul'*, respectively.

3.3 Outlook

The M2M system relies on lexical similarity between pairs of mentions instead of the similarity between mentions and clusters. Thus, the system is fragile to lexical variations because of the generated distance vector. However, the same vector increases the performance of the *Self Model* because of the speaker names. Therefore, in order to exploit the distance vector for personal pronoun resolution in the *Self Model*, we need to also apply clustering, to avoid the variations between mentions in *Pronoun Model* and *Noun Model*. Therefore, we plan to combine M2M and WCS (Section 2) to benefit from their complementary strengths.

4 Discourse Deixic Resolution (DDR)

Next we present a cross-team comparison of the discourse deixis resolution systems submitted to CCST, as well as some difficulties we had with the gold discourse deixis annotations. We discuss the *Eval-DD(Pred)* track, as we did not participate in *Eval-DD(Gold)*. There were only two submissions, from us and from the UTD_NLP team.

4.1 System overview

At first sight the two approaches look very different. We utilize machine learning using a Siamese network together with hand-crafted rules (Anikina et al., 2021). The UTD_NLP system is purely machine learning based. It extends the model by Xu and Choi (2020), originally designed for entity coreference resolution. While we perform discourse deixis mention detection and resolution separately, the UTD_NLP system does it jointly.

Despite these differences, both systems actually exploit the same idea – given an anaphor to resolve, they rank several antecedent candidates using neural networks. The two realizations of this idea are more similar than it may seem. We check antecedent-anaphor 'compatibility' by replacing the anaphor with an antecedent candidate and comparing the encoding of the resulting utterance with the encoding of the original utterance containing the anaphor. The UTD_NLP system encodes anaphors and antecedent candidates separately from the utterances they are part of (incorporating context with SpanBERT instead) and afterwards ranks their joint 'compatibility' using only distance as a feature. Nevertheless, the UTD_NLP system achieves twice as high F-scores.

4.2 Performance Analysis

Table 2 shows the results of discourse deixis mention extraction of both systems. We use a simple *SpaCy*-based method to find anaphors. This gives us moderate recall; according to our rules many anaphors (e.g., all noun phrases and personal pronoun *it*) are simply omitted. Because the approach is greedy, the precision is really low, which leads to low F-scores. In our case the choice of antecedent candidates for each anaphor is also rule-based. Because of erroneous or missed anaphors, as well as mistakes made by our Siamese Net-based scorer and sometimes strange gold annotations (see examples in Section 4.4) the scores for antecedents are even worse than for anaphors.

Table 2 shows that the anaphor identification method employed by the UTD_NLP team achieves better recall for the Light and Switchboard test sets, but for the other two it is lower than ours. Having analysed the recall tables prepared by the CCST organizers we noticed that while our system simply ignores all the anaphors that have a *SpaCy* POS tag different from DET, the UTD_NLP system also has difficulties recognizing anaphors other than *'this'* and *'that'*. E.g., both systems miss absolutely all anaphors represented by NPs (with an exception of one case of *'the same'* recognized by UTD_NLP). Additionally, the winning system misses many anaphors represented by *'it'*, all cases of *'which'*, as well as all capitalized anaphors. This behavior can be caused by the insufficient amount of such markables in the training data.

Interestingly, UTD_NLP's recall of antecedent identification is worse than ours for all the files. One possible explanation of this can be the fact that the UTD_NLP system seems to omit all split antecedent cases, i.e. they probably do not consider antecedents consisting of several utterances, and thus miss a certain number of markables. This hypothesis is supported by very low F-scores for singleton clusters reported by the team in their system description paper. As far as we can judge, gold annotations use singleton clusters as containers for parts of split antecedents, and low F-scores may mean that split antecedents are disregarded. Still, due to a much better precision of both anaphor and antecedent recognition, UTD_NLP achieves higher F-scores for discourse deixis mention extraction.

To compare clustering results of both teams we refer to the recall and precision files provided by the CCST organizers. Table 3 compares the number of (in)correct pairs identified by each system. The numbers are disjoint, e.g., the Light test set contains 67 antecedent-anaphor pairs, of which 6 pairs were correctly predicted by both systems, other 19 pairs only by the UTD_NLP system, and different 5 ones only by our system. At the same time, of 133 incorrectly predicted pairs in the Light test set 10 were found in the output of both systems, 25 pairs were predicted only by the UTD_NLP system, and 98 pairs only by our system.

One can notice rather poor recall of both systems, with ours being often (but not always) worse than by UTD_NLP's. Our system has especially low recall on the Light test set. This probably happens, because Light contains quite a number of cases, where an anaphor is parts of its antecedent, and our approach does not consider this possible. Table 3 also shows that our system, in contrast to the UTD_NLP's approach, creates really many wrong antecedent-anaphor pairs. This is probably due to the fact that our system has very low precision for anaphor identification, and thus tries to resolve too many false anaphors. Also, having taken a closer look at our output files and gold annotations, we saw that our approach was able to correctly recognize only a small number of split antecedents. As far as we can judge, no anaphors referring to split antecedents are present in the recall/precision files prepared by the CCST organizers. Still, it is obvious that detecting split antecedents is very challenging for our system.

4.3 Outlook

The UTD_NLP system demonstrates that a model originally designed for entity coreference resolution can be rather successfully adapted for discourse deixis resolution without adding any sophisticated features. It is difficult to tell what exactly helps their model to achieve better scores in comparison with our approach. It can be the usage of SpanBERT, more refined scoring method (it includes three components), longer training with better chosen parameters, a combination of these

		Light			AMI			Persuasion			Swbd		
		P	R	F	P	R	F	P	R	F	P	R	F
Anaphor	UTD_NLP	71.4	68.8	70.1	58.0	64.4	61.0	76.7	64.2	69.9	65.7	70.7	68.1
	DFKI_TR	24.2	57.8	34.1	17.3	79.8	28.5	37.0	69.4	48.3	25.2	66.5	36.6
Antecedent	UTD_NLP	50.8	27.7	35.8	66.0	20.5	31.3	59.6	21.2	31.3	60.8	21.5	31.7
	DFKI_TR	19.1	37.5	25.3	11.5	37.3	17.5	21.8	49.3	30.2	20.9	39.4	27.3

Table 2: Markable extraction results (UTD_NLP's scores come from Kobayashi et al. (2021))

	Corpus	Light	AMI	Persuasion	Swbd
Recall	UTD_NLP	19	13	18	31
	DFKI_TR	5	14	13	36
	Both	6	12	7	26
	Total	67	100	113	224
Precision	UTD_NLP	25	36	27	142
	DFKI_TR	98	316	108	358
	Both	10	4	8	16
	Total	133	356	143	516

Table 3: Discourse deixis resolution results

reasons, or something else. We also think that both systems can be improved at least in terms of markable identification. It is clear that in our case the most obvious step is the improvement of precision. The UTD_NLP team could, on the other hand, rather easily incorporate split antecedents. Currently they limit the width of a span by 70 tokens, so that spans consisting of several utterances are not considered. Allowing larger spans would help identifying split antecedents, and probably improve the recall for antecedent identification.

4.4 Observations on Gold Annotations

We highly appreciate the efforts that were invested into the discourse reference annotation of the data sets provided for the CCST. However, some aspects could be improved.

First, the available brief description of the corpus format,[3] is very useful, but it does not provide an annotation manual with enough explanations of the annotation principles (e.g., no clear definition of a markable) and examples. The instructions that were used by the annotators have not been published. So we needed to infer these principles from data/examples themselves. In some cases it was difficult to correctly determine markables and their spans. Especially, when the data contains inconsistent examples. E.g., in the *Light_dev* file in the utterance *"I will do my best to spread your kind words around , my god ."* the noun phrase *'your kind words'* is annotated as a discourse deixis markable, but the phrase *'your words'* in *"You are the wisest merchants in these lands , and I shall heed your words - ..."* is not, despite the fact that it has an antecedent.

Also, some antecedents' spans seem to be too long. E.g., according to the gold annotations of the same *Light_dev* file, *'That'* in *"That certainly scared the eternal daylights out of me !"* has the whole utterance *"I myself happened to look out from the kitchen and see his dangling legs in front of the window ."* as the antecedent, while logically only the part *'see his dangling legs in front of the window'* should be considered as such. Sometimes the anaphor is annotated as a part of the antecedent, like the pronoun *'this'* in *"You are a good man , I can recognize this ."* from the same file.

Second, some files with gold annotations have markables with mismatched closing brackets. Thus, in the file *Pear_Stories* some markables span over several utterances, and may even contain nested markables. E.g., *"Then a kid came along on a bicycle"* (which is actually one of the fragments of a larger utterance) is a separate discourse deixis markable, and at the same time it is the beginning of a larger markable whose closing bracket can be found three fragments later. At the same time both these markables (together with eight other ones that follow) are split antecedents of an anaphor that occurs later in the dialogue.

5 Conclusions and CCST Outlook

We compared our systems and their results to the systems and results by other teams. We also presented some ideas that this analysis gave us for the further development of our systems. Besides improvements of mention detection we also plan to combine WCS and M2M to benefit from their complementary strengths. As the analysis showed, M2M did well on resolving personal pronoun coref-

[3]See https://github.com/UniversalAnaphora/UniversalAnaphora/blob/main/UA_CONLL_U_Plus_proposal_0.1.md

erence, whereas WCS' clustering approach is better than M2M at noun coreference cases. Another interesting challenge to consider is to also account for discourse deixis in one integrated system or even by the same approach, similarly to the UTD_NLP system.

Admittedly, the difficult examples that we have pointed out are ones that every state-of-the-art system finds hard. In the scope of the analysis that we were able to carry out given the time and resources, we could not identify properties of examples that different system configurations are able to handle versus not, in order to draw generalizations on what kinds of examples are handled well by what approaches, and why. Such analysis is also complicated by the fact that the systems differ in markable detection. A systematic deeper analysis is an interesting topic for future research.

To conclude, we would like to make a few suggestions for the future of the shared task. We think that the shared task is very useful and it would be good to continue running it, because anaphora resolution is far from being a solved task.

First, we suggest to have separate tracks for the evaluation of systems trained only on the provided data vs. systems (pre-)trained on external/additional data. This would help not only to achieve a fair comparison but also to see whether improvements are due to (pre-)training with more data and transfer or due to better feature engineering and modeling. In order to study what specifically was learned from the external data that could not be learned by the training data provided in CCST it would be useful to compare the results of models trained with the same approach on only the external data vs. only the CCST data vs. using all data.

Second, we would like to see a separate comparison of mention detection and anaphor identification results for the different systems. Our experience showed that finding correct mentions is crucial for the overall performance and we believe that this stage should be evaluated separately. It would also be interesting to compare results on both dialogues and narrative texts.

Third, future competitions might consider using more fine-grained evaluation metrics because different cases of coreference have different difficulty levels. E.g., *'a black cat'* and *'the black cat'* are much easier to resolve compared to *'a black cat'* and *'the dark and furry creature'*. We believe that a more differentiated evaluation could be done (at least partially) in an automated way. For instance, similarly to the sieve-based approach (Raghunathan et al., 2010) one could compare a referent and its true antecedent using exact string matching vs. head matching, compute similarity between the corresponding mention embeddings or count the number of candidates (valid markables) between the anaphor and its antecedent. Our analysis showed that some tricky cases of coreference, e.g., *'this sword'* and *'your gift to us, the soldiers'* were missed by all participating systems and we expect that weighting each pair w.r.t. the difficulty level and/or distinguishing difficulty levels in the presentation of the results would help to shift the focus towards resolving 'harder' cases. The evaluation could also report results on pronominal and nominal anaphora separately, and distinguish the different syntactic types of antecedents.

Finally, we have some suggestions for the organization of the shared task. Namely, it would be helpful to have a more detailed description of the task, its tracks, test data format (with a couple of input-output examples). For instance, it was unclear that for the *Eval-DD(Gold)* track we would only get anaphors in the IDENTITY column and would need to distinguish between discourse deixis and 'standard' anaphora markables. More information regarding the submission procedure would also be useful, for example for the case that a team has more than one system for one track. Quality control of the annotations should be improved, or gold vs. silver (vs. bronze) data should be distinguished. Data quality is very important, because we are making conclusions about the correctness of models based on the annotations. One possibility could be to ask participating teams to provide annotations or additional data sets annotated according to uniform guidelines.

As for new challenges to include in the shared task in the future, there is no shortage of smaller steps and giant leaps. The easiest ones were already mentioned above, i.e., evaluation of the contribution of external training data, separate evaluation of mention detection and anaphor identification, as well as a more finegrained evaluation scheme, in order to obtain more insight into the capabilities of the different models. Other potential extensions depend on the availability of annotated data, and even agreed annotation standards. Thanks to existing datasets it would probably be most feasible to extend the task, on the one hand, to zero pronouns and other forms of implicit entity reference and/or event references, and on the other hand, to other languages. Multimodal reference would also be interesting, but more challenging, from reference to visual objects embedded in text to reference to physical situations, for example in cooking or physical activity videos, which are used in the language-and-vision community. Finally, non-verbal forms or reference, such as pointing, are in our view the most challenging, due to lack of data as well as annotation standards, and the difficulty of annotation.

Acknowledgements

The authors have been supported by the German Ministry of Education and Research (BMBF): T. Anikina and I. Kruijff-Korbayová through project CORA4NLP (grant Nr. 01IW20010); C. Oguz through project IMPRESS (grant Nr. 01IS20076) and N. Skachkova through project A-DRZ (grant No. I3N14856).

References

Tatiana Anikina, Cennet Oguz, Natalia Skachkova, Siyu Tao, Sharmila Upadhyaya, and Ivana Kruijff-Korbayová. 2021. Anaphora Resolution in Dialogue: Description of the DFKI-TalkingRobots System for the CODI-CRAC 2021 Shared-Task.

Mandar Joshi, Danqi Chen, Yinhan Liu, Daniel S. Weld, Luke Zettlemoyer, and Omer Levy. 2020. Spanbert: Improving pre-training by representing and predicting spans. *Trans. Assoc. Comput. Linguistics*, 8:64–77.

Sopan Khosla, Juntao Yu, Ramesh Manuvinakurike, Vincent NG, Massimo Poesio, Michael Strube, and Carolyn Rosé. 2021. The CODI-CRAC 2021 Shared Task on Anaphora, Bridging, and Discourse Deixis in Dialogue. In *Proceedings of the CODI-CRAC 2021 Shared Task on Anaphora, Bridging, and Discourse Deixis in Dialogue*. Association for Computational Linguistics.

Hideo Kobayashi, Shengjie Li, and Vincent Ng. 2021. Neural Anaphora Resolution in Dialogues.

Ivana Kruijff-Korbayová, Francis Colas, Mario Gianni, Fiora Pirri, Joachim de Greeff, Koen V. Hindriks, Mark A. Neerincx, Petter Ögren, Tomás Svoboda, and Rainer Worst. 2015. TRADR project: Long-term human-robot teaming for robot assisted disaster response. *Künstliche Intell.*, 29(2):193–201.

Jonathan K. Kummerfeld and Dan Klein. 2013. Error-driven analysis of challenges in coreference resolution. In *Proceedings of the 2013 Conference on Empirical Methods in Natural Language Processing, EMNLP 2013, 18-21 October 2013, Grand Hyatt Seattle, Seattle, Washington, USA, A meeting of SIGDAT, a Special Interest Group of the ACL*, pages 265–277.

Kenton Lee, Luheng He, and Luke Zettlemoyer. 2018. Higher-order coreference resolution with coarse-to-fine inference. In *Proceedings of the 2018 Conference of the North American Chapter of the Association for Computational Linguistics: Human Language Technologies, NAACL-HLT, New Orleans, Louisiana, USA, June 1-6, 2018, Volume 2 (Short Papers)*, pages 687–692.

Karthik Raghunathan, Heeyoung Lee, Sudarshan Rangarajan, Nate Chambers, Mihai Surdeanu, Dan Jurafsky, and Christopher D. Manning. 2010. A multi-pass sieve for coreference resolution. In *Proceedings of the 2010 Conference on Empirical Methods in Natural Language Processing, EMNLP 2010, 9-11 October 2010, MIT Stata Center, Massachusetts, USA, A meeting of SIGDAT, a Special Interest Group of the ACL*, pages 492–501.

Natalia Skachkova and Ivana Kruijff-Korbayová. 2020. Reference in team communication for robot-assisted disaster response: An initial analysis. In *Proceedings of the 3rd Workshop on Computational Models of Reference, Anaphora and Coreference. (CRAC-2020), COLING'2020, Virtual, Spain*. Association for Computational Linguistics.

Liyan Xu and Jinho D. Choi. 2020. Revealing the myth of higher-order inference in coreference resolution. In *Proceedings of the 2020 Conference on Empirical Methods in Natural Language Processing (EMNLP)*, pages 8527–8533, Online. Association for Computational Linguistics.

The CODI-CRAC 2021 Shared Task on Anaphora, Bridging, and Discourse Deixis Resolution in Dialogue: A Cross-Team Analysis

Shengjie Li* and **Hideo Kobayashi*** and **Vincent Ng**
Human Language Technology Research Institute
University of Texas at Dallas
Richardson, TX 75083-0688
{sxl180006,hideo,vince}@hlt.utdallas.edu

Abstract

The CODI-CRAC 2021 shared task is the first shared task that focuses exclusively on anaphora resolution in dialogue and provides three tracks, namely entity coreference resolution, bridging resolution, and discourse deixis resolution. We perform a cross-task analysis of the systems that participated in the shared task in each of these tracks.

1 Introduction

The CODI-CRAC 2021 shared task (Khosla et al., 2021), which focuses on anaphora resolution in dialogue, provides three tracks, namely entity coreference resolution, bridging resolution, and discourse deixis/abstract anaphora resolution. Among these three tracks, bridging resolution and discourse deixis resolution are relatively under-studied problems. This is particularly so in the context of dialogue processing. This shared task is therefore of potential interest to researchers in the discourse and dialogue communities, particularly researchers in anaphora resolution who intend to work on problems beyond identity coreference.

Our goal in this paper is to perform a cross-team analysis of the systems participating in the three tracks of the shared task. Our analysis is partly quantitative, where we attempt to draw conclusions based on statistics computed using the outputs of the systems, and partly qualitative, where we discuss the strengths and weaknesses of the systems based on our manual inspection of these outputs. While several attempts have been made to perform an analysis of different coreference systems (e.g., Kummerfeld and Klein (2013), Lu and Ng (2020)), we note that conducting an insightful analysis of these systems is inherently challenging for at least two reasons. First, for entity coreference resolution and discourse deixis resolution, the latter of which is treated as a general case of event coreference, the system outputs on which we perform our analysis is in the form of clusters. Hence, we do not have information about which *links* were posited by a system and used to create a given cluster. This makes it impossible to pinpoint the mistakes (i.e., the erroneous linking decisions) made by a system and fundamentally limits our ability to *explain* the behavior of a system. Second, even if we could pinpoint the mistakes, existing models for anaphora resolution have become so complex that it is virtually impossible to explain why a particular mistake was made. For instance, a mention extraction component is so closely tied to a resolution model that it is not always possible to determine whether a mistake can be attributed to erroneous mention extraction or resolution. Worse still, since the participants have the freedom to partition the available training and development datasets in any way they want for model training and parameter tuning and are even allowed to exploit external training corpora, it makes it even harder to determine whether a system performs better because of a particular way of partitioning the data or because external training data are used.

The rest of this paper is structured as follows. The next three sections describe our cross-team analysis for the three tracks, namely entity coreference (Section 2), bridging (Section 3), and discourse deixis (Section 4). We present our conclusions and observations in Section 5.

2 Entity Coreference Resolution

In this section, we analyze the results of the four teams that participated in the anaphora resolution track and submitted a shared task paper, namely the team from Emory University (Xu and Choi, 2021) (henceforth Emory), the team from the University of Texas at Dallas (Kobayashi et al., 2021) (henceforth UTD), the team from Korea University (Kim et al., 2021) (henceforth KU), and the DFKI team (Anikina et al., 2021) (henceforth DFKI).

*Equal contribution

Proceedings of the CODI-CRAC 2021 Shared Task on Anaphora, Bridging, and Discourse Deixis in Dialogue, pages 71–95
Punta Cana, Dominican Republic, November 10, 2021.

	LIGHT			AMI			Persuasion			Switchboard		
	P	R	F	P	R	F	P	R	F	P	R	F
Emory	89.2	92.5	90.8	82.2	90.2	86.0	90.6	90.7	90.6	85.3	89.8	87.5
UTD	92.3	91.6	92.0	86.6	78.6	82.4	91.3	89.7	90.5	89.2	86.1	87.6
KU	85.6	92.8	89.1	79.4	89.3	84.0	83.3	92.5	87.7	78.7	89.8	83.8
DFKI	84.8	82.6	83.7	75.4	65.8	70.3	79.8	77.5	78.6	79.3	77.9	78.6

Table 1: Entity coreference resolution: mention extraction results.

2.1 Mention Extraction

Since mention extraction has a large impact on coreference resolution performance (Pradhan et al., 2011, 2012), let us first consider the mention extraction performance of the participating systems.

Table 1 presents the mention extraction results in the standard manner, expressing the results of each system on each corpus in terms of recall, precision, and F-score. Specifically, a mention is considered correctly detected if it has an exact match with a gold mention in terms of boundary. In terms of F-score, Emory and UTD achieve comparable performance, and both of them outperform KU and DFKI. Except for DFKI, all the systems achieve an average mention extraction F-score of more than 85%. These mention extraction results are much better than those achieved by traditional coreference resolvers, and are consistent with Lu and Ng's (2020) observation that mention detection performance has improved significantly over the years, particularly after the introduction of span-based neural coreference models (Lee et al., 2017, 2018). Considering the recall and precision numbers, we see that Emory and KU are recall-oriented, whereas UTD and DFKI are precision-oriented. Specifically, Emory and KU achieve the highest recall, whereas UTD achieves the highest precision.

To gain additional insights into the mention extraction results achieved by these systems, we present these results from a different point of view in Table 2. We first divide the mentions into 10 groups, which are shown in Table 3. As can be seen, the first nine groups focus on different kinds of pronouns, whereas the last group is composed of non-pronominal mentions. We note that the classification of the mentions in the test corpus into these 10 groups is not error-free: since we rely on part-of-speech tags and the surface forms to identify pronouns, words that appear in the corpus such as "well" (which corresponds to "we'll") and "were" (which corresponds to "we're") should belong to Group 1 but are being misclassified as non-pronominal.

Consider first Table 2a, where results are aggregated over the four datasets. The "%" and "count" columns show the percentage and number of gold mentions that belong to each group. "none" shows the fraction of mentions that are not detected by any of the four participating systems. E (Emory), T (UTD), K (KU), and D (DFKI) show the percentage of gold mentions successfully extracted by each of these systems. E-only, T-only, K-only, and D-only show the percentage of gold mentions that are successfully extracted by exactly one of the systems. For instance, E-only shows the fraction of mentions successfully extracted by the Emory resolver but not the other three.

A few points deserve mention. First, despite the fact that Group 10 (non-pronominal mentions) is the largest group, approximately half of the mentions are pronominal. The largest pronoun groups are Group 1 (1st and 2nd person pronouns (e.g., "I", "we")), Group 3 (3rd person ungendered pronouns (e.g., "it", "they")), Group 5 (reflexive pronouns (e.g., "myself", "yourself")), and Group 7 (demonstrative pronouns (e.g., "this", "that")). This should not be surprising given the prevalence of these pronouns in dialogue, but their prevalence suggests the importance of pronoun resolution in the shared task. Second, considering the "only" columns, we see that the percentage of mentions that are uniquely identified by one of the systems is relatively small. Third, Emory and KU extract more gold mentions than UTD and DFKI. As can be seen in the "Overall" row, Emory and KU manage to extract more than 90% of the gold mentions. These results are consistent with those shown in Table 1. Perhaps the biggest difference among the systems lies in the extraction of non-pronominal mentions: Group 10 is the group for which Emory and KU clearly demonstrate superior extraction performance.

While Table 2a focuses on gold mention extraction, Table 2b focuses on the extraction of erroneous mentions. Specifically, we take the union of the set of erroneous mentions extracted by the

(a) Coverage of gold mentions

Group	%	count	none	E	T	K	D	E-only	T-only	K-only	D-only
Overall	100.0	19051	4.1	90.5	86.1	90.7	76.0	1.0	0.5	1.5	0.9
1	28.5	5433	0.0	99.8	99.6	99.0	99.7	0.0	0.0	0.0	0.0
2	1.6	308	0.0	99.4	99.7	99.4	100.0	0.0	0.0	0.0	0.3
3	8.8	1670	0.0	98.3	97.1	99.8	100.0	0.0	0.0	0.0	0.1
4	5.2	986	0.0	98.5	98.7	99.4	94.7	0.0	0.0	0.5	0.0
5	0.3	65	0.0	95.4	89.2	93.8	100.0	0.0	0.0	0.0	0.0
6	0.9	172	2.3	79.7	68.6	88.4	56.4	0.6	0.0	3.5	3.5
7	5.1	974	1.3	97.8	96.6	96.9	0.0	0.2	0.1	0.5	0.0
8	0.3	61	6.6	70.5	63.9	78.7	45.9	0.0	0.0	0.0	3.3
9	0.6	115	3.5	77.4	75.7	94.8	93.0	0.0	0.9	0.9	0.0
10	48.6	9267	8.1	82.3	74.0	82.4	63.3	2.0	0.9	2.9	1.7

(b) Coverage of wrong mentions

Group	%	count	E	T	K	D	E-only	T-only	K-only	D-only
Overall	100.0	7072	39.0	26.7	57.7	52.4	10.0	4.2	18.8	20.7
1	0.5	32	75.0	71.9	87.5	87.5	3.1	0.0	9.4	0.0
2	0.0	0	0.0	0.0	0.0	0.0	0.0	0.0	0.0	0.0
3	6.2	439	58.3	45.3	99.8	100.0	0.0	0.0	0.0	0.2
4	0.9	67	61.2	58.2	92.5	55.2	0.0	0.0	17.9	3.0
5	0.0	0	0.0	0.0	0.0	0.0	0.0	0.0	0.0	0.0
6	2.4	173	23.7	16.8	66.5	69.4	3.5	0.6	22.0	28.9
7	0.7	52	82.7	53.8	50.0	0.0	32.7	3.8	5.8	0.0
8	5.3	376	17.0	14.1	39.4	90.7	0.5	0.5	5.1	56.6
9	3.7	262	16.4	9.5	99.2	83.2	0.4	0.0	8.8	0.0
10	80.2	5671	39.6	26.3	52.9	44.5	12.0	5.1	21.7	21.1

Table 2: Entity coreference resolution: per-class mention extraction results.

Group	Description
1	1st and 2nd person pronouns
2	3rd person gendered pronouns
3	3rd person ungendered pronouns
4	Possessive pronouns
5	Reflexive pronouns
6	Indefinite pronouns
7	Demonstrative pronouns
8	Relative and interrogative pronouns
9	Other pronouns
10	Non-pronominal noun phrases

Table 3: Division of mentions into groups.

four resolvers and compute statistics based on the resulting set, which we refer to as S. The columns in Table 2b can be interpreted in the same way as those in Table 2a. For instance, E, T, K, and D show the percentage of mentions in S extracted by each of the systems, and E-only, T-only, K-only, and D-only show the percentage of mentions in S extracted by exactly one of the systems.

A few points deserve mention. First, approximately 80% of the erroneous mentions belong to Group 10. This should perhaps not be surprising given that the extraction of non-pronominal mentions, which are often composed of multiple tokens, is typically more challenging than that of pronouns. Note that a complication involved in the extraction process concerns the detection of non-referring mentions: according to the shared task guidelines, any non-referring mention extracted will be considered erroneous. The second largest group is Group 3, whose mentions account for 6.2% of the number of erroneous mentions. This again should not be surprising. This group is composed of pronouns such as "it", many of which may not be referring because of its use as an expletive or a pleonastic pronoun. Second, considering the "Overall" row, we can see that UTD has the smallest coverage of erroneous mentions, which translates to a higher mention extraction precision., whereas KU has the highest coverage of erroneous mentions. While Table 2a shows that Emory and KU both achieve high mention extraction recall, Table 2b shows that KU does so at the expense of precision and that Emory is clearly superior to KU for mention extraction. While DFKI's coverage of gold mentions is the lowest among the four systems, its coverage of erroneous mentions is relatively high. Third, considering the group specific results, we can get a better idea of what makes a particular system better for mention extraction. UTD extracts fewer erroneous mentions

	MUC			B^3			$CEAF_e$			
	P	R	F	P	R	F	P	R	F	CoNLL
					LIGHT					
Emory	90.6	89.5	90.0	74.2	84.9	79.2	68.1	75.9	71.8	80.3
UTD	87.8	89.1	88.5	72.7	82.6	77.3	74.5	73.9	74.2	79.6
KU	89.3	75.3	81.7	64.9	54.9	59.5	55.7	78.4	65.1	68.8
DFKI	86.2	70.9	77.8	75.3	59.0	66.2	52.8	64.1	57.9	67.3
					AMI					
Emory	72.4	69.0	70.7	57.2	66.2	61.4	53.5	67.9	59.8	64.0
UTD	66.7	65.5	66.0	48.5	58.3	53.0	51.1	46.4	48.6	57.4
KU	69.0	53.0	60.0	63.6	49.5	55.7	46.5	72.4	56.6	57.4
DFKI	59.1	41.9	49.1	48.1	41.3	44.4	37.0	39.7	38.3	43.9
					Persuasion					
Emory	80.4	88.0	84.0	76.9	82.5	79.6	74.7	68.8	71.6	78.4
UTD	78.7	87.8	83.0	76.6	80.4	78.5	76.2	74.8	75.5	77.5
KU	76.5	77.2	76.9	65.6	70.4	67.9	61.9	73.1	67.0	70.6
DFKI	69.8	65.2	67.4	65.2	55.1	59.7	52.6	52.7	52.6	59.9
					Switchboard					
Emory	82.2	79.1	80.6	72.4	76.5	74.4	64.1	73.4	68.5	74.5
UTD	77.5	79.5	78.5	70.7	74.3	72.4	71.5	69.0	70.2	72.6
KU	80.9	66.4	72.9	66.3	58.2	62.0	52.0	75.8	61.7	65.5
DFKI	62.7	60.2	61.4	55.6	56.9	56.3	42.8	43.1	43.0	53.5

Table 4: Entity coreference resolution: official resolution results.

than other teams except for Groups 4 and 7, both of which are relatively small. By contrast, KU extracts considerably more erroneous possessive pronouns (Group 4) than other teams, Emory extracts considerably more erroneous demonstrative pronouns (Group 7) than other teams, DFKI extracts more erroneous relative and interrogative pronouns (Group 8) than other teams, and both KU and DFKI extract considerably more erroneous indefinite pronouns (Group 6) and other pronouns (Group 9) than other teams. Finally, considering the "only" columns, we see that 10% of the erroneous mentions are only extracted by Emory, 18.8% by KU, and 20.7% by DFKI. This shows that the systems are quite different in terms of mention extraction.

2.2 Resolution

Next, we consider the coreference results. Table 4 shows the official results obtained using the official scorer. These results are expressed in terms of MUC (Vilain et al., 1995), B^3 (Bagga and Baldwin, 1998), and $CEAF_e$ (Luo, 2005) recall (R), precision (P), and F-score (F), as well as the CoNLL score, which is the unweighted average of the MUC, B^3, and $CEAF_e$ F-scores.

The four participating systems show a clear difference in performance in terms of CoNLL F-score: Emory performs the best, UTD and KU rank second and third respectively, and DFKI achieves the lowest performance. The performance difference between Emory and UTD is smaller compared to that between any other pair of systems: UTD underperforms Emory roughly by 0.7–6.6% in the CoNLL score. This could be explained in part by the fact that both systems were built upon coref-hoi, which is Xu and Choi's (2020) entity coreference system. Nevertheless, as we will see below, the two systems behave quite differently.

Next, we consider the performance of these systems w.r.t. each scorer. As a link-based metric, MUC focuses on link identification and does not reward successful identification of singleton clusters. Hence, by looking at the MUC recall, we can get a better idea of how well a resolver does in terms of link identification. As can be seen, Emory and UTD are substantially better than KU and DFKI in terms of link identification. To gain a better understanding of the extent to which the singleton clusters and the non-singleton clusters contribute to the overall performance of the systems, we show the corresponding results in Table 5. Specifically, in the "F" columns we show the CoNLL score. The "ns-F" columns show the CoNLL scores obtained by removing the singleton clusters from the output prior to scoring, meaning that the scorers are applied to score only the non-singleton clusters. Similarly, the "s-F" columns show the CoNLL scores obtained by removing the non-singleton clusters from the output prior to scoring, effectively allow-

	LIGHT			AMI			Persuasion			Switchboard		
	F	ns. F	s. F	F	ns. F	s. F	F	ns. F	s. F	F	ns. F	s. F
Emory	80.3	60.5	32.4	64.0	45.0	29.3	78.4	56.6	35.8	74.5	53.6	33.7
UTD	79.6	60.2	32.9	57.4	42.9	25.2	77.5	56.5	35.3	72.6	53.7	32.5
KU	68.8	49.4	28.0	57.4	38.5	27.5	70.6	48.0	33.1	65.5	44.8	30.7
DFKI	67.3	51.2	27.0	43.9	32.2	19.1	59.9	43.2	27.3	53.5	41.6	20.7

Table 5: Entity coreference resolution: results on singleton and non-singleton cluster identification.

ing the scorers to score only the singleton clusters.

As we can see from the results in Table 5, Emory and UTD achieve comparable performance w.r.t. both non-singleton and singleton cluster identification, except on the AMI dataset where Emory clearly demonstrates its superior performance w.r.t. both tasks. In addition, while Emory and UTD are generally better than KU w.r.t. both tasks, the difference stems more from non-singleton cluster identification than singleton cluster identification. Comparing KU and DFKI, we see that KU is better than DFKI on both tasks on all but the LIGHT dataset.

Next, we measure system performance, specifically link identification performance, at the *pairwise* level. For each non-singleton coreference cluster in the gold output, we extract every pair of mentions in the cluster, and denote the set of pairs extracted from all non-singleton clusters as G_p. We similarly extract all the pairs from the non-singleton clusters produced by each of the four systems, and denote the resulting sets as E_p, T_p, K_p and D_p. The recall, precision, and F-scores in Table 6 are computed based on the pairwise links in these sets.

From the "Overall" row in Table 6, we can see that approximately 120K pairs can be extracted from the gold clusters of the four test datasets. As we can see, except for KU, all systems have higher recall than precision. In particular, UTD has the highest recall but the lowest precision. Comparing Emory and UTD, we see that while the two systems achieve comparable recall, UTD's precision is much lower, which in turn results in a lower F-score. Though precision-oriented, KU's precision is not as high as Emory's, which has the highest precision among the systems.

To gain a better understanding of how these systems perform w.r.t. identifying difficult vs. easy links, we divide the pairs into three groups based on an intuitive notion of hardness. Group A is composed of pairs where the two mentions are lexically identical. A pair appears in Group B if (1) both mentions in the pair are pronouns or (2) both mentions are non-pronominal and have a content word overlap. Finally, a pair appears in Group C if (1) the anaphor is pronominal but the antecedent is not or (2) the two mentions have no content word overlap.

Results are shown in the rows labeled A, B, and C. The easiest links (Group A) account for nearly half of all pairs while the hardest links (Group C) have a much lower representation, accounting for only 15% of all pairs. Emory achieves the best results in all three groups, indicating its robustness in identifying both easy and hard links. UTD ranks second in Groups A and B, and the performance gap between Emory and UTD widens as hardness increases. DFKI ranks third in Groups A and B, and largely fails to identify the links in Group C. Finally, while KU does poorly for Groups A and B, it performs slightly better than UTD w.r.t. Group C. We speculate that KU chooses to resolve only those pairs it is most confident about regardless of hardness, yielding a low recall but a higher precision.

To understand how well each system does in resolving the anaphors in each of the 10 groups we defined earlier, we show the per-group results in the rows labeled 1 through 10. As can be seen, the links involving 1st or 2nd pronouns as anaphors (Group 1) form the largest group, accounting for 70% of all links. This is followed by links involving non-pronominal mentions (Group 10) and possessive pronouns (Group 4), both of which account for slightly more than 10% of all links. Emory achieves the best performance on these three largest groups. Comparing Emory and UTD, we can see that the two systems are indeed different: Emory achieves a higher precision than UTD on all 10 groups, and its precision and recall are both higher than UTD's on Groups 6, 7, and 10. Comparing KU and DFKI, we see that DFKI outperforms KU in resolving 1st and 2nd pronouns (Group 1), possessive pronouns (Group 4) and reflexive pronouns (Group 5). Though achieving the lowest overall performance, KU outperforms UTD in resolving

			Emory			UTD			KU			DFKI		
Group	%	count	P	R	F	P	R	F	P	R	F	P	R	F
Overall	100.0	120045	60.4	78.9	68.4	45.2	80.2	57.8	57.9	30.6	40.1	49.1	58.7	53.5
A	46.4	55702	63.4	84.3	72.4	55.4	90.5	68.7	64.6	28.1	39.2	54.4	79.9	64.8
B	38.6	46357	62.8	80.7	70.6	41.3	83.1	55.2	55.5	35.5	43.3	44.5	54.9	49.1
C	15.0	17986	44.5	57.2	50.1	25.8	41.0	31.6	48.4	25.9	33.7	10.1	2.5	4.0
1	70.0	84000	62.2	84.3	71.6	48.1	87.0	61.9	57.5	28.2	37.8	49.1	71.1	58.1
2	2.4	2835	81.6	68.8	74.7	59.4	78.6	67.6	87.1	51.2	64.5	58.4	35.1	43.9
3	5.0	5990	47.2	53.9	50.3	27.1	59.1	37.2	57.1	44.2	49.8	29.9	14.0	19.1
4	10.1	12124	62.3	82.2	70.9	46.1	84.6	59.7	60.5	42.2	49.7	55.3	62.6	58.7
5	0.7	862	67.2	68.6	67.9	56.9	74.9	64.7	49.3	20.6	29.1	51.1	49.9	50.5
6	0.1	158	38.4	27.2	31.9	24.1	21.5	22.7	59.0	22.8	32.9	7.7	0.6	1.2
7	0.9	1051	37.9	40.9	39.3	18.7	34.1	24.1	44.8	29.6	35.6	nan	0.0	nan
8	0.0	37	15.6	13.5	14.5	11.5	18.9	14.3	23.3	18.9	20.9	0.0	0.0	nan
9	0.2	259	50.1	74.9	60.1	28.2	78.4	41.5	37.5	47.5	41.9	26.7	3.1	5.5
10	10.6	12729	49.2	58.7	53.5	33.1	46.5	38.6	52.9	25.2	34.2	31.3	6.6	10.9
1A	39.7	47641	63.0	86.7	73.0	56.0	93.2	69.9	62.1	25.1	35.7	53.8	88.1	66.8
1B	26.2	31414	64.2	84.2	72.8	42.0	85.2	56.2	54.4	33.7	41.6	41.9	56.4	48.1
1C	4.1	4945	43.4	61.6	50.9	21.7	39.2	27.9	46.1	23.6	31.2	2.0	0.5	0.8
2A	0.9	1108	91.3	74.2	81.9	66.4	94.7	78.0	94.2	58.8	72.4	79.2	46.4	58.5
2B	0.9	1097	79.6	64.4	71.2	54.2	85.9	66.5	85.2	49.2	62.4	46.4	32.7	38.4
2C	0.5	630	70.1	67.0	68.5	54.6	37.5	44.4	76.1	41.4	53.6	43.5	19.5	26.9
3A	1.9	2322	53.4	63.3	57.9	36.3	67.4	47.2	67.0	53.7	59.6	56.0	22.3	31.9
3B	1.1	1289	40.7	45.5	43.0	13.8	51.0	21.8	46.3	40.6	43.2	22.3	9.3	13.1
3C	2.0	2379	44.2	49.3	46.6	33.0	55.3	41.4	53.4	36.9	43.7	14.9	8.4	10.8
4A	1.1	1271	71.3	87.3	78.5	55.9	91.3	69.3	68.9	46.7	55.7	68.4	75.0	71.5
4B	7.9	9499	63.4	83.9	72.2	46.9	88.3	61.2	60.9	43.0	50.4	54.9	69.3	61.3
4C	1.1	1354	47.2	65.4	54.8	31.1	52.1	39.0	49.7	33.1	39.7	15.7	4.2	6.6
5A	0.0	11	42.9	27.3	33.3	80.0	36.4	50.0	0.0	0.0	nan	46.2	54.5	50.0
5B	0.6	750	68.4	73.1	70.7	57.5	79.2	66.6	50.0	20.5	29.1	52.8	56.3	54.5
5C	0.1	101	56.3	39.6	46.5	49.5	47.5	48.5	48.0	23.8	31.8	6.9	2.0	3.1
6A	0.1	69	50.0	37.7	43.0	32.1	37.7	34.7	69.7	33.3	45.1	8.3	1.4	2.5
6B	0.0	38	0.0	0.0	nan	0.0	0.0	nan	0.0	0.0	nan	0.0	0.0	nan
6C	0.0	51	39.5	33.3	36.2	17.8	15.7	16.7	59.1	25.5	35.6	nan	0.0	nan
7A	0.2	280	53.8	60.0	56.8	38.6	51.1	44.0	59.8	53.6	56.5	nan	0.0	nan
7B	0.3	318	33.0	36.2	34.5	12.5	36.8	18.6	34.8	21.7	26.7	nan	0.0	nan
7C	0.4	453	30.9	32.5	31.7	16.1	21.6	18.5	37.6	20.3	26.4	nan	0.0	nan
8A	0.0	1	0.0	0.0	nan	0.0	0.0	nan	100.0	100.0	100.0	0.0	0.0	nan
8B	0.0	6	14.3	16.7	15.4	5.6	16.7	8.3	16.7	16.7	16.7	0.0	0.0	nan
8C	0.0	30	16.7	13.3	14.8	14.6	20.0	16.9	21.7	16.7	18.9	nan	0.0	nan
9A	0.0	42	49.2	76.2	59.8	42.7	76.2	54.7	40.0	33.3	36.4	46.7	16.7	24.6
9B	0.1	125	62.6	87.2	72.9	30.4	92.0	45.7	38.2	58.4	46.2	0.0	0.0	nan
9C	0.1	92	35.8	57.6	44.2	21.0	60.9	31.2	35.3	39.1	37.1	100.0	1.1	2.2
10A	2.5	2957	70.3	70.0	70.2	64.9	67.3	66.1	81.5	34.4	48.4	75.3	18.5	29.7
10B	1.5	1821	43.8	49.9	46.6	33.7	52.6	41.0	43.5	25.5	32.1	30.0	13.8	18.9
10C	6.6	7951	44.1	56.6	49.6	24.8	37.3	29.8	46.0	21.8	29.6	3.7	0.5	0.9

Table 6: Entity coreference resolution: resolution results at the pairwise level.

3rd person ungendered pronouns (Group 3), indefinite pronouns (Group 6), demonstrative pronouns (Group 7), relative and interrogative pronouns (Group 8), and other pronouns (Group 9). The remaining rows of the table show the results when each of the ten groups is further subdivided into three groups based on the three levels of hardness. Space limitations preclude a discussion of these results, however.

Table 7a shows each system's coverage of gold coreferent pairs. The rows can be interpreted in the same way as those in Table 6, whereas the columns can be interpreted in the same way as those in Table 2. As a quick reminder, "none" shows the percentage of gold pairs that are not extracted by any of the four systems; "E", "T", "K", and "D" show the percentage of gold pairs extracted by each of the four systems; and the "x-only" columns show the percentage of gold pairs that are extracted only by system x.

A few points deserve mention. First, consider the "none" results. As can be seen, only 10.5% of the links are not recovered by any of the four systems. Taking into account link hardness, we see that 31.9% of the hardest links (Group C) are not extracted while only 4.9% of the easiest links (Group A) are not extracted. These results provide suggestive evidence that our intuition notion of link hardness is consistent with what a resolver would perceive as hard. Considering the per-group results (Group i, where $1 \leq i \leq 10$), approximately 65% of the links involving indefinite pronouns (Group 6) and relative and interrogative pronouns (Group 8), 47% of the links involving demonstrative pronouns (Group 7), and 29% of the links involving 3rd person ungendered pronouns (Group 3) and non-pronominal mentions (Group 10) are missed by all four systems. These are traditionally the harder groups of anaphors to resolve. Second, consider the "x-only" results. While the "Overall" results suggest that Emory and UTD may not very different from each other in terms of the links they recover, the "x-only" results suggest otherwise. Specifically, 18% of the hardest links (Group C) and 16.6% of the non-pronominal links (Group 10) are uniquely identified by Emory, whereas 15.1% of the links involving 3rd person gendered pronouns (Group 2) are uniquely identified by UTD.

While Table 7a focuses on the extraction of gold coreferent pairs, Table 7b focuses on pairs that are erroneously posited as coreferent. Specifically, we take the union of the set of pairs that are erroneously posited as coreferent by the four resolvers and compute statistics based on the resulting set, which we refer to as S. The columns in Table 7b can be interpreted in the same way as those in Table 2. For instance, E, T, K, and D show the percentage of pairs in S extracted by each of the systems, and the "x-only" columns show the percentage of pairs in S that are extracted only by system x.

As can be seen in Table 7b, approximately 19.4K erroneous links are established by the four systems, of which 60.2% are established by UTD, 37.7% by DFKI, 32% by Emory, and 13.8% by KU; in addition, 32.4% of these erroneous links are only established by UTD and 20.4% are only established by DFKI. Combining the results in Tables 7a and 7b, we see that UTD is the most aggressive among the four systems in link identification: it has the highest recall but the lowest precision, which is consistent with the results in Table 6, and a large percentage of erroneous links are only established by UTD. In fact, a closer examination of the results reveals that the percentage of erroneous links established by UTD is higher than that by any other system w.r.t. each of the ten groups and each of the three hardness groups. Furthermore, recall from Table 7a that Emory manages to correctly extract many hard links (Group C) and non-pronominal links (Group 10), but from Table 7b we can see that this success comes at the expense of extracting a fairly large number of erroneous links in these groups. Finally, the "only" columns show that the errors made by the four systems are quite different from each other.

2.3 Discussion

In this subsection, we manually analyze the pairwise links that are correctly and incorrectly established by the participating systems.

We begin by examining the coreference links that are not identified by any system. The mention pairs that are most frequently missed are: ("I", "I"), ("I", "you"), ("you", "I"), and ("it", it"), where the first mention in each pair is the anaphor and the second mention is its antecedent. It should perhaps not be surprising that these pairs all involve links between pronouns given their prevalence in spoken dialogues. More than 3000 instances of these four mention pairs are not extracted by any of the participating systems. The other major types

(a) Coverage of correct links

Group	%	count	none	E	T	K	D	E-only	T-only	K-only	D-only
Overall	100.0	120045	10.5	78.9	80.2	30.6	58.7	4.6	3.7	1.1	0.7
A	46.4	55702	4.8	84.3	90.5	28.1	79.9	1.3	2.6	0.6	0.6
B	38.6	46357	9.0	80.7	83.1	35.5	54.9	3.3	3.7	1.3	1.0
C	15.0	17986	31.9	57.2	41.0	25.9	2.5	18.0	7.1	2.4	0.1
1	70.0	84000	6.2	84.3	87.0	28.2	71.1	2.9	2.4	0.7	0.7
2	2.4	2835	9.7	68.8	78.6	51.2	35.1	5.4	15.1	0.5	1.1
3	5.0	5990	29.1	53.9	59.1	44.2	14.0	4.0	9.3	3.4	0.6
4	10.1	12124	7.1	82.2	84.6	42.2	62.6	3.2	2.7	1.3	1.1
5	0.7	862	13.6	68.6	74.9	20.6	49.9	2.6	5.3	1.6	2.7
6	0.1	158	65.8	27.2	21.5	22.8	0.6	4.4	1.9	1.9	0.0
7	0.9	1051	47.4	40.9	34.1	29.6	0.0	9.3	5.2	4.5	0.0
8	0.0	37	64.9	13.5	18.9	18.9	0.0	8.1	5.4	8.1	0.0
9	0.2	259	12.7	74.9	78.4	47.5	3.1	5.8	9.3	0.8	0.0
10	10.6	12729	29.3	58.7	46.5	25.2	6.6	16.6	7.8	2.4	0.2
1A	39.7	47641	3.1	86.7	93.2	25.1	88.1	0.6	1.6	0.3	0.7
1B	26.2	31414	7.3	84.2	85.2	33.7	56.4	3.4	3.0	1.0	0.8
1C	4.1	4945	29.4	61.6	39.2	23.6	0.5	22.3	6.1	1.9	0.0
2A	0.9	1108	1.8	74.2	94.7	58.8	46.4	1.7	17.6	0.0	1.0
2B	0.9	1097	8.3	64.4	85.9	49.2	32.7	1.9	20.2	0.3	1.5
2C	0.5	630	26.0	67.0	37.5	41.4	19.5	17.8	1.6	1.9	0.5
3A	1.9	2322	20.6	63.3	67.4	53.7	22.3	3.7	7.8	3.1	0.4
3B	1.1	1289	36.5	45.5	51.0	40.6	9.3	4.1	8.7	5.0	0.9
3C	2.0	2379	33.3	49.3	55.3	36.9	8.4	4.2	11.1	2.9	0.7
4A	1.1	1271	2.8	87.3	91.3	46.7	75.0	0.8	4.0	0.6	0.5
4B	7.9	9499	5.3	83.9	88.3	43.0	69.3	1.8	1.8	1.4	1.3
4C	1.1	1354	23.7	65.4	52.1	33.1	4.2	15.1	7.5	2.0	0.1
5A	0.0	11	36.4	27.3	36.4	0.0	54.5	9.1	0.0	0.0	18.2
5B	0.6	750	10.9	73.1	79.2	20.5	56.3	1.7	2.9	1.3	2.7
5C	0.1	101	30.7	39.6	47.5	23.8	2.0	7.9	23.8	4.0	1.0
6A	0.1	69	47.8	37.7	37.7	33.3	1.4	5.8	4.3	2.9	0.0
6B	0.0	38	100.0	0.0	0.0	0.0	0.0	0.0	0.0	0.0	0.0
6C	0.0	51	64.7	33.3	15.7	25.5	0.0	5.9	0.0	2.0	0.0
7A	0.2	280	29.6	60.0	51.1	53.6	0.0	6.4	3.2	5.7	0.0
7B	0.3	318	47.8	36.2	36.8	21.7	0.0	8.5	7.2	5.3	0.0
7C	0.4	453	58.1	32.5	21.6	20.3	0.0	11.7	5.1	3.1	0.0
8A	0.0	1	0.0	0.0	0.0	100.0	0.0	0.0	0.0	100.0	0.0
8B	0.0	6	66.7	16.7	16.7	16.7	0.0	16.7	0.0	0.0	0.0
8C	0.0	30	66.7	13.3	20.0	16.7	0.0	6.7	6.7	6.7	0.0
9A	0.0	42	11.9	76.2	76.2	33.3	16.7	11.9	9.5	0.0	0.0
9B	0.1	125	4.0	87.2	92.0	58.4	0.0	4.0	8.8	0.0	0.0
9C	0.1	92	25.0	57.6	60.9	39.1	1.1	5.4	9.8	2.2	0.0
10A	2.5	2957	18.1	70.0	67.3	34.4	18.5	9.1	7.7	1.6	0.2
10B	1.5	1821	30.2	49.9	52.6	25.5	13.8	10.5	12.7	2.7	0.9
10C	6.6	7951	33.3	56.6	37.3	21.8	0.5	20.8	6.7	2.6	0.0

(b) Coverage of wrong links

Group	%	count	E	T	K	D	E-only	T-only	K-only	D-only
Overall	100.0	193827	32.0	60.2	13.8	37.7	9.6	32.4	7.3	20.4
A	34.6	66992	40.5	60.5	12.8	55.6	6.7	18.5	7.1	23.2
B	46.8	90794	24.4	60.4	14.6	35.0	7.1	37.7	7.4	22.3
C	18.6	36041	35.6	59.0	13.8	11.1	21.2	44.7	7.3	10.1
1	70.0	135593	31.7	58.2	12.9	45.6	7.6	27.6	7.3	24.4
2	1.1	2207	19.9	69.0	9.8	32.2	4.5	48.7	2.5	20.5
3	7.3	14074	25.7	67.5	14.1	14.0	12.9	53.9	5.7	11.6
4	9.4	18316	33.0	65.4	18.3	33.5	8.3	34.2	8.5	14.0
5	0.6	1069	26.9	45.7	17.1	38.5	8.8	27.6	8.2	33.0
6	0.1	168	41.1	63.7	14.9	7.1	20.8	46.4	5.4	6.0
7	1.2	2290	30.8	68.0	16.7	0.0	18.9	58.1	9.7	0.0
8	0.0	88	30.7	61.4	26.1	6.8	13.6	48.9	9.1	6.8
9	0.3	631	30.6	81.9	32.5	3.5	8.9	47.9	5.9	2.2
10	10.0	19391	39.9	61.7	14.8	9.5	21.3	42.9	7.4	7.3
1A	30.6	59401	40.8	58.9	12.3	60.8	5.9	15.2	7.4	25.5
1B	33.3	64556	22.9	57.3	13.7	38.0	6.7	35.6	7.4	25.9
1C	6.0	11636	34.2	60.2	11.8	11.0	21.2	46.7	6.2	10.3
2A	0.3	566	13.8	94.0	7.1	23.9	0.5	64.8	0.0	4.8
2B	0.6	1179	15.4	67.4	8.0	35.2	2.5	48.5	2.4	27.1
2C	0.2	462	39.0	42.4	17.7	34.6	14.5	29.2	5.8	22.9
3A	2.0	3866	33.1	71.0	15.9	10.5	14.7	51.4	4.8	6.5
3B	2.7	5227	16.4	78.2	11.6	8.0	8.6	69.2	5.3	6.5
3C	2.6	4981	29.7	53.6	15.4	23.0	16.1	39.9	6.9	20.9
4A	0.6	1197	37.3	76.6	22.4	36.8	4.9	33.2	7.4	6.5
4B	7.4	14350	32.0	66.3	18.3	37.6	5.9	32.5	8.5	15.6
4C	1.4	2769	35.8	56.4	16.4	11.0	22.1	43.2	8.7	9.3
5A	0.0	12	33.3	8.3	25.0	58.3	16.7	0.0	16.7	41.7
5B	0.5	942	26.9	46.6	16.3	40.1	7.5	27.3	7.5	34.3
5C	0.1	115	27.0	42.6	22.6	23.5	18.3	33.0	13.0	21.7
6A	0.0	74	35.1	74.3	13.5	14.9	8.1	48.6	1.4	12.2
6B	0.0	29	58.6	51.7	20.7	3.4	31.0	31.0	6.9	3.4
6C	0.0	65	40.0	56.9	13.8	0.0	30.8	50.8	9.2	0.0
7A	0.2	375	38.4	60.5	26.9	0.0	20.5	45.3	12.5	0.0
7B	0.6	1080	21.6	75.9	11.9	0.0	13.9	69.4	8.5	0.0
7C	0.4	835	39.3	61.1	18.3	0.0	24.6	49.2	10.1	0.0
8A	0.0	6	16.7	33.3	0.0	50.0	16.7	33.3	0.0	50.0
8B	0.0	26	23.1	65.4	19.2	11.5	7.7	57.7	3.8	11.5
8C	0.0	56	35.7	62.5	32.1	0.0	16.1	46.4	12.5	0.0
9A	0.0	55	60.0	78.2	38.2	14.5	14.5	30.9	5.5	0.0
9B	0.2	300	21.7	87.7	39.3	4.7	4.0	50.0	2.7	4.7
9C	0.1	276	34.4	76.4	23.9	0.0	13.0	48.9	9.4	0.0
10A	0.7	1440	60.7	74.7	16.0	12.4	15.4	27.6	1.8	5.4
10B	1.6	3105	37.5	60.7	19.4	19.0	15.9	39.1	8.9	10.5
10C	7.7	14846	38.4	60.7	13.7	7.3	23.0	45.1	7.7	6.9

Table 7: Entity coreference resolution: coverage of wrong links at the pairwise level.

of missing links involve demonstrative pronouns, wh-pronouns, and one-anaphora.

As for missing links that involve non-pronominal expressions, some appear to be easy to identify as the two mentions involved are synonyms, such as ("the super market", "the grocery store"), ("the school", "the college"), and ("kids", "children"). Since we do not examine the context in which they appear or consider how far apart they are from each other, we cannot conclude why these seemingly simple cases are being missed by all systems.

Some missing links are difficult to identify because the two mentions involved appear to have different semantic types. Examples include: ("your destination", "the king of the goolehops"), ("your donation", "the organization"), ("this very reputable charity", "you"), ("this school your son goes to", "private"), ("the battery", "the standard"), ("sixty-six", "the street"), and ("Michael", "a").

There are links that are missed because one or both of the mentions involved are simply not extracted. Examples include: ("your husband", "a wonderful man, you know, who treats me very, you know, with a, with as") and ("your grandfathers of past", "the kings of old: my great-grandfather kind leonidas, the pious baylor the blessed, and maegor the cruel"). Note that the antecedents in these examples are very long and certainly pose challenges to a mention detection system.

Next, we take a closer look at the top-performing system, the Emory system, in an attempt to understand why it works better than the other systems. First, there are more than 1700 links in the AMI test corpus that involve "well" (i.e., "we'll") and "were" (i.e., "we're") and are correctly identified by Emory but not the other systems. In fact, the large discrepancy in resolution performance between Emory and UTD on AMI can primarily be attributed to UTD's failure to even extract "well" and "were" as mentions (probably because of the missing apostrophe). Second, Emory appears to be better than the other systems at exploiting context to determine when two mentions are coreferent. Consider a lexical pair that appears frequently in the data such as ("I", "I"). While many instances of it are coreferent, there are also many instances that are not coreferent. The coreferent and non-coreferent instances can only be distinguished by factors such as distance and the surrounding context. While Emory and UTD achieve similar recall numbers, Emory achieves higher precision scores because of its ability to better exploit context to distinguish the coreferent and non-coreferent cases of a frequently-occurring lexical pair than UTD.

We also examine the erroneous links established by Emory. A major type of error involves links between nouns that are synonymous or semantically similar. Examples include ("contrast", "brightness") and ("the cash", "budget"). Another major type of error involves the frequently occurring lexical pairs discussed in the previous paragraph: while Emory is comparatively better than the other systems in exploiting context to distinguish the coreferent and non-coreferent instances, it is still far from being perfect in doing so. For instance, while it correctly identifies more than 1700 links involving "well" and "were", it incorrectly identifies more than 1500 links involving these two pronouns. Determining how to effectively exploit context to distinguish the coreferent instances from their non-coreferent counterparts is by no means trivial, but it is a problem that must be addressed in order to bring entity coreference resolvers to the next level of performance.

Table 8 shows examples of the most frequent gold coreferent pairs in the four test sets as well as the predictions made by the four systems on these pairs. Specifically, the first block shows the results of the five most frequent coreferent pairs. Perhaps not surprisingly, each pair involves two pronouns. The "count" column shows the number of times the two pronouns are coreferent in the test data. In addition, we show the number of times each system correctly predicts each pair as coreferent as well as the number of times each system incorrectly predicts each pair as coreferent. As can be seen, Emory and UTD establish a lot more correct links but also a lot more erroneous links than KU and DFKI. Moreover, the number of wrong links posited by Emory is considerably smaller than that by UTD. These results provide empirical support for our earlier claim that determining how to effectively exploit context to distinguish the coreferent instances of a frequent pair from their non-coreferent counterparts is a challenging but important problem for coreference researchers.

The second block shows results involving pairs in which one is a pronominal mention and the other is a non-pronominal mention, whereas the last block shows results involving pairs in which both mentions are non-pronominal. The first two blocks of results are similar in terms of the ob-

anaphor	antecedent	count	Emory Correct	Emory Wrong	UTD Correct	UTD Wrong	KU Correct	KU Wrong	DFKI Correct	DFKI Wrong
				Most frequent pairs						
i	i	34534	31110	13677	32175	17729	8120	5420	29747	6515
i	you	8500	7053	3484	6866	7438	2697	2120	2607	7056
we	we	8148	5957	8829	8049	12885	1412	264	7858	12793
you	i	7472	6155	3778	6113	7676	2642	2131	3402	10122
you	you	4713	3996	1647	3962	4241	2304	1557	4148	16741
			Most frequent (pronoun, non-pronoun) or (non-pronoun, pronoun) pairs							
they	people	114	88	55	107	141	26	8	23	36
it	the remote	109	23	24	59	181	9	0	1	0
i	william	96	0	0	0	0	0	0	0	0
people	them	93	78	13	90	15	6	0	0	0
people	they	89	61	75	85	73	17	11	0	0
			Most frequent (non-pronoun, non-pronoun) pairs							
texas	here	19	0	0	0	0	0	1	0	0
texas	down here	18	0	0	0	0	0	0	0	0
the product	the remote	18	0	0	10	2	1	1	0	0
here	raleigh	15	0	0	15	41	0	0	0	0
childrens	children	12	6	3	6	3	2	3	0	0

Table 8: Entity coreference resolution: examples of frequent gold coreferent pairs and the results of the systems on them.

servations we can draw. The last block of results indicate how challenging it is to correctly establish links between two non-pronominal mentions.

3 Bridging Resolution

The shared task divides the evaluation of bridging resolution into two phases: (1) the *Predicted* phase, where a system needs to first identify all of the entity mentions that likely correspond to anaphors and antecedents, then perform bridging resolution on the predicted mentions; and (2) the *Gold* phase, which is essentially the same as the Predicted phase except that bridging resolution is performed on the given gold mentions.

In this section, we analyze the performance of the teams that participated in the bridging resolution track. The UTD team (Kobayashi et al., 2021) and the KU team (Kim et al., 2021) participated in both phases, whereas the INRIA team (Renner et al., 2021) only participated in the Gold phase. In other words, two teams participated in the Predicted phase, and three teams participated in the Gold phase. We will use their team name to refer to the bridging resolution systems they developed. To make it clear which phase a system was developed for, we will augment the team name with a superscript that encodes the phase. For instance, we will use UTD^P and UTD^G to refer to the systems the UTD team developed for the Predicted phase and the Gold phase respectively.

3.1 Anaphor Extraction

The "Recognition" rows in Table 9 show the official anaphor extraction results on each of the four test sets, where results are expressed in terms of recall (R), precision (P), and F-score. An anaphor is considered correctly detected if it has an exact match with a gold bridging anaphor in terms of boundary. Comparing the two systems developed for the Predicted phase, we see that KU^P beats UTD^P on three datasets, LIGHT, AMI, and Switchboard. Perhaps impressively, on these three datasets, KU^P outperforms UTD^P in terms of both precision and recall, showing its firm superiority over UTD^P. Note that KU^P is a pipelined system where anaphor extraction is performed as an explicit step prior to resolution, whereas UTD^P is a span-based system where the spans corresponding to anaphors are jointly learned as part of the resolution process. These results seem to suggest that better results can be achieved if one designs a model specifically for anaphor extraction.

Among the three Gold systems, UTD^G outperforms KU^G on all datasets, and KU^G in turn outperforms INRIA^G on all datasets. One difference between UTD^G and UTD^P is that the former has an explicit anaphor extraction component whereas the latter does not. The better anaphor extraction results achieved by UTD^G in comparison to KU^G could be therefore be attributed to the introduction of this anaphor extraction component, providing further empirical support for our earlier hypoth-

	LIGHT			AMI			Persuasion			Switchboard		
	P	R	F	P	R	F	P	R	F	P	R	F
					UTD^P							
Recognition	21.8	44.3	29.2	26.8	32.9	29.5	29.6	38.9	33.6	28.9	32.2	30.4
Resolution	10.4	21.2	14.0	12.1	14.8	13.3	19.3	25.3	21.9	14.5	16.1	15.3
					KU^P							
Recognition	28.8	54.7	37.7	32.3	38.4	35.1	20.9	60.4	31.1	29.7	43.4	35.3
Resolution	10.3	19.5	13.5	9.4	11.2	10.3	8.3	24.0	12.3	9.3	13.5	11.0
					UTD^G							
Recognition	34.7	40.7	37.5	37.0	42.2	39.4	43.0	52.1	47.1	37.7	50.9	43.3
Resolution	18.3	21.4	19.7	18.4	21.0	19.6	28.7	34.7	31.4	18.4	24.8	21.1
					KU^G							
Recognition	38.2	34.7	36.4	41.9	30.8	35.5	31.3	53.1	39.4	41.2	30.9	35.3
Resolution	17.5	15.9	16.7	18.1	13.3	15.3	14.9	25.3	18.8	21.4	16.1	18.3
					INRIA^G							
Recognition	34.8	11.8	17.6	34.1	14.4	20.2	46.7	17.0	24.9	34.2	24.9	28.8
Resolution	18.4	6.3	9.4	10.1	4.3	6.0	30.5	11.1	16.3	9.2	6.7	7.8

Table 9: Bridging resolution: official anaphor recognition and resolution results.

esis that better anaphor extraction results could be achieved via an anaphor extraction component. While one would generally expect to see better anaphor extraction performance in the Gold phase than in the Predicted phase, it is interesting to see that this is not necessarily the case for KU. Specifically, except on Persuasion where KU^G achieves considerably better performance than KU^P, the two systems achieve similar F-scores on the remaining three datasets. While their F-scores are similar, the recall and precision scores are not: KU^P has dramatically higher recall and substantially lower precision than KU^G. INRIA^P is roughly on par with the other systems in terms of precision, but its recall is much lower than the other systems: the best recall it achieves on any of the datasets is only 24.9%. This level of extraction performance will likely limit its resolution performance severely.

Tables 10 and 11 show each system's coverage of correct and wrong anaphors in the Predicted phase and the Gold phase respectively. The rows and columns in these tables can be interpreted in the same way as those in Table 2. As a quick reminder, "none" shows the percentage of gold anaphors that are not extracted by any of the systems, and the "x-only" columns show the percentage of correct/wrong anaphors extracted by system x and not any of the other systems.

Consider first the left half of Table 10, which shows each Predicted system's coverage of gold anaphors. As we can see, 40.4% of the gold anaphors are not extracted by any of the two systems. More specifically, 38.4% of the non-pronominal anaphors (the largest group), 50.7% of the 1st+2nd person pronouns (one of the second largest groups) and 67.6% of the 3rd person ungendered pronouns (the other second largest group) are not extracted by any of them. These results suggest that anaphor extraction in the Predicted phase is rather challenging. In terms of the coverage of gold anaphors, the "x-only" columns show that the two Predicted systems are quite different: while many of the anaphors extracted by KU^P are not extracted by UTD^P, there are also a number of anaphors that are extracted by UTD^P but not by KU^P.

The right half of Table 10 shows each Predicted system's coverage of mentions that are erroneously extracted as anaphors. As can be seen, KU^P extracts nearly half of the erroneously extracted anaphors, whereas the corresponding percentage for UTD^P is slightly lower (38.9%). The number of mistakes uniquely made by KU^P is larger than that by UTD^P on all but Groups 4 (possessive pronouns) and 7 (demonstrative pronouns). These results suggest that the two systems are very different from each other in terms of anaphor extraction.

Next, consider the three Gold systems in Table 11. Somewhat surprisingly, when the gold mentions are provided, the percentage of anaphors that cannot be extracted by any of the three systems increases for all but two groups (Group 10 (non-pronominal mentions) and Groups 6 (indefinite pronouns)) in comparison to the corresponding percentages in the Predicted phase. The remaining

Group	%	Coverage of gold anaphors count	none	T-only	K-only	%	Coverage of wrong anaphors count	T-only	K-only
Overall	100.0	2526	40.4	14.5	25.1	100.0	4863	38.9	49.5
1	2.8	71	50.7	8.5	26.8	9.4	459	14.6	80.4
2	0.0	1	100.0	0.0	0.0	0.2	10	0.0	100.0
3	2.8	71	67.6	2.8	25.4	3.3	159	8.2	85.5
4	0.9	23	39.1	26.1	30.4	1.1	55	58.2	30.9
5	0.0	0	100.0	0.0	0.0	0.1	3	33.3	66.7
6	1.8	46	26.1	17.4	30.4	2.0	97	58.8	34.0
7	1.9	49	73.5	0.0	22.4	1.9	94	6.4	91.5
8	0.0	1	100.0	0.0	0.0	0.1	4	25.0	75.0
9	1.3	32	62.5	9.4	21.9	0.8	39	33.3	64.1
10	88.4	2232	38.4	15.3	25.0	81.1	3943	43.1	43.8

Table 10: Bridging resolution (Predicted phase): coverage of correct and wrong anaphors.

Group	%	Coverage of gold anaphors count	none	T-only	K-only	I-only	%	Coverage of wrong anaphors count	T-only	K-only	I-only
Overall	100.0	2526	35.6	20.2	12.3	3.5	100.0	3338	37.5	26.4	12.3
1	2.8	71	56.3	11.3	5.6	8.5	8.9	297	26.3	37.0	19.2
2	0.0	1	100.0	0.0	0.0	0.0	0.1	5	0.0	60.0	40.0
3	2.8	71	73.2	5.6	7.0	2.8	3.5	117	47.0	31.6	12.8
4	0.9	23	56.5	13.0	0.0	0.0	1.0	35	48.6	5.7	31.4
5	0.0	0	100.0	0.0	0.0	0.0	0.0	1	0.0	100.0	0.0
6	1.8	46	17.4	19.6	15.2	2.2	1.9	62	30.6	40.3	9.7
7	1.9	49	83.7	2.0	12.2	0.0	1.0	35	20.0	71.4	8.6
8	0.0	1	100.0	0.0	0.0	0.0	0.1	3	0.0	0.0	100.0
9	1.3	32	75.0	6.2	3.1	3.1	0.6	20	40.0	55.0	5.0
10	88.4	2232	32.2	21.7	12.9	3.5	82.8	2763	38.7	24.1	11.3

Table 11: Bridging resolution (Gold phase): coverage of correct and wrong anaphors.

columns provide suggestive evidence that the three systems are quite different from each other in terms of anaphor extraction. Specifically, among the gold anaphors, 20.2% are extracted only by UTD^G, 12.3% only by KU^G, and 3.5% only by INRIA^G, and among the erroneously extracted anaphors, 37.5% are only extracted by UTD^G, 26.4% only by UTD^G, and 12.3% only by INRIA^G.

3.2 Resolution

The "Resolution" rows in Table 9 show the official resolution results on each of the four test sets, where results are expressed in terms of recall (R), precision (P), and F-score at the *entity* level. In other words, an anaphor is considered correctly resolved if it is resolved to its antecedent or any preceding mention that is coreferent with its antecedent. Comparing the two Predicted systems, we see that UTD^P beats KU^P on all datasets in terms of recall, precision, and F-score. Given that UTD^P's anaphor extraction performance is poorer than that of KU^P, its superior resolution results can be attributed solely to better resolution and not better anaphor extraction. We speculate that KU^P's poorer resolution performance can be attributed to its attempt to establish links, many of which are wrong, more aggressively than UTD^P.

Among the three Gold systems, UTD^G outperforms KU^G on all datasets in terms of F-score, and with the exception of its precision on Switchboard, it outperforms KU^G on both recall and precision on all datasets. It is worth noting that both Gold systems outperform their Predicted counterparts on all datasets, which is consistent with our expectation that the Gold setting is easier than the Predicted setting. INRIA^G's performance is much lower than the other two systems in terms of both recall and precision, but primarily because of recall. We believe that its low recall can be attributed in part to its fairly poor anaphor extraction performance.

To gain a better understanding of how these systems perform w.r.t. identifying difficult vs. easy links, we divide the bridging pairs based on how hard we believe it is to resolve them. Specifically, we partition the bridging pairs into five groups: same string (the two mentions are the same string), same head (the two mentions have the same head), same head lemma (the two mentions have the same lemma head), word overlap (the two mentions have at least one content word overlap), and other (pairs

(a) Coverage of correct links

Group	all		none		T		K		T-only		K-only	
	%	cnt	%	cnt	%	cnt	%	cnt	%	cnt	%	cnt
Overall	100.0	2526	77.4	1954	14.4	364	12.1	306	10.5	266	8.2	208
Same string	1.1	28	89.3	25	10.7	3	0.0	0	10.7	3	0.0	0
Same head	18.8	475	58.5	278	32.0	152	17.7	84	23.8	113	9.5	45
Same head lemma	6.6	167	61.1	102	30.5	51	15.6	26	23.4	39	8.4	14
Word overlap	4.2	105	79.0	83	13.3	14	13.3	14	7.6	8	7.6	8
Other	69.3	1751	83.7	1466	8.2	144	10.4	182	5.9	103	8.1	141

(b) Coverage of wrong links

Group	all		T		K		T-only		K-only	
	%	cnt	%	cnt	%	cnt	%	cnt	%	cnt
Overall	100.0	6604	44.8	2961	57.6	3807	42.4	2797	55.2	3643
Same string	7.0	462	54.1	250	45.9	212	54.1	250	45.9	212
Same head	16.0	1055	74.3	784	31.2	329	68.8	726	25.7	271
Same head lemma	4.3	287	71.1	204	39.0	112	61.0	175	28.9	83
Word overlap	5.2	346	46.5	161	55.8	193	44.2	153	53.5	185
Other	67.4	4454	35.1	1562	66.5	2961	33.5	1493	64.9	2892

Table 12: Bridging resolution (Predicted phase): coverage of correct and wrong links.

that have no lexical overlap).

Two points deserve mention. First, the groups are listed in ascending order of resolution difficulty: intuitively, a pair of mentions having the same head lemma is easier to resolve than one that does not have any lexical overlap, for instance. Second, if a pair belongs to a group (e.g., same head lemma), then it should also belong to all subsequent groups (i.e., word overlap and other), but since we are *partitioning* the pairs, we will assign a pair to only the first group that is applicable to it.

Tables 12a and 13a show the results for the Predicted systems and the Gold systems respectively. The rows correspond to the five groups. The columns can be interpreted in the same way as those in Table 7a. "all" expresses the size of a group in terms of the number of pairs it covers and the corresponding percentage. "none" shows the number and percentage of pairs that are not resolved by any of the systems. The "T", "K", and "I" columns show the number and percentage of pairs correctly resolved by the individual systems, whereas the "x-only" columns show the number and percentage of pairs that can be resolved by system x and not any of the other systems.

We begin by noting that the percentage of anaphors that belong to the "same string" group is much smaller in bridging than in coreference. This is understandable: this group contains pairs in which the mentions are lexically identical. While many coreferent mentions are lexically identical, relatively few bridging pairs are composed of lexically identical mentions. In addition, approximately only 30% of the links (i.e., those that connect the pairs in the first four groups) can be established using string-matching facilities. This makes bridging resolution more challenging than entity coreference resolution.

Next, consider the Predicted systems. As we can see in the "overall" row, the overall resolution performance of KU^P is worse than that of UTD^P. However, this by no means implies that UTD^P is better than KU^P in all categories. Generally, UTD^P performs much better than KU^P on the easier categories, and as we move down the table, the performance gap between the two systems continues to shrink, to the point that KU^P starts to outperform UTD^P on "other", the most difficult category. Overall, these results suggest that while UTD^P is better than KU^P at resolving the easier-to-resolve pairs, the reverse is true when it comes to resolving the difficult-to-resolve pairs. Considering the results in the "x-only" columns, we see that the links recalled by the two systems are largely different from each other. Finally, considering the results in the "none" column, we note that 77.4% of the links are not recalled by any of the two systems. Even for simpler categories such as "same head" and "same head lemma", around 60% of the pairs are not recalled. These results provide suggestive evidence that the Predicted setting is indeed very challenging.

Consider the Gold systems. A few points deserve mention. First, the performance differences that

(a) Coverage of correct links

Group	all %	all cnt	none %	none cnt	T %	T cnt	K %	K cnt	I %	I cnt	T-only %	T-only cnt	K-only %	K-only cnt	I-only %	I-only cnt
Overall	100.0	2526	70.2	1773	19.3	488	13.5	342	5.3	134	12.5	315	7.7	195	1.9	49
Same string	1.1	28	89.3	25	0.0	0	0.0	0	10.7	3	0.0	0	0.0	0	10.7	3
Same head	18.8	475	47.4	225	42.5	202	19.8	94	7.6	36	27.2	129	7.8	37	1.5	7
Same head lemma	6.6	167	46.1	77	37.7	63	27.5	46	10.8	18	21.6	36	12.6	21	1.2	2
Word Overlap	4.2	105	64.8	68	21.9	23	17.1	18	5.7	6	16.2	17	8.6	9	1.9	2
Other	69.3	1751	78.7	1378	11.4	200	10.5	184	4.1	71	7.6	133	7.3	128	2.0	35

(b) Coverage of wrong links

Group	all %	all cnt	T %	T cnt	K %	K cnt	I %	I cnt	T-only %	T-only cnt	K-only %	K-only cnt	I-only %	I-only cnt
Overall	100.0	5400	49.5	2675	34.9	1883	23.0	1244	43.2	2333	30.2	1629	19.6	1060
Same string	7.7	414	77.1	319	11.8	49	17.6	73	70.5	292	11.8	49	11.1	46
Same head	15.7	847	74.0	627	29.0	246	11.1	94	61.4	520	19.0	161	6.6	56
Same head lemma	4.6	250	71.6	179	32.0	80	11.2	28	58.0	145	21.6	54	6.4	16
Word overlap	7.7	416	34.9	145	31.5	131	39.7	165	30.3	126	27.4	114	37.5	156
Other	64.3	3473	40.5	1405	39.6	1377	25.5	884	36.0	1250	36.0	1251	22.6	786

Table 13: Bridging resolution (Gold phase): coverage of correct and wrong links.

we have observed above between UTD^P and KU^P are also applicable to UTD^G and KU^G, except that UTD^G outperforms KU^G on all categories. In other words, UTD^G manages to do better than KU^G on the difficult categories. Second, INRIA^G underperforms UTD^G and KU^G on all but the easiest group, "same string". Third, considering the results in the "x-only" columns, we see that the links recalled by UTD^G and KU^G are quite different, but the links recalled by INRIA^G are for the most part similar to those recalled by the other two systems. Finally, considering the results in the "none" column, we see that 70.2% of the links are not recalled by any of the three systems, which is smaller than the corresponding percentage in the Predicted setting. In fact, the percentage associated with nearly every group in the Gold phase is smaller than the corresponding percentage in the Predicted phase. This again provides suggestive evidence that the Gold setting is indeed less challenging than the Predicted setting.

While Tables 12a and 13a focus on the extraction of gold pairs, Tables 12b and 13b focus on the extraction of wrong pairs (i.e., wrong links). Specifically, in Table 12b, we take the union of the set of wrong pairs extracted by the two Predicted systems and compute statistics based on the resulting set, which we refer to as S. The columns in Table 12b can be interpreted in the same way as those in Table 12a. Table 13b is essentially the same as Table 12b except that it shows the results of the three Gold systems.

Consider first the Predicted systems (Table 12b). As can be seen, 6604 erroneous links are established by the two systems, of which 44.8% are established by UTD^P and 57.6% by KU^P; in addition, 42.4% of these erroneous links are only established by UTD^G and 55.2% are only established by UTD^P. Comparing Tables 12a and 12b, we see that each system identifies a lot more erroneous links than correct links. Moreover, while Table 12a shows that UTD^P performs better than KU^P on the easy categories and worse than it on the harder categories, Table 12b shows the reverse trend. Specifically, UTD^P extracts more erroneous pairs that belong to the easy categories than KU^P, whereas KU^P extracts more erroneous pairs that belong to the harder categories than UTD^P. Finally, considering the "x-only" columns, we see that there is very little overlap in the erroneous links predicted by the two systems.

Next, consider the Gold systems (Table 13b). We can see that 5400 erroneous links are established by the three systems, which is smaller than the corresponding number in Table 12b. This again suggests that the provision of gold mentions has made the task somewhat easier. Of these 5400 erroneous links, 49.5% are established by UTD^G, 34.9% by KU^G, and 23.0% by INRIA^G; in addition, 43.2% of these erroneous links are only established by UTD^G, 30.2% are only established by UTD^G, and 19.6% are only established by INRIA^G. Some of the observations we made on the Predicted results in Table 12b are applicable to the Gold results. For

relation/category	Recalled							Missed	
	anaphor	antecedent	T^P	K^P	T^G	K^G	I^G	anaphor	antecedent
Part-whole	these waters	the sea	✓	✓	✓	✓	✓	a bird	a beak
Is-a	a parent	the father	✓		✓			a chrysler	car
Instance-of (same head)	a car	cars	✓		✓			a college	colleges
Instance-of (diff heads)	a highway	the road		✓		✓		humans	i
Related/Associated	any amount	your payment	✓	✓	✓	✓	✓	sound	volume
Number	fifteen	seventeen	✓	✓		✓		fifty	the tenth
Pronoun pairs	we	you		✓				we	we
Pro, non-pro pairs	they	texas				✓		people	they
Demonstrative pronouns	this	an adventure		✓		✓		conceptual design	this

Table 14: Bridging resolution: examples of gold bridging pairs that belong to different relations/categories.

instance, UTD^G extracts a lot more erroneous pairs that belong to the easy categories than KU^P. What is different is that UTD^G extracts more erroneous pairs than KU^G on the hard categories as well, even though the difference in the number of erroneous pairs they extract is smaller as the hardness level increases. INRIA^G generally extracts fewer erroneous pairs than the other two systems, but it extracts more erroneous pairs in the "word overlap" group than the other systems. Finally, considering the "x-only" columns, we see that the three systems are quite different from each other in terms of their prediction of erroneous pairs.

3.3 Discussion

In this subsection, we manually analyze the pairwise links that are correctly and incorrectly established by the participating systems.

A bridging relation in this data typically involves two mentions where one is a specific instance of a generic concept referred to by the other via the use of semantic relations such as *set-subset*, *part-whole*, and *is-a*. There are no noticeable differences between the Predicted systems and the Gold systems in terms of the *kind* of semantic relations they extract. Specifically, both the Predicted systems and the Gold systems are able to extract a variety of semantic relations as bridging relations, such as *is-a* (e.g., ("an eagle", "bird"), ("a light blue", "standard color")), set-subset (e.g., ("I", "we"), ("charities", "Save the Children")) and *part-whole* (e.g., ("the engine", "the car"), ("New Orleans", "the United States")). In addition, both are able to extract less well-defined relations in which one mention is simply associated with or is a specific instance of the other (e.g., ("one chip", "two"), ("a child", "kid"), ("people", "customers"), ("it", "a new one, the phone"), ("the place", "a restaurant"), ("some", "animals"), ("That", "a special flower to show you"), ("dresses", "Levi's), ("people who have killed police officers", "murderers")). Additional examples that are successfully recalled by the systems are shown in Table 14. Specifically, the "Recalled" column shows successfully recalled pairs that are instances of different semantic relations or categories as well as the system(s) that identified these pairs. As discussed before, while some relations can be identified via string-matching facilities (e.g., ("the function", "a desired function"), ("two batteries", "battery")), the majority of them cannot.

In addition, we do not observe any noticeable differences between the systems submitted by different teams in terms of the kinds of semantic relations they extract. As discussed before, the UTD systems achieve better resolution results than the KU systems because (1) the UTD systems are more conservative in positing bridging links between two mentions than the KU systems, and (2) the UTD systems focus more on the relations that can be identified via string-matching facilities, which presumably are easier to identify.

Examining the links that are missed by all of the systems, we do not find any noticeable differences between the kinds of semantic relations that exist in the correctly extracted pairs and those that exist in the pairs that fail to be extracted. Table 14 shows several gold pairs that are not extracted by any of the systems in the "Missed" column. While a deeper analysis is needed in order to understand why some instances of a particular semantic relation are being extracted and others are not, we speculate that the distance between the two mentions involved, their surrounding contexts, and whether a given mention pair is seen in the training data as having a bridging relation may have played a role.

While it is encouraging to see from Table 14 that the systems can successfully recall pairs that belong to the "Other" (i.e., most difficult-to-resolve) category, a large percentage of bridging links in this category are still not extracted by any of the systems. To improve system recall for these difficult cases, existing work has explored the use of information extracted from manually constructed resources such as knowledge graphs (Pandit et al., 2020) as well as bridging pairs (Hou, 2018) and bridging-annotated data (Hou, 2020) automatically constructed using lexico-syntactic patterns. These and other ideas (see Kobayashi and Ng (2020) for an overview) could be explored to improve the recall of the participating systems. Note, however, that these manually and automatically constructed resources are not likely to be helpful for resolving bridging links that involve pronouns as well as nouns that are semantically poor (e.g., "here"). Currently, demonstrative pronouns such as "this" and "that" have a resolution recall of 14.2% and 4.5% respectively, and the word "here" has a resolution recall of 6.3%. Given that these anaphors cannot be resolved via string matching, the only way to resolve them is to exploit the contexts in which they appear. While the mention representations acquired by existing mechanisms are supposed to be contextualized, the contextual information encoded in them is arguably quite limited and insufficient as far as making accurate linking decisions is concerned. Hence, learning effective context representations is a key challenge for state-of-the-art bridging resolvers. As discussed earlier, learning effective context representations is also an issue surrounding state-of-the-art entity coreference resolvers. However, we believe that this issue is likely to be more challenging for bridging resolution than for entity coreference. The reason is that determining whether two mentions are *associated* based on context is in general a lot more challenging than determining whether they refer to the same entity.

4 Discourse Deixis Resolution

The shared task divides the evaluation of discourse deixis resolution into two phases: (1) the *Predicted* phase, where a system needs to first identify all of the entity mentions that likely correspond to anaphors and antecedents, then perform discourse deixis resolution on the predicted mentions; and (2) the *Gold* phase, which is essentially the same as the Predicted phase except that the mentions corresponding to anaphors are to be extracted from the given gold mentions.

In this section, we analyze the performance of the teams that participated in the discourse deixis resolution track. The UTD team (Kobayashi et al., 2021) participated in both phases, whereas the DFKI team (Anikina et al., 2021) participated in the Predicted phase only. In other words, two teams participated in the Predicted phase, and one team participated in the Gold phase. As in bridging, we will use their team name to refer to the discourse deixis resolution systems they developed, augmenting the team name with a superscript that encodes the phase the system was developed for.

4.1 Mention Extraction

Mention extraction results of the four test sets, which are expressed in terms of R, P, and F, are shown in the "Overall" row of Table 15. As in the other tracks, a mention is considered correctly extracted if it has an exact match with a gold mention in terms of boundary.

Consider first the two systems developed for the Predicted phase, UTD^P and DFKI^P. DFKI^P achieves a much higher recall (9–17% points) than UTD^P on three of the four datasets, and on the remaining dataset (LIGHT), the two systems achieve comparable recall. These results suggest that DFKI^P is a lot more aggressive in extracting mentions than UTD^P. The high recall scores achieved by DFKI^P, however, come at the expense of precision. As can be seen, DFKI^P's precision scores are substantially lower than UTD^P's, with a difference of 37–42% points. Consequently, the mention extraction F-scores achieved by DFKI^P are also lower than those achieved by UTD^P: there is a 12–22% point difference in F-score between the two systems.

Next, consider the two UTD systems, UTD^P and UTD^G. The performance difference between these two systems is less than that between the two systems for the Predicted phase. In terms of F-score, while UTD^G outperforms UTD^P by nearly 12% points on Persuasion, the two differ from each other by only 2–3% points on the remaining datasets. The difference between their recall and precision values, however, provides some evidence that they may not be as similar to each other as their F-scores suggest. Specifically, UTD^G's mention extraction system seems to be recall-oriented: on three of the four datasets, UTD^G has a much higher recall (6–26% points) but a much lower precision (6–16% points) than UTD^P.

To better understand whether these systems dif-

		LIGHT			AMI			Persuasion			Switchboard		
		P	R	F	P	R	F	P	R	F	P	R	F
Overall	UTD^G	66.2	49.0	56.3	54.5	45.2	49.4	61.8	67.3	64.4	48.2	61.8	54.2
	UTD^P	65.2	46.9	54.5	60.2	39.1	47.4	72.3	41.6	52.8	64.4	42.2	51.0
	DFKI^P	25.2	44.3	32.1	18.5	56.3	27.8	31.5	58.4	40.9	27.7	51.3	36.0
Anaphor	UTD^G	–	65.0	–	–	61.9	–	–	77.2	–	–	74.9	–
	UTD^P	–	73.8	–	–	64.4	–	–	65.9	–	–	71.1	–
	DFKI^P	–	56.2	–	–	81.4	–	–	69.1	–	–	68.1	–
Antecedent	UTD^G	–	37.5	–	–	32.9	–	–	58.9	–	–	52.4	–
	UTD^P	–	27.7	–	–	20.5	–	–	21.2	–	–	21.5	–
	DFKI^P	–	35.7	–	–	37.9	–	–	49.3	–	–	39.4	–

Table 15: Discourse deixis resolution: mention extraction results.

fer in terms of how well they extract anaphors and antecedents, we also show in the last two rows of Table 15 their results on anaphor and antecedent extraction. Since each mention in the test sets is annotated as "anaphor" or"antecedent", we can easily compute recall. However, since the systems did not label each of the extracted mentions as "anaphor" or "antecedent" in the outputs, we cannot compute precision. As can be seen, DFKI^P extracts more mentions as antecedents and anaphors than UTD^P on all datasets, with the exception on LIGHT and Switchboard, where UTD^P achieves better recall on anaphor extraction. Comparing UTD^P and UTD^G, we can see that while UTD^G lags behind UTD^P by 3–9% points in anaphor extraction on LIGHT and AMI, UTD^G achieve superior mention extraction performance to UTD^P in the remaining cases. In particular, the difference between their recall in antecedent extraction is much bigger than that in anaphor extraction.

To gain additional insights into the difference between the systems w.r.t. mention extraction, we show in Table 16a their performance on extracting the five gold mentions that occur most frequently on the four test sets combined. More specifically, in the "mention" column, "overall" shows the results aggregated over all gold mentions, "The rest" aggregates the results of all but the top five gold mentions, and the remaining rows show the results of each of the top five gold mentions. The "%" and "count" columns show the percentage and number of gold mentions that belong to each category. The remaining columns can be interpreted in the same way as those in Table 2. For instance, "none" shows the percentage of gold mentions that cannot be extracted by any of the three systems, UTD^G shows the percentage of gold mentions extracted by UTD^G, and UTD^G-only shows the percentage of gold mentions that are extracted by UTD^G but not by the other two systems.

Perhaps not surprisingly, the most frequent categories of mentions are all anaphor categories. Specifically, the most frequent category is "that", accounting for 29.3% of the gold mentions. This is followed by "it" (6.9%) and "this" (1.8%). These three categories of anaphors account for nearly 38% of the gold mentions in the test data. From the "none" column, we see that the worst-performing category is "The rest". This should perhaps not be surprising either: the majority of the mentions in this category are antecedents, which may not have appeared in the training data at all. In addition, 55.8% of the anaphor "it" were missed by the systems. We believe that this can be attributed to two reasons. First, DFKI^P gave up on handling "it". Second, we speculate that it is challenging to determine whether "it" is used deictically: while "this", "that" and "it" can all be used as coreferent anaphors, bridging anaphors, and deictic expressions, it is more likely for "it" to be a coreferent or bridging anaphor than a discourse deixis compared to "this" and "that". Moving on to the performance of the systems (UTD^G, UTD^P, and DFKI^P), we see that the systems are indeed better at extracting "this" and "that" than "it". Note that DFKI^P's recall scores on the anaphors that the system is able to handle are substantially higher than those of the UTD systems. In particular, considering the "x-only" columns, we see that there are many instances of these anaphors that are extracted only by DFKI^P.

While Table 16a focuses on gold mention extraction, Table 16b focuses on the extraction of erroneous mentions. Specifically, we take the union of the set of erroneous mentions extracted by the three resolvers and compute statistics based on the

(a) Coverage of gold mentions

mention	%	count	none	UTD^G	UTD^P	DFKI^P	UTD^G-only	UTD^P-only	DFKI^P-only
Overall	100.0	1371	65.0	30.4	28.9	29.5	1.7	0.8	2.4
that	29.3	402	2.2	86.6	85.3	92.3	1.2	0.7	6.0
it	6.9	95	55.8	36.8	32.6	0.0	11.6	7.4	0.0
this	1.8	25	0.0	76.0	60.0	100.0	0.0	0.0	20.0
which	0.7	10	10.0	50.0	30.0	70.0	10.0	0.0	40.0
the same	0.3	4	25.0	75.0	25.0	0.0	50.0	0.0	0.0
The rest	60.9	835	99.0	0.8	0.4	0.1	0.5	0.1	0.0

(b) Coverage of wrong mentions

mention	%	count	UTD^G	UTD^P	DFKI^P	UTD^G-only	UTD^P-only	DFKI^P-only
Overall	100.0	1202	43.3	17.4	61.6	29.8	4.1	49.9
that	43.3	520	25.8	23.5	90.6	2.7	2.1	67.7
this	6.3	76	17.1	23.7	89.5	3.9	2.6	71.1
it	4.5	54	61.1	81.5	0.0	18.5	38.9	0.0
which	3.5	42	9.5	11.9	95.2	2.4	2.4	81.0
that way	0.4	5	80.0	60.0	0.0	40.0	20.0	0.0
The rest	42.0	505	65.7	3.4	31.9	65.0	2.6	31.7

Table 16: Discourse deixis resolution: per-anaphor mention extraction results.

resulting set, which we refer to as S. The columns in Table 16b can be interpreted in the same way as those in Table 16a. For instance, UTD^G, UTD^P, and DFKI^P show the percentage of mentions in S extracted by each of the systems, and the "x-only" columns show the percentage of mentions in S extracted by exactly one of the systems.

A few points deserve mention. First, the five most frequently occurring categories of mentions that are erroneously extracted are likely mentions that are incorrectly posited by the systems as discourse deixis, as the top four categories are the same as the top four categories of gold mentions. The erroneously extracted antecedents will likely appear in the "The rest" category. Second, DFKI^P covers more than 90% of the mistakes made for the top categories of anaphors that it can handle (i.e., "that", "this", "which"), suggesting that the system is very aggressive in positing the occurrences of these words as anaphors. In contrast, it only extracts one-third of the mentions in the "The rest" category, which, as noted above, should mostly contain erroneously extracted antecedents, while UTD^G and UTD^P extract two-thirds and 3% of the erroneously extracted antecedents respectively. These results imply that UTD^P is a lot more cautious in positing mentions as antecedents compared to the other two systems, while UTD^G is the most liberal in positing mentions as antecedents. These differences can also be observed when considering the "x-only" columns.

4.2 Resolution

A discourse deixis resolver is expected to output clusters, each of which contains a deixis and all of its antecedents. As far as scoring is concerned, discourse deixis resolution is viewed as a generalized case of event coreference, and hence the scorer used for scoring entity coreference chains is used to score the output of a discourse deixis resolver.

Table 17 shows the official results obtained using the official scorer. Again, the results are expressed in terms of MUC, B^3, and CEAF$_e$ R, P, and F, as well as the CoNLL score.

A few points deserve mention. First, there is a clear difference in performance between the two systems developed for the Predicted phase, UTD^P and DFKI^P, in terms of CoNLL F-score, where the scores achieved by UTD^P almost double those achieved by DFKI^P. In comparison, the difference in the CoNLL score between UTD^G and UTD^P is smaller: less than 2% points on LIGHT and AMI, 12.5% points on Persuasion, and 5.0% points on Switchboard. We speculate that the particularly large difference in performance between the two systems on Persuasion can be attributed in part to mention extraction, where UTD^G has a considerably higher mention extraction F-score on this dataset than UTD^P (64.4 vs. 52.8). Second, DFKI^P's MUC recall scores are lower than the other systems for all but the Switchboard dataset. This implies that DFKI^P is not able to recall as many links as the other systems. However, a closer

	MUC			B^3			$CEAF_e$			
	P	R	F	P	R	F	P	R	F	CoNLL
					LIGHT					
UTD^G	49.0	30.0	37.2	56.3	39.1	46.2	51.7	42.9	46.9	43.4
UTD^P	44.6	31.2	36.8	56.2	37.0	44.6	55.3	40.5	46.7	42.7
DFKI^P	9.2	12.5	10.6	21.1	31.3	25.2	19.3	42.1	26.5	20.8
					AMI					
UTD^G	44.6	21.2	28.7	49.7	34.6	40.8	39.6	43.0	41.2	36.9
UTD^P	45.5	21.2	28.9	52.4	29.5	37.8	44.9	35.1	39.4	35.4
DFKI^P	7.5	16.9	10.4	14.5	39.1	21.2	12.6	49.5	20.1	17.2
					Persuasion					
UTD^G	53.3	45.5	49.1	54.9	55.7	55.3	46.0	59.3	51.8	52.1
UTD^P	45.5	20.3	28.1	64.9	30.2	41.2	61.0	41.8	49.6	39.6
DFKI^P	14.7	14.6	14.7	26.9	37.2	31.2	16.9	46.7	24.8	23.6
					Switchboard					
UTD^G	39.4	31.2	34.8	41.6	48.5	44.8	33.7	55.0	41.8	40.4
UTD^P	35.2	21.3	26.5	52.3	30.4	38.5	50.5	34.9	41.3	35.4
DFKI^P	14.2	21.3	17.1	22.6	37.2	28.1	18.9	42.8	26.2	23.8

Table 17: Discourse deixis resolution: official resolution results.

	LIGHT			AMI			Persuasion			Switchboard		
	F	ns. F	s. F	F	ns. F	s. F	F	ns. F	s. F	F	ns. F	s. F
UTD^G	43.4	43.9	7.7	36.9	35.2	8.4	52.1	52.0	4.2	40.4	36.6	9.5
UTD^P	42.7	47.0	2.2	35.4	37.9	2.6	39.6	42.1	1.0	35.4	39.1	2.0
DFKI^P	20.8	17.1	6.9	17.2	15.3	3.4	23.6	22.8	2.1	23.8	22.6	3.8

Table 18: Discourse deixis resolution: results on singleton and non-singleton cluster identification.

examination of the results reveals that precision seems to play a bigger role in the observed performance difference between DFKI^P and the other systems: DFKI^P's precision scores are generally very poor. We speculate that this can be attributed to the fact that the system is overly aggressive in positing "that", "this", and "which" as anaphors and attempts to resolve them, which in turn yields a lot of erroneous links. Third, comparing UTD^G and UTD^G, we see that the considerably better results achieved by UTD^G on Persuasion can be attributed to not only mention extraction but also resolution, as reflected in the 25.2% point difference in MUC recall between the two systems.

To further our understanding of how the systems perform w.r.t. non-singleton cluster and singleton cluster identification, we show the corresponding results in Table 18, whose rows and columns can be interpreted in the same manner as those in Table 5. Comparing the two Predicted systems, we see that while DFKI^P is considerably worse than UTD^P in non-singleton cluster identification, it performs slightly and consistently better than UTD^P in singleton cluster identification. This again could be attributed to its being aggressive in extracting anaphors. Comparing the two UTD systems, we see that UTD^G is always better than UTD^P in singleton cluster identification, but UTD^P is better than UTD^G in non-singleton cluster identification on all but the Persuasion dataset. These results further reveal why UTD^G performs substantially better than UTD^P on Persuasion: UTD^G are better than UTD^P in both non-singleton and singleton cluster identification on Persuasion.

Next, we measure system performance, specifically link identification performance, at the pairwise level. For each non-singleton cluster in the gold output, we extract every pair of mentions in the cluster. We similarly extract all the pairs from the non-singleton clusters produced by each of the three systems. The recall, precision, and F-scores in Table 19 are computed based on the pairwise links in these sets.

From the "Overall" row in Table 19, we can see that 504 pairs can be extracted from the gold clusters of the four test sets. As we can see, all systems have higher recall than precision. Comparing the two Predicted systems, we see that while

anaphor	%	count	UTD^G P	UTD^G R	UTD^G F	UTD^P P	UTD^P R	UTD^P F	DFKI^P P	DFKI^P R	DFKI^P F
Overall	100.0	504	25.0	37.7	30.1	17.2	26.2	20.7	9.4	23.6	13.5
that	68.1	343	30.1	47.8	36.9	21.4	33.5	26.1	11.8	33.5	17.5
it	17.7	89	12.7	16.9	14.5	9.1	13.5	10.9	0.0	0.0	0.0
this	4.4	22	18.9	31.8	23.7	10.5	18.2	13.3	2.9	13.6	4.8
which	2.0	10	20.0	30.0	24.0	0.0	0.0	0.0	1.9	10.0	3.1
the same	0.8	4	0.0	0.0	0.0	25.0	25.0	25.0	0.0	0.0	0.0
The rest	7.1	36	2.5	2.8	2.6	0.0	0.0	0.0	0.0	0.0	0.0

Table 19: Discourse deixis resolution: per-anaphor resolution results at the pairwise level.

(a) Coverage of correct links

anaphor	%	count	None	UTD^G	UTD^P	DFKI^P	UTD^G-only	UTD^P-only	DFKI^P-only
Overall	100.0	504	46.0	37.7	26.2	23.6	14.3	8.3	6.3
that	68.1	343	31.8	47.8	33.5	33.5	16.0	9.3	8.7
it	17.7	89	76.4	16.9	13.5	0.0	10.1	6.7	0.0
this	4.4	22	45.5	31.8	18.2	13.6	22.7	13.6	9.1
which	2.0	10	70.0	30.0	0.0	10.0	20.0	0.0	0.0
the same	0.8	4	75.0	0.0	25.0	0.0	0.0	25.0	0.0
The rest	7.1	36	97.2	2.8	0.0	0.0	2.8	0.0	0.0

(b) Coverage of wrong links

anaphor	%	count	UTD^G	UTD^P	DFKI^P	UTD^G-only	UTD^P-only	DFKI^P-only
Overall	100.0	1330	19.5	20.2	69.0	13.7	15.6	63.9
that	69.5	925	21.8	21.1	68.1	14.5	15.6	61.2
this	7.8	104	14.4	15.4	78.8	9.6	10.6	75.0
it	5.0	67	43.3	64.2	0.0	35.8	56.7	0.0
which	4.4	59	8.5	16.9	74.6	8.5	16.9	74.6
the	1.7	22	0.0	0.0	100.0	0.0	0.0	100.0
The rest	11.5	153	5.9	2.6	91.5	5.9	2.6	91.5

Table 20: Discourse deixis resolution: per-anaphor resolution results at the pairwise level.

DFKI^P achieves lower overall recall and precision than UTD^P, the difference in their recall scores is comparatively smaller than the difference in their precision scores. In particular, the two systems achieve the same recall in the resolution of "that", the most frequent anaphor, and the slightly lower overall recall achieved by DFKI^P can be largely attributed to its decision of not resolving "it" and some other anaphors. Comparing the two UTD systems, we see that UTD^G achieves better recall and precision than UTD^P in resolving the top anaphors. Perhaps more interesting, while the two Predicted systems cannot resolve any of the anaphors in "The rest" category, UTD^G manages to achieve a non-zero F-score on this category, though precision and recall are both low.

Table 20a shows each system's coverage of gold pairs. The rows can be interpreted in the same way as those in Table 19, whereas the columns can be interpreted in the same way as those in Table 7a. As a quick reminder, "none" shows the percentage of gold pairs that are not extracted by any of the three systems; "UTD^G", "UTD^P", and "DFKI^P" show the percentage of gold pairs extracted by each of the three systems; and the "x-only" columns show the percentage of gold pairs that are extracted only by system x.

A few points deserve mention. First, consider the "none" results. As can be seen, 46.0% of the links are not recovered by any of the three systems. In particular, 97.2% of the links involving the anaphors in the "The rest" category are not recovered. This is followed by "it", where 76.4% of the links involving "it" are not recovered. In contrast, the recovery rate is higher for "that", probably because of the larger representation of links involving "that" in the training set. Second, consider the "x-only" results, which suggest that the three systems are more different from each other than we may think. Examining the "that" links, we see that 16% are only identified by UTD^G, 9.3% only by UTD^P, and 8.7% only by DFKI^P. Similarly for "this": 22.7% are only identified by UTD^G, 13.6% only by UTD^P, and 9.1% only by DFKI^P.

	0	1	2	3	4	5	6	7	8	9	10	>10
Distribution of links over sentence distances												
Gold	90	216	98	49	21	9	4	2	0	1	3	11
UTD^G	122	339	141	70	28	10	7	5	0	3	6	33
UTD^P	106	278	132	77	32	16	10	14	3	5	8	91
DFKI^P	386	573	261	151	21	9	4	2	0	1	3	11
Distribution of correctly predicted links over sentence distances												
UTD^G	11	126	39	13	1	0	0	0	0	0	0	0
UTD^P	28	64	23	10	4	2	0	0	0	1	0	0
DFKI^P	0	78	23	18	0	0	0	0	0	0	0	0
Distribution of incorrectly predicted links over sentence distances												
UTD^G	111	213	102	57	27	10	7	5	0	3	6	33
UTD^P	78	214	109	67	28	14	10	14	3	4	8	91
DFKI^P	386	495	238	133	21	9	4	2	0	1	3	11

Table 21: Discourse deixis resolution: distribution of gold/predicted links over the sentence distances between the anaphor and the antecedents.

While Table 20a focuses on the extraction of gold pairs, Table 20b focuses on the extraction of wrong pairs (i.e., wrong links). Specifically, we take the union of the set of wrong pairs extracted by the three resolvers and compute statistics based on the resulting set, which we refer to as S. The columns in Table 20b can be interpreted in the same way as those in Table 20a. For instance, UTD^G shows the percentage of pairs in S extracted by UTD^G, and UTD^G-only shows the percentage of pairs in S that are extracted by UTD^G but not the other two systems.

As can be seen in Table 20b, 1330 erroneous links are established by the three systems, of which 19.5% are established by UTD^G, 20.2% by UTD^P, and 69.0% by DFKI^P; in addition, 13.7% of these erroneous links are only established by UTD^G, 15.6% are only established by UTD^P, and 63.9% are only established by DFKI. These results again reveal that DFKI^P establishes a lot more erroneous links than the UTD systems in each category of anaphors it handles. Interestingly, it attempts to resolve "the", which should not have appeared in the training data as an anaphor. Considering the "x-only" results, we see that there is a fairly large percentage of links in each category that are identified by only one of the three systems, suggesting that the three systems are quite different from each other in their resolution behavior.

To get a better idea of how far a discourse deixis can be from its antecedent, we show in Table 21 the relevant statistics collected from the four test sets. Specifically, the row labeled "Gold" shows the distribution of gold links over the number of sentences between a deixis and its antecedent. (If the sentence distance is 0, it means that the deixis refers to the sentence in which it appears.) As can be seen, the results are consistent with our intuition: a deictic expression most likely has the immediately preceding sentence (i.e., distance = 1) as its referent; in addition, the number of links drops as distance increases. More than 90% of the antecedents are at most four sentences away from their anaphors. In other words, if a discourse deixis resolver simply employs the closest five sentences preceding an anaphor as its candidate antecedents, they should cover more than 90% of the correct antecedents.

The next three rows of Table 21 show the distributions of the links identified by the three resolvers, UTD^G, UTD^P, and DFKI^P. Interestingly, these three distributions all have similar shapes to the gold distribution: they all peak at distance = 1 and generally drop as the sentence distance increases. Next, we tease apart the correct links from the wrong links. The distributions of the correctly predicted links as well as the distributions of the incorrectly predicted links created by the three resolvers over sentence distances are shown in the next two blocks of results. Comparing UTD^P and DFKI^P, we see that DFKI^P does not posit any links between an anaphor and the sentence in which it appears, but it establishes more correct links than UTD^P when the sentence distance is between 1 and 3. Nevertheless, as discussed before, it posits a substantially larger number of erroneous links than the two UTD resolvers.

4.3 Discussion

At first glance it appears that discourse deixis resolution is more challenging the entity coreference resolution and bridging resolution. The reason is that while various string-matching facilities can be used to identify some of the entity coreference relations and bridging relations, they cannot be applied to resolve deictic expressions as there is no content word overlap between a deixis and its antecedent. However, this task has certain characteristics that make it somewhat easier that it seems. First, for antecedents, the unit of annotation is a sentence/utterance; moreover, an antecedent cannot be bigger than a turn (i.e., the utterances produced by a speaker within a turn). These constraints on antecedent annotation can be exploited to significantly reduce the search space of candidate antecedents. Better still, as discussed in the previous subsection, there is a recency constraint that can be exploited to further reduce this search space: a deixis's antecedent typically appears close to it. In contrast, any multi-word expression can be a valid antecedent for an anaphor in entity coreference and bridging; moreover, in some of the entity coreference relations and bridging relations, the two mentions involved can be far apart from each other. Hence, to achieve good performance, a coreference/bridging resolver typically needs to work with a larger search space than a discourse deixis resolver.

The key factor that appears to be limiting the performance of the participating systems is anaphor recognition. The most frequent deictic expressions such as "that", "this", and "it" can also serve as an identity or bridging anaphor, and determining whether a mention is deictic is a key challenge in discourse deixis resolution. As discussed earlier, the low recognition and resolution results achieved by DFKI's system can largely be attributed to its being weak at determining whether a given expression such as "this" or "that" is used deictically and its being overly liberal in classifying these words as deictic and resolving them.

5 Concluding Remarks

We presented a cross-team analysis of the systems that participated in each of the three tracks of the CODI-CRAC 2021 shared task. As noted in the introduction, conducting a systematic analysis that can provide insightful observations is by no means a trivial task. We believe that future cross-team analyses can be improved in a number of ways.

First, any analysis should be based on the *links* identified by a system rather than the output *clusters* they generated. The reason is that a cluster contains both the links identified by a system and the links automatically created via transitive closure. Hence, to better understand the mistakes made by a resolver, we should request the teams to provide the links their systems identify in addition to the clusters they produce so that we can conduct cross-team analyses on the links instead. We do note, however, that this may not be easy for entity-based systems, where a link is established between an anaphor and one of its preceding clusters. For these systems, assumptions may need to be made. For example, when merging takes place, we may assume that a link is established between the anaphor and the member of the cluster that is closest to the anaphor.

Second, to facilitate cross-team comparisons, the teams should be asked to run diagnostic tests provided by the organizers on their systems so that additional insights into their behavior can be gained. For instance, since mention extraction performance has a significant correlation with resolution performance, we will not be able to quantify its impact on resolution performance or directly compare different models in terms of their *resolution* performance that is not affected by their mention detection performance unless we provide a system with *gold* mentions. Hence, a useful diagnostic test, which was employed in the CoNLL-2012 shared task on Unrestricted Multilingual Coreference (Pradhan et al., 2012), involves running the systems on the test data when gold mentions are given. Another useful diagnostic test, which involves running the bridging resolvers and the discourse deixis resolvers on the test data when gold anaphors are given, would allow us to directly compare the resolvers in terms of their antecedent selection performance. While this shared task has a Gold phase for the bridging track and the discourse deixis track in which gold mentions are given, these gold mentions are somewhat different from what one would expect. Specifically, while the participants expected to be given task-specific gold mentions, they were instead provided with gold mentions that were created by taking the union of the three sets of gold mentions collected from the three tracks. Worse still, the gold mentions provided in the discourse deixis track did not even include the antecedents.

Unfortunately, this somewhat unconventional definition of gold mentions was not clearly communicated to the participants and has caused some confusion among them.

Third, our analysis could be improved with an analysis of annotation quality. Strictly speaking, an analysis of annotation quality should not be part of a cross-team analysis, but for this shared task annotation quality may have played a role in the performance of the participating systems given that there are linking decisions that we do not agree with based on our casual inspection of the annotated data. Having said that, we are not sure whether it is possible for us to assess annotation quality since the annotation guidelines are not made available to the participants.

Fourth, from an analysis point of view, it may be a good idea to include LEA (Moosavi and Strube, 2016) as one of the evaluation metrics. As Moosavi and Strube point out, it is not easy to interpret the scores provided by existing scorers such as MUC, B^3, and $CEAF_e$ and LEA is designed to partially address this problem.

Fifth, our analysis did not focus on the differences among the four datasets. For instance, in discourse deixis resolution, UTD^G achieved significantly better results than UTD^P on Persuasion but not the other datasets. A cross-dataset analysis could shed light on why systems exhibit different trends on different datasets. Having said that, the organizers should take an active role in explaining to the participants the differences among the different datasets and the unique challenges associated with each of them so that the participants know why these four datasets were chosen, rather than have them figure these differences out on their own.

Finally, to facilitate cross-team analyses, the organizers should include as much relevant information in the system prediction files that they make available to the participants as possible. Currently, these files merely contain the pairwise predictions made by the systems as well as the gold links they missed. Some potentially useful information that can also be provided in these files includes the sentence/turn distance between the mention pairs and their surrounding contexts. While this information can be extracted by the participants from the raw system outputs, simply laying the burden on them will likely deter them from conducting an analysis.

Acknowledgments

This work was supported in part by NSF Grant IIS-1528037. Any opinions, findings, conclusions or recommendations expressed in this paper are those of the authors and do not necessarily reflect the views or official policies, either expressed or implied, of the NSF.

References

Tatiana Anikina, Cennet Oguz, Natalia Skachkova, Siyu Tao, Sharmila Upadhyaya, and Ivana Kruijff-Korbayova. 2021. Anaphora resolution in dialogue: Description of the DFKI-TalkingRobots system for the CODI-CRAC 2021 shared-task. In *Proceedings of the CODI-CRAC 2021 Shared Task on Anaphora, Bridging, and Discourse Deixis in Dialogue*, Punta Cana, Dominican Republic. Association for Computational Linguistics.

Amit Bagga and Breck Baldwin. 1998. Algorithms for scoring coreference chains. In *Proceedings of the First International Conference on Language Resources and Evaluation Workshop on Linguistic Coreference*, pages 563–566.

Yufang Hou. 2018. Enhanced word representations for bridging anaphora resolution. In *Proceedings of the 2018 Conference of the North American Chapter of the Association for Computational Linguistics: Human Language Technologies, Volume 2 (Short Papers)*, pages 1–7, New Orleans, Louisiana. Association for Computational Linguistics.

Yufang Hou. 2020. Bridging anaphora resolution as question answering. In *Proceedings of the 58th Annual Meeting of the Association for Computational Linguistics*, pages 1428–1438, Online. Association for Computational Linguistics.

Sopan Khosla, Juntao Yu, Ramesh Manuvinakurike, Vincent Ng, Massimo Poesio, Michael Strube, and Carolyn Rosé. 2021. The CODI-CRAC 2021 shared task on anaphora, bridging, and discourse deixis in dialogue. In *Proceedings of the CODI-CRAC 2021 Shared Task on Anaphora, Bridging, and Discourse Deixis in Dialogue*, Punta Cana, Dominican Republic. Association for Computational Linguistics.

Hongjin Kim, Damrin Kim, and Harksoo Kim. 2021. The pipeline model for resolution of anaphoric reference and resolution of entity reference. In *Proceedings of the CODI-CRAC 2021 Shared Task on Anaphora, Bridging, and Discourse Deixis in Dialogue*, Punta Cana, Dominican Republic. Association for Computational Linguistics.

Hideo Kobayashi, Shengjie Li, and Vincent Ng. 2021. Neural anaphora resolution in dialogue. In *Proceedings of the CODI-CRAC 2021 Shared Task on Anaphora, Bridging, and Discourse Deixis in Dialogue*, Punta Cana, Dominican Republic. Association for Computational Linguistics.

Hideo Kobayashi and Vincent Ng. 2020. Bridging resolution: A survey of the state of the art. In *Proceedings of the 28th International Conference on Computational Linguistics*, pages 3708–3721, Barcelona, Spain (Online). International Committee on Computational Linguistics.

Jonathan K. Kummerfeld and Dan Klein. 2013. Error-driven analysis of challenges in coreference resolution. In *Proceedings of the 2013 Conference on Empirical Methods in Natural Language Processing*, pages 265–277, Seattle, Washington, USA. Association for Computational Linguistics.

Kenton Lee, Luheng He, Mike Lewis, and Luke Zettlemoyer. 2017. End-to-end neural coreference resolution. In *Proceedings of the 2017 Conference on Empirical Methods in Natural Language Processing*, pages 188–197, Copenhagen, Denmark. Association for Computational Linguistics.

Kenton Lee, Luheng He, and Luke Zettlemoyer. 2018. Higher-order coreference resolution with coarse-to-fine inference. In *Proceedings of the 2018 Conference of the North American Chapter of the Association for Computational Linguistics: Human Language Technologies, Volume 2 (Short Papers)*, pages 687–692, New Orleans, Louisiana. Association for Computational Linguistics.

Jing Lu and Vincent Ng. 2020. Conundrums in entity coreference resolution: Making sense of the state of the art. In *Proceedings of the 2020 Conference on Empirical Methods in Natural Language Processing (EMNLP)*, pages 6620–6631, Online. Association for Computational Linguistics.

Xiaoqiang Luo. 2005. On coreference resolution performance metrics. In *Proceedings of Human Language Technology Conference and Conference on Empirical Methods in Natural Language Processing*, pages 25–32, Vancouver, British Columbia, Canada. Association for Computational Linguistics.

Nafise Sadat Moosavi and Michael Strube. 2016. Which coreference evaluation metric do you trust? a proposal for a link-based entity aware metric. In *Proceedings of the 54th Annual Meeting of the Association for Computational Linguistics (Volume 1: Long Papers)*, pages 632–642, Berlin, Germany. Association for Computational Linguistics.

Onkar Pandit, Pascal Denis, and Liva Ralaivola. 2020. Integrating knowledge graph embeddings to improve mention representation for bridging anaphora resolution. In *Proceedings of the Third Workshop on Computational Models of Reference, Anaphora and Coreference*, pages 55–67, Barcelona, Spain (online). Association for Computational Linguistics.

Sameer Pradhan, Alessandro Moschitti, Nianwen Xue, Olga Uryupina, and Yuchen Zhang. 2012. CoNLL-2012 shared task: Modeling multilingual unrestricted coreference in OntoNotes. In *Joint Conference on EMNLP and CoNLL - Shared Task*, pages 1–40, Jeju Island, Korea. Association for Computational Linguistics.

Sameer Pradhan, Lance Ramshaw, Mitchell Marcus, Martha Palmer, Ralph Weischedel, and Nianwen Xue. 2011. CoNLL-2011 shared task: Modeling unrestricted coreference in OntoNotes. In *Proceedings of the Fifteenth Conference on Computational Natural Language Learning: Shared Task*, pages 1–27, Portland, Oregon, USA. Association for Computational Linguistics.

Joseph Renner, Priyansh Trivedi, Gaurav Maheshwari, Rémi Gilleron, and Pascal Denis. 2021. An end-to-end approach for full bridging resolution. In *Proceedings of the CODI-CRAC 2021 Shared Task on Anaphora, Bridging, and Discourse Deixis in Dialogue*, Punta Cana, Dominican Republic. Association for Computational Linguistics.

Marc Vilain, John Burger, John Aberdeen, Dennis Connolly, and Lynette Hirschman. 1995. A model-theoretic coreference scoring scheme. In *Sixth Message Understanding Conference (MUC-6): Proceedings of a Conference Held in Columbia, Maryland, November 6-8, 1995*.

Liyan Xu and Jinho D. Choi. 2020. Revealing the myth of higher-order inference in coreference resolution. In *Proceedings of the 2020 Conference on Empirical Methods in Natural Language Processing (EMNLP)*, pages 8527–8533, Online. Association for Computational Linguistics.

Liyan Xu and Jinho D. Choi. 2021. Adapted end-to-end coreference resolution system for anaphoric identities in dialogues. In *Proceedings of the CODI-CRAC 2021 Shared Task on Anaphora, Bridging, and Discourse Deixis in Dialogue*, Punta Cana, Dominican Republic. Association for Computational Linguistics.

Association for Computational Linguistics
209 N. Eighth Street
Stroudsburg, Pennsylvania 18360

ISBN 978-1-7138-9173-4

CURRAN ASSOCIATES INC.
proceedings.com

9 781713 891734